THE LEGACY OF HIROSHIMA

THE LEGACY OF HIROSHIMA

by Edward Teller with Allen Brown

DOUBLEDAY & COMPANY, INC., GARDEN CITY, NEW YORK
1962

CONTENTS

CONTENTS

INTRODUCTION

THE CATASTROPHE of World War II could have been avoided. If
we had not pressed for reparations after World War I, if we had
used foreign aid as we are now using it, Hitler might never have
come to power. If we had supported the League of Nations as
we now are supporting the United Nations, lawless conquest
would not have become rampant in the 1930s. If we had spent as
much on military preparedness as we now are spending, Hitler
could have been defeated in the first year of the war.

But what would have sufficed a few decades ago is not enough
today. The world has become smaller; time has become shorter;
changes and revolutions have become more frequent. And in
Russian Communism we have met an opponent that is more
powerful, more patient, and incomparably more dangerous than
German Nazism.

What we are doing today would have seemed impossible in
1930. What we actually should be doing, similarly, seems beyond
our reach at present. By being one generation behind our times,
we are endangering peace; we may bring about World War III.

It has become necessary to create a lawful world community.
Most people agree that our globe has become too small, too
crowded, too dangerous to accommodate many sovereign governments—each of them a law unto itself. This is the chief obstacle
to peace, the central problem of the world today. It is futile to

present a blueprint for the solution of this problem; it cannot be solved at one stroke. The solution requires many contributions from many quarters.

The main purpose of this book is to make my contribution to the cause of peace. I shall not limit myself to a single aspect of this problem. How to teach science, how to use science to conquer misery and provide more stability are questions that must be discussed and can be discussed in the spirit of hope.

Owing to my experience in the field of atomic explosives, it is proper that I should particularly emphasize the influence that these powerful instruments have on all questions of war and peace. One fact seems inescapable to me: It will not be possible to preserve peace unless we are willing to think carefully and in detail about war.

My contention is not that our preparation for war is insufficient. My main point is that our preparation is misdirected. We have been frightened by the display of our own power at Hiroshima, and we have lost our sense of proportion. On the one hand, we think of an all-out war as a cataclysm that will wipe out mankind. On the other hand, we think of an abolition of nuclear weapons as a means to restore stability and to avoid a future war. These two patterns of ideas are driving us toward a tragedy which, when it comes, will be of our own making.

There are a few points which are obvious, but which are rejected by the majority of our people.

In a dangerous world we cannot have peace unless we are strong.

We cannot be strong unless we are fully prepared to exploit the biggest modern power, nuclear explosives.

Nuclear weapons can be used with moderation on all scales of serious conflict. Nuclear weapons do not mean the end of the world, but they do mean the end of non-nuclear power.

World War III would be much worse than anything we can remember. But it would not destroy mankind. If we do not prepare, it would do to us what wars have done to many nations. It would kill the United States.

The atomic age has brought fears, and it has brought a challenge. Unless we respond to the challenge, unless we create a world of tomorrow better than anything we can imagine or describe, too many of our fears will be justified.

The validity of these statements should be evident. Talking with my friends, reading books and newspapers, listening to the speeches of politicians and scientists have convinced me that the opposite of some of these statements is widely believed and that none of them are fully accepted. That is why these statements have been expanded into a book.

None of these statements can be proved. The world is much more involved than a mathematical demonstration. And, outside of mathematics, it is too often possible to prove both a statement and its opposite. So I shall not attempt to prove. I can only describe and discuss.

Much of the description will be personal. I am eager to state both my reasons and my motives. Much of the discussion will be detailed. Familiarity does help understanding, and details slow us down enough to prevent us from making false generalizations. Some of the conclusions will be erroneous; in discussing difficult questions, this is unavoidable. Yet I am fully convinced of the correctness of my statements, and I will present my conclusions in terms of my own full convictions.

PART ONE:
The Work of Many People

CHAPTER ONE:

The Secret of Los Alamos

AT SIXTEEN MINUTES PAST eight o'clock on the morning of August 6, 1945, an atomic bomb exploded 1850 feet above Hiroshima.

The 245,000 people in the city were not prepared. They already had been inconvenienced by an apparently unnecessary air raid warning that morning. The warning had come at 7:09 A.M., when a B-29 acting as weather scout for history's first atomic bomb run had approached the city. The scout plane made two passes over Hiroshima and flew away at 7:25 A.M. The all clear sounded. The annoying warning had gone almost unobserved in the teeming city, where people were more concerned with getting to work than with sheltering themselves from a single plane.

No new alert was sounded when Hiroshima was approached by the *Enola Gay*, the bomber carrying the atomic weapon, and its two trailing B-29s that were loaded with instruments to measure and photograph the atomic blast. Japanese officials assumed the three B-29s were on a reconnaissance flight. Unchallenged, the *Enola Gay* flew to the heart of the city with its load of death and destruction.

The atomic bomb created a succession of terrors. Its sudden, frighteningly intense heat burned people who were more than two miles from the point of the explosion.

The blast of the shock wave followed the heat almost immediately. The shock toppled buildings all over Hiroshima and was so severe that people in widely separated areas of the city thought their homes had suffered a direct hit by a conventional bomb.

Then came fire. The bomb's heat started many fires spontaneously. Thousands of others were caused by the shock wave that overturned fire-filled *habachis* that had been used to cook breakfasts in nearly all of the city's wood-and-paper houses. The thousands of individual fires spread and joined, creating a huge updraft and the greatest terror: the fire storm. Ground winds whipped through Hiroshima, converting the city into a gigantic funeral pyre. This fire storm did more damage than the atomic bomb itself.

Few people were spared. Some were killed outright by the bomb. More were burned by the explosion's radiated heat. Still more were crushed to death in buildings collapsed by the bomb's blast. But most of Hiroshima's victims were trapped in the gigantic fire storm.

The official statistics: 78,150 people killed, 13,983 missing, 37,425 injured; 62,000 out of the city's 90,000 buildings destroyed, and 6000 other buildings damaged beyond repair.

The destruction of Hiroshima and the awful suffering of the city's people, however, were not the most significant consequences of history's first atomic attack. Five months before, on the night of March 9, about sixteen square miles of Tokyo had been set afire by 2000 tons of incendiaries dropped from our massed B-29s. The same number of people killed at Hiroshima, 78,000 Japanese, died in that Tokyo raid. The dreadful significance of Hiroshima was that such damage could be inflicted by a single bomb dropped from a single plane.

Hiroshima changed the course of history. The actions, thoughts, and emotions of men during the years after Hiroshima would be more and more influenced by the tragedy that ended a war and started a new age. But on that sixth day of August the world was unprepared for these consequences of Hiroshima. The world was stunned by the sudden revelation of the secret of Los Alamos.

In Santa Fe, the city closest to the Los Alamos Laboratory where the atomic weapon had been developed, the reaction to the bombing was incongruous, provincial, and at the same time understandable. But the burning ruins in Hiroshima and the reaction in New Mexico were in glaring contrast; that I cannot forget.

New Mexicans for years had speculated about the mysterious, secret activities at the former Los Alamos School on the slope of Jemez Mountain. On August 6, 1945, the pent-up curiosity of the people erupted with the vigor of a one-track mind. That day's top headline in the Santa Fe *New Mexican* was concerned neither with the actual bombing of Hiroshima nor with the effect it would have upon the world. The headline read: LOS ALAMOS SECRET DISCLOSED BY TRUMAN.

The paper reported the news with obvious and understandable relish. Its staff for years had been sniffing at one of the world's great news stories, but had been working under a censorship that the *New Mexican* called, without rancor, "the greatest ever imposed."

The newspaper's most difficult day had come exactly three weeks before Hiroshima, when the world's first atomic bomb was experimentally exploded before dawn at Alamogordo in the New Mexican desert. The explosion's bright, brilliant flash startled a blind girl, Georgia Green, who was riding in a car 120 miles away from Alamogordo. And over on the Arizona-New Mexico state line, 150 miles west of the test site, Mrs. H. E. Weiselman described the flash: "It was just like the sun had come up and then suddenly gone down again."

At Alamogordo, our security officer watched the cloud of atomic dust rise to a height of 40,000 feet and lamented: "You might as well try to keep the Mississippi River a secret." The switchboard at the *New Mexican* lighted up with inquiries that day, but the newspaper could print only the official cover-up press release saying that the brilliant flash and mushroom cloud were caused by an accidental explosion in a remote ammunition dump.

But on August 6, the fiery cat was out of the bag. Even then few dared to think what the bombing of Hiroshima and the beginning of the atomic age might mean to us. Instead, the *New Mexican* that day reported with peculiar humor the speculations of people outside Los Alamos' gates about our work. It had been thought that the Los Alamos scientists were working night and day on jet fuels, on death rays, or on development of windshield wipers for submarines. Some Santa Fe women had convinced themselves that Los Alamos really was nothing more than a hospital for expectant WAVES and WACS.

The newspaper did take an oblique look into the future in reporting a conversation between two ladies at the Santa Fe library: "One said, 'Oh, gracious, I'm afraid to live in such a dangerous place!' 'But, dear,' said the other, 'maybe this new whatchamacallit will heat our homes. Think how nice that would be. You must look on the bright side of things.'"

There were those who had wondered, more seriously, about the mysterious secret of Los Alamos. The military personnel, the guards, and the WACS had seen us daily—but still were in the dark.

One day I was driven down the winding mountain road to the airport by an obviously disgruntled WAC. I asked her if she liked her work.

She replied frankly: "No!"

"Why not?"

"Look," she said. "My girl friend is in Egypt. I am here. When the war ends, we'll both go home, and people will ask us what our jobs were. She will say she was in El Alamein.

"'And what were you doing there?'

"'Driving a truck loaded with explosives.'

"'What for?'

"'We had to get the explosives to Montgomery so he could beat Rommel.'

"And then they will ask me, 'What did *you* do?'

"'I was in New Mexico in a place called Los Alamos.'

"'What did you do?'

"'I drove someone name of Teller to the airport.'

"'What for?'

"'I don't know.'"

Her attitude was typical of the military people at Los Alamos. They did not know what we were doing, and they yearned for an active part in the fighting of the war. On the day Hiroshima was bombed, their attitude changed completely. They knew, then, what we had been doing, and they felt that they had been a part of it. After that day, when I showed my pass to the guard at the Los Alamos gate, he smiled.

The occurrences of many years prepared me for the day of Hiroshima. But I am sure that I had not been prepared sufficiently.

I was a member—and proudly so—of a group of Hungarian scientists who came to the United States during the decade preceding World War II. The oldest of us is Theodore von Karman, the great hydrodynamitian with a twinkle in his eye and many good stories in his conversations, who contributed immeasureably toward improvements of American airplanes. Leo Szilard, who prodded us into working on atomic energy, never would be caught saying or doing anything that was expected of him. Eugene Wigner, who did the most toward developing the theory of the nucleus and our nuclear reactors, is so absurdly courteous that he has created a legend of Hungarian politeness. John von Neumann, who pioneered the development of computers, was said to be the only human with a mind faster than an electronic brain.

The members of this group are quite different, and yet people say they see similarities. Perhaps this is because we all were survivors of the shipwreck of Hungary. We all escaped Nazism and Communism after having had a horrifying look at a world that was not free.

I started my scientific work in Germany during the declining years of the Weimar Republic. For as long as I could remember, I had wanted to do one thing: to play with ideas and find out how the world is put together. Then, in Göttingen in 1932, I heard something from a Russian mathematician that puzzled me, warned me, and started me on a long road.

I vividly remember taking a long walk in Göttingen with my Russian friend. He also had been fascinated by pure science. To my surprise and shock, he told me that he was returning to Russia to work on airplane designs. I asked how a man of his interests could possibly abandon pure mathematical research. I shall not forget his reply: "With Hitler on the rise, we scientists no longer can be frivolous. We cannot play around with ideas and theories. We must go to work."

Three years later I came to the United States. I still was playing with theories. But, year by year, I had become more worried. I was teaching at George Washington University in the nation's capital. It was there, subsequently, that I decided to devote my energies to the development of nuclear weapons.

The decision began to take shape in January 1939. That month I helped organize a scientific conference on low temperatures, a subject far removed from nuclear weapons. But on the night before the conference began, George Gamow, whom I respect as a scientist and enjoy as a friend with an uninhibited sense of humor, called on the telephone: "Bohr has just come in. He has gone crazy. He says a neutron can split uranium."

I knew that Niels Bohr, the great Danish scientist who taught all of us our atomic physics, could not be crazy. And I remembered that when Enrico Fermi, working in Italy, had bombarded uranium with neutrons, a great variety of radioactive substances were produced. Like hundreds of other physicists before me, I suddenly understood the obvious. The next day, as Bohr talked at the conference about a subject very different from low temperatures, I knew what was coming. He explained in detail that when a neutron hits the nucleus of a uranium atom, the entire nucleus is split into two pieces, and the two fragments are forced away from each other with a tremendous velocity.

Although I had been prepared for Bohr's description of fission, I was completely unprepared for the reaction of one scientist at the conference. Obviously concerned, he took me aside: "Let's be careful. Let's not talk about this too much." I agreed, and concentrated on returning the conference to the subject of low temperatures.

On the night the conference ended—when my wife, Mici, and I were ready to collapse under the strain of our social-scientific burdens as hostess and host of the meeting—Leo Szilard, who we thought was far from Washington, telephoned: "I am at the railroad station. Can you pick me up?"

Mici protested: "No! We both are much too tired. He must go to a hotel." But we did meet him at the depot, and, to my surprise, Mici said: "You must, of course, stay with us."

We drove to our home, and I showed Szilard to his room. He felt the bed suspiciously, then turned to me suddenly and said: "Is there a hotel nearby?" There was, and he continued: "Good! I have just remembered sleeping in this bed before. It is much too hard."

But before he left, he sat on the edge of the hard bed and talked excitedly: "You heard Bohr on fission?"

"Yes," I replied.

Szilard continued: "You know what that means!" Perhaps the splitting of the uranium nucleus might, itself, create more neutrons. These could split additional nuclei. We might have a chain reaction and release many more neutrons and, in the end, a fantastic amount of energy. The question was whether a splitting nucleus would create more neutrons, and the answer to this question was important. Said Szilard: "Hitler's success could depend on it."

A few weeks later I was at my piano, attempting with the collaboration of a friend and his violin to make Mozart sound like Mozart, when the telephone rang. It was Szilard, calling from New York. He spoke to me in Hungarian, and he said only one thing: "I have found the neutrons." I was unhappy about those neutrons. They presented, to me, an inescapable challenge. I guessed, then, that I would be unable to continue playing with theories.

Later that summer I was given my first atomic assignment. I was drafted as chauffeur for Szilard, who never had descended to the mechanical skill of driving a car. He had an appointment with Albert Einstein at Peconic Bay, N.Y., that was to have a profound effect on the future of the United States. It was August 2, 1939, and during their meeting Szilard and Einstein discussed a letter addressed to "F. D. Roosevelt" at the White House. It read:

Sir:
Some recent work by E. Fermi and L. Szilard, which has been communicated to me in manuscript, leads me to expect that the element uranium may be turned into a new and important source of energy in the immediate future.

Certain aspects of the situation which has arisen seem to call for watchfulness and, if necessary, quick action on the part of the Administration. I believe therefore that it is my duty to bring to your attention the following facts and recommendations:

In the course of the last four months it has been made probable —through the work of Joliot as well as Fermi and Szilard, in America—that it may become possible to set up a nuclear chain reaction in a large mass of uranium, by which vast amounts of power and large quantities of new radium-like elements would be generated. Now it appears almost certain that this could be achieved in the immediate future.

This new phenomenon would also lead to the construction of bombs, and it is conceivable—though less certain—that extremely powerful bombs of a new type may thus be constructed. A single bomb of this type, carried by boat and exploded in a port, might very well destroy the whole port together with some of the surrounding territory. However, such bombs might well prove to be too heavy for transportation by air.

The United States has only very poor ores in uranium in moderate quantities. There is some good ore in Canada and the former Czechoslovakia, while the most important source of uranium is Belgian Congo.

In view of this situation you may think it desirable to have some permanent contact maintained between the Administration and the group of physicists working on chain reactions in America. One possible way of achieving this might be for you to entrust with this task a person who has your confidence and who could perhaps serve in an unofficial capacity. His task might comprise the following:

A—To approach Government departments, keep them informed of the further development, and put forward recommendations for Government action, giving particular attention to the problem of securing a supply of uranium ore for the United States.

B—To speed up the experimental work, which at present is being carried on within the limits of the budgets of university laboratories, by providing funds, if such funds are required, through his contacts with private persons who are willing to make contributions for this cause, and perhaps also by obtaining the co-operation of industrial laboratories which have the necessary equipment.

I understand that Germany has actually stopped the sale of uranium from the Czechoslovakian mines which she has taken over. That she should have taken such early action might perhaps be understood on the ground that the son of the German under-secretary of state, Von Weizsacker, is attached to the Kaiser-Wilhelm Institute in Berlin where some of the American work on uranium is now being repeated.

Yours very truly,

The letter was signed with the name that would carry the greatest scientific impact for President Roosevelt: "A. Einstein."

This letter launched the atomic bomb project in the United States.

I still had not decided that I should devote myself to work on weapons. The war already was raging in Europe, and I knew that I could make a contribution toward weapons development. But I worried, on moral grounds, about whether I should.

Almost a year after the Einstein-Szilard letter had been drafted on Long Island, President Roosevelt was scheduled to speak briefly at the Eighth Congress of Pan-American Scientists in Washington. Even though I knew the President was to speak, I did not plan to attend. I had made it a practice to avoid politics, and I considered any political speech a waste of time. But The Netherlands was invaded on the day Roosevelt was to talk. This changed my mind, and I went to hear him.

He spoke for only about twenty minutes. This was the first of his famous timetable talks. Discussing geographical distances, he made it clear that we were living in a small and dangerous world: He talked of distances between cities and nations, and of how few hours were required by bombers to cover those distances.

I knew he had received the Einstein letter, and I knew the government's atomic project already was in its beginning stages. So some of President Roosevelt's remarks carried a special significance for me. He said: "The great achievements of science . . . are only instruments by which men try to do the things they most want to do. . . . Surely it is time for our Republics . . . to use every knowledge, every science we possess. . . . You and I, in the long run, if it be necessary, will act together to protect and defend by every means at our command our science, our culture, our American freedom and our civilization."

I concluded that President Roosevelt was telling us that the duty of scientists was to see that the most effective weapons would be available for use if necessary, that we would stand morally guilty before the free world if we refused to lend our talents to the cause of the free world.

President Roosevelt's talk answered my last doubts. I left the meeting feeling that I was committed to do whatever I could— regardless of the ultimate consequences—to help provide the instruments of strength for the defense of freedom.

So it was that I felt no qualms of personal conscience about my work on the atomic bomb. My moral decision had been made in 1941. That was the year I joined the effort to produce an atomic bomb. That was the year I became an American citizen.

But, in the spring of 1945, I did become worried about the way the atomic bomb might be used. My apprehension reached a high plateau several months before Hiroshima when I received a letter at Los Alamos from Szilard. He asked my support for a petition urging that the United States would not use the atomic bomb in warfare without first warning the enemy.

I was in absolute agreement, and prepared to circulate Szilard's petition among the scientists at Los Alamos. But it was my duty, first, to discuss the question with the director of the Los Alamos Laboratory, Dr. J. Robert Oppenheimer. He was the constituted authority at Los Alamos. But he was more: His brilliant mind, his quick intellect, and his penetrating interest in everyone at the laboratory made him our natural leader as well. He seemed to be the obvious man to turn to with any formidable problem, particularly political.

Oppenheimer told me, in a polite and convincing way, that he thought it improper for a scientist to use his prestige as a platform for political pronouncements. He conveyed to me in glowing terms the deep concern, thoroughness, and wisdom with which these questions were being handled in Washington. Our fate was in the hands of the best, the most conscientious men of our nation. And they had information which we did not possess. Oppenheimer's words lifted a great weight from my heart. I was happy to accept his word and his authority. I did not circulate Szilard's petition. Today I regret that I did not.

I can appreciate the reasons for the fateful decision to drop an atomic bomb without warning. The men who made the decision thought that a quick end to the war would save many lives, Japanese and American. But I do regret that decision. I am convinced that the tragic surprise bombing was not necessary. We could have exploded the bomb at a very high altitude over Tokyo in the evening. Triggered at a high altitude, the bomb would have created a sudden, frightening daylight over the city. But it would have killed no one. After the bomb had been demonstrated—after we were sure that it was not a dud—we could have told the Japanese what it was and what would happen if another atomic bomb were detonated at low altitude.

Implicit in our decision to drop the atomic bomb without warning was the hope that a surprise attack of such magnitude would frighten the Japanese into surrender. A nighttime atomic explosion high over Tokyo, in full sight of Emperor Hirohito and his Cabinet, would have been just as terrifying as Hiroshima. And it would have frightened the right people.

After the Tokyo demonstration, we could have delivered an ultimatum for Japan's surrender. The ultimatum, I believe, would have been met, and the atomic bomb could have been used more humanely but just as effectively to bring a quick end to the war. But, to my knowledge, such an unannounced, high-altitude demonstration over Tokyo at night was never proposed.

The recommendation that the atomic bomb should be used against Japan without specific warning was made in June 1945 by an Interim Committee appointed to advise President Truman on nuclear policy. Chairman of the committee was Secretary of War Henry L. Stimson. Nuclear physicists advising the Interim Committee were Drs. Oppenheimer, Fermi, Arthur H. Compton, and Ernest O. Lawrence.

The advisory panel of nuclear physicists was instructed to investigate the possibility of demonstrating the bomb's terrible destructive powers without killing anyone. Lawrence pressed for a demonstration explosion of the bomb before international observers. New Mexico, desert islands, and evacuated areas of Japan itself were all suggested as locations for the atomic show. But the panel could not agree on a concrete and foolproof demonstration plan, and so submitted its final report: "We can propose no technical demonstration likely to bring an end to the war; we can see no acceptable alternative to direct military use."

Before the advisory panel's report was received, weeks before the Alamogordo test had proved beyond doubt that we actually had a workable atomic bomb, members of the Interim Committee reached a unanimous decision on the way the bomb should be used. After this recommendation had been carried to President Truman and after the physicists' report had been received, one member of the Interim Committee began having serious second thoughts; Navy Undersecretary Ralph A. Bard declared in a secret memo: "Japan should have some preliminary warning for say two or three days in advance of use. The position of the United States as a great humanitarian nation and the fair play attitude of our people generally is responsible in the main for this feeling."

But the Interim Committee's recommendations, already transmitted to President Truman, had been unanimous: The bomb should be used against Japan—without specific warning—as soon as possible.

We learned the facts about an atomic explosion at Alamogordo. Los Alamos, in the days and weeks immediately before this climax of our two-billion-dollar experiment, was alive with feverish activity. We were on the verge, in the New Mexican desert, of making a laboratory test on a scale never before attempted in the history of science. The time finally had come for us to know, beyond doubt, whether our calculations were correct, whether we really knew what we were doing.

Before Alamogordo, I asked for and obtained a most important assignment, one that many considered superfluous. There had been some suggestions that we might have miscalculated, that the explosion could be much larger than we had anticipated. Could the enormity of the atomic bomb be even more enormous? Might we set off a chain reaction that would encircle the globe in a sea of fire? It was my job to make a last check and review.

I spent a great deal of time indulging in controlled fantasies, trying to dream up new, undiscovered laws of nature that a sudden release of atomic energy might bring into play. There was a possibility that the test blast might touch off a natural phenomenon that was not contrary to our knowledge, but perhaps beyond our experience. The possibility of error, most of the time, could be tolerated in our conclusions. But in this case the last vestige of doubt had to be removed.

I could find no reason to believe that the test shot would touch off the destruction of the world, no reason to think that our advance calculations were not entirely correct, no reason to say that the Alamogordo experiment should not be made. The effects of the nuclear experiment would be limited; this was a mathematical certainty.

Most of the Los Alamos scientists, however, were not concerned with such grim thoughts as the possible end of the world. There was, instead, a general feeling of relief and exhilaration among the men on the slopes of our mesa. We were, after all, nearing the end of an intensive effort. We were about to discover, once and for all, whether we had been right or wrong.

Early on the morning of July 16, 1945, I was one of a group watching the explosion of the world's first atomic bomb. Our observation post was about twenty miles from the Alamogordo test site. We were told to lie down on the sand, turn our faces away from the blast, and bury our heads in our arms. No one complied. We were determined to look the beast in the eye.

But, having practiced to expect the impossible, I was cautious. Beneath the welder's glasses provided us, I wore an extra pair of dark glasses. I smeared my face with sun-tan lotion and offered some to the others. I wore a heavy pair of gloves. Holding the welder's glasses securely to my face with both gloved hands, I converted the glasses into goggles.

The test, delayed ninety minutes by a desert rainstorm, was rescheduled for 5:30 A.M. Twenty minutes before, our observation post was tied in with the control center by radio. The count-down began: "It now is minus twenty minutes, nineteen minutes, eighteen minutes, seventeen minutes . . . It now is minus thirty seconds, twenty-five, twenty, fifteen." At ten, the count-down was second by second: "Nine . . . eight . . . seven . . . six . . . five." Then there was silence.

The five seconds of quiet stretched out until I thought the explosion had failed. I was almost ready to take off my protective glasses. But then, through the glasses, I saw a tiny pin point of light. I was disappointed: "Is this all? Is this what we have worked so hard to develop?"

In a second, I remembered that I was wearing a double thickness of dark glasses. The pin point of light grew and then faded. I tipped my right hand away from my face to allow a crack of light beneath my glasses. It was like opening the heavy curtains of a darkened room to a flood of sunlight. Then I was impressed.

In a minute, the explosion's noise and pressure wave reached us. William H. Lawrence, the well-known and competent science reporter, was alarmed: "What was that?"

I took off both pairs of dark glasses to watch the explosion's remarkable mushroom cloud swell into the atmosphere, stop when it hit a layer of warm air, and then shoot up again. As the cloud towered 40,000 feet above us, we trooped back toward our bus, and we realized that the next atomic explosion would be something very different from an experiment.

The desert winds, blowing in varying directions at different altitudes, shaped the mushroom cloud into a giant question mark.

It was midmorning, three weeks later, before I learned about Hiroshima.

I left my apartment to walk along the Jemez Mesa to the Los Alamos Laboratory. On the way, I saw one of the laboratory's scientists sitting in a jeep parked beneath the Los Alamos water tower. His face was exuberant. He was as exhilarated as a victorious boxer. He called to me excitedly: "One down!"

I did not know what he meant, and walked on toward the laboratory. There I heard the news. But the news of Hiroshima created no exuberance, no exhilaration, no elation among most of the Los Alamos scientists that morning. There was, instead, a clear and strong feeling of worry, a deep concern, a great anxiety. A new force was in the world. What this new force would do to our thoughts, actions, and lives, no one could guess.

The United States Strategic Bombing Survey learned after the war's end that Emperor Hirohito and his senior statesmen agreed in February of 1945—six months before we bombed Hiroshima— that Japan faced certain defeat and should seek peace.

One week after American troops landed on Okinawa in April 1945, Admiral Baron Kantaro Suzuki was named Japan's premier. He later told the Survey team: "It was the Emperor's desire to make every effort to bring the war to a conclusion as quickly as possible, and that was my purpose."

In May of 1945, Emperor Hirohito's representatives in Moscow asked Russia to help negotiate a peace between Japan and the United States. Prince Fumimaro Konoye was selected as a special Japanese emissary to Russia to press for a negotiated peace. On

July 12, Emperor Hirohito called Prince Konoye into private audience and gave him explicit and secret instructions to agree to end the war at any cost, no matter how severe the surrender terms. But the next day, on July 13, Moscow told Tokyo that both Stalin and Molotov were leaving for the Potsdam Conference and Russia could not consider intercession until after their return.

At Potsdam on July 26—just ten days after we tested our first atomic bomb at Alamogordo—the Allied Powers issued an ultimatum for Japan to surrender unconditionally or face "prompt and utter destruction."

The Potsdam ultimatum sent the six members of Emperor Hirohito's Inner Cabinet into intensive deliberations. Not a single member of the Inner Cabinet had any objections to ending the war. But the War Minister and two chiefs of staff thought the terms of unconditional surrender were "too dishonorable." Premier Suzuki and other members of the Inner Cabinet had decided, even before the Potsdam Declaration was issued, that they probably could end the war only by broadcasting a direct appeal to the United States. But the dissidents in the Inner Cabinet continued to hope that Russia would intercede to negotiate a peace.

Even after the atomic bombs exploded over Japan, the Inner Cabinet remained divided as before—three to three—on the Potsdam ultimatum. Then Emperor Hirohito himself intervened. He laid the question of unconditional surrender before his full Cabinet. And the Cabinet decided to sue for peace.

Would the course of history have been different had we demonstrated an atomic bomb over Tokyo? Would such a nighttime demonstration have convinced the Emperor and the dissidents in his Inner Cabinet that they should seek peace immediately and unconditionally? Could we have avoided the tragedy of Hiroshima? Could we have started the atomic age with clean hands?

No one knows. No one can find out.

This we do know: Hiroshima has haunted many scientists and has distorted the judgment of quite a few United States policy makers. The idea has become fixed in the minds of our people that atomic weapons are instruments of indiscriminate destruction.

The atomic age presents us with opportunities, challenges, and dangers. Hiroshima stands at the beginning of this age. This fact has made our hard task even more difficult. In 1945, we used too much force. Later we were to turn away from our new power at a time when nuclear instruments would be most important to ourselves and to the free world.

We cannot expect that our society and our government never should make mistakes in times of crisis. Even if Hiroshima was a mistake, I continue to place my confidence in our democratic society and in our methods of reaching decisions. The most vital decisions can and must be made by our people and by their elected representatives. Still, if a mistake has been made, it is important to recognize this fact. My purpose is to make a contribution toward right decisions in the future.

The first act of the atomic drama has brought me to two convictions:

It was necessary and right to develop the atomic bomb.

It was unnecessary and wrong to bomb Hiroshima without specific warning.

CHAPTER TWO

The Vanishing Advantage

THE MOUNTAIN QUIET of Los Alamos was shattered suddenly on the evening of August 14, 1945. A wild racket broke upon the serenity of Jemez Mesa in a single instant, as if by prearranged signal. Sirens whined. Bells rang. Dozens of automobile horns blasted. I thought a giant traffic jam somehow had developed in the quiet streets. The cacophony was completed by the sounds of people running and shouting to each other. I rushed from my apartment to investigate the commotion, and soon discovered its cause: Japan had surrendered. The war was over.

The 10,000 people at Los Alamos, to varying degrees, thought of the Japanese capitulation as a personal victory. Nearly everyone—the guard at the gate, the scientist in the laboratory, my WAC driver—was intensely proud of Los Alamos' contribution to the rapid and dramatic ending of the war. Each knew, finally, that his wartime effort had been meaningful.

The victory over Japan was celebrated at a score of Los Alamos parties, jubilant affairs feeding on the first flush of victory. No one at Los Alamos slept that night.

But even while the party-goers congratulated themselves and toasted the peaceful future, we knew that the vigorous work at Los Alamos was coming to an end and that the laboratory itself was facing a deadly crisis.

After Hiroshima, most Los Alamos scientists were profoundly disturbed by the questionable morality of using the atomic bomb without first warning the Japanese. After Nagasaki, the moral doubts deepened. After the war's end, relieved scientists who wanted no more of weapons work began fleeing to the sanctuary of university laboratories and classrooms.

Los Alamos scientists were not the only people, after the war, to lose their appetites for weapons development. Government officials in Washington did, too. Comfortable in the easy assurances that no other nation could develop an atomic bomb for at least 20 years, the government after World War II all but abandoned its support of weapons work. To emphasize the fact that the United States no longer was interested in working on nuclear weapons, the birthplace of the atomic bomb was given a new name: the Los Alamos Scientific Laboratory.

I could understand those at Los Alamos who wanted to get back to pure science. I also was most anxious to return to the kind of pure scientific research that was my first love. And I had been invited to join the faculty of the University of Chicago to work with Enrico Fermi, the brilliant Italian winner of the Nobel Prize who had begun experiments in the bombardment of uranium atoms as early as 1934. But I was torn in two directions. I knew that disintegration of the Los Alamos Laboratory could be a threat to America's future.

Before I could accept or reject the Chicago offer, I was approached by the new director of the Los Alamos Scientific Laboratory, Norris Bradbury. He asked me to stay at Los Alamos as chief of the laboratory's theoretical division. I said I would remain only if the laboratory's intensive level of theoretical work could be maintained and channeled toward either of two goals: Development of a hydrogen bomb or refinement of atomic explosions. I said we either should make a great effort to build a hydrogen bomb in the shortest possible time or develop new models of fission explosives and speed progress by at least a dozen tests a year. Bradbury said he would like to see either program, but that neither was realistic. There no longer was governmental support for weapons work. No one was interested.

I took my problem to Oppenheimer, seeking his advice and support. I told him about my conversation with Bradbury, and then said: "This has been your laboratory, and its future depends upon you. I will stay if you tell me that you will use your influence to help me accomplish either of my goals, if you will help enlist support for work toward a hydrogen bomb or further development of the atomic bomb."

Oppenheimer's reply was quick: "I neither can nor will do so."

It was obvious and clear to me that Oppenheimer did not want to support further weapons work in any way. It was equally obvious that only a man of Oppenheimer's stature could arouse governmental interest in either program. I was not willing to work without backing, and told Oppenheimer that I would go to Chicago. He smiled: "You are doing the right thing."

That evening both Oppenheimer and I attended a party at a friend's home. Oppenheimer approached and asked: "Now that you have decided to go to Chicago, don't you feel better?"

I really did not feel better, and said so. I felt that our wartime work had been only a beginning.

Oppenheimer closed the subject by saying: "We have done a wonderful job here, and it will be many years before anyone can improve on our work in any way."

On February 1, 1946, I left Los Alamos for Chicago.

The United States, immediately after World War II, had a unique opportunity to ensure peace. The people of the world were sick of war, and the ending of history's greatest conflict produced world-wide elation. At the same time, the world was shocked and frightened by the atomic bomb. Only the United States had the bomb. Only the United States had the opportunity to use this big atomic stick to back up a proposal that would ensure peace. But we let the opportunity slip by, and it never can return.

When the war ended, the United States had no blueprint for pressing its atomic advantage. We stumbled forward with no concrete plan, no national policy outlining the conversion of our awesome weapon of war into a significant instrument for peace. I cannot believe that President Roosevelt, who spent two billion dollars in secret to develop the atomic bomb, intended to use the weapon only to end the war. He was a man who thought ahead, and he made concessions to Russia at Yalta that could be carried out only in a peaceful world. He nursed the plans for a new world organization, the United Nations. I cannot rid myself of the thought that President Roosevelt may have planned to use the existence of the atomic bomb, after the war, as a powerful driving force toward world government.

But Roosevelt died. No one could replace him. He was the leader who had victoriously defended the free world. He had the most powerful country in the world behind him, and he was trusted throughout the world. He was irreplaceable. But he made a terrible and unforgivable mistake: He left the United States with an uninformed Vice President who had been kept completely in the dark about our atomic work and plans for our atomic future.

Harry Truman knew nothing about the atomic bomb project until after he took the oath as President on the night of April 12, 1945. An hour after becoming President, Truman was told by Secretary of War Stimson that the United States was developing a weapon of fantastic power. Days passed before Truman learned the details of the atomic bomb project. When Truman became President, that project was only five months from completion.

At Hyde Park on the previous September 18, Roosevelt and Winston Churchill had agreed: "When a 'bomb' is finally available, it might perhaps, after mature consideration, be used against the Japanese, who should be warned that this bombardment would be repeated until they surrender." Eventual use of the bomb thus was broadly outlined before Truman became President, before he even knew that an atomic bomb was being developed. Inheriting the tremendous responsibility of a wartime presidency with no knowledge of the atomic project, anyone would be inclined to let events develop as planned. This Truman did.

But this was a tragic mistake: We used the bomb without warning. A plan for the atomic future laid before the United Nations on the day of Hiroshima would have had a wonderful effect, but we made a second mistake: We ended the war without a complete and clear-cut plan of what to do next.

Seven months after Hiroshima, the United States finally developed a workable plan for world-wide control of atomic energy. This report from a special Board of Consultants, appointed on January 23, 1946, by Dean Acheson, was presented "not as a final plan, but as a place to begin, a foundation on which to build."

The Board of Consultants was headed by David E. Lilienthal, chairman of the Tennessee Valley Authority. But the one person on the five-man board who really understood the issues and problems, and who emerged as chief author of the board's report, was J. Robert Oppenheimer. When the board's report was made public by the Secretary of State in March 1946, it was known as the Acheson-Lilienthal Report. Later, when Bernard Baruch fought for adoption of the plan in the United Nations, it became known as the Baruch Plan. It might well have been called the Oppenheimer plan.

The plan was a good one. It "concluded that there is no prospect of security against atomic warfare in international agreements controlled only by inspection and other police-like methods." Instead of confining its report to inspection procedures and other negative phases of the control problem, the board maintained: "Only if the dangerous aspects of atomic energy are taken out of national hands and placed in international hands is there any reasonable prospect of devising safeguards against the use of atomic energy for bombs, and only if the international agency was engaged in development and operation could it possibly discharge adequately its functions as a safeguarder of the world's future."

The board, in short, recommended establishment of an Atomic Development Authority that literally would control atomic energy from the cradle to the grave, from the mine to the bomb. The board held that the international agency should own or control the world's supplies of the raw materials of atomic energy, uranium and thorium; it should own and operate the world's atomic reactors and separation plants; it should co-operate with nations and private institutions in atomic research, but through the licensing of raw materials necessary for research it should maintain rigid inspection standards and control of all atomic work.

The board's plan for an international atomic authority was complex, and it was a bold departure from prevailing public opinion. It was ingenious, reasonable, and workable. Most important, the plan offered an opportunity for true international co-operation that could have led to exclusively peaceful, beneficial uses of atomic power.

The final conclusion of the report gave an inspiring view of the future: "When fully in operation, the plan . . . can provide a great measure of security against surprise attack. It can do much more than that. It can create deterrents to the initiation of schemes of aggression, and it can establish patterns of co-operation among nations, which may contribute to the solution of the problem of war itself. When the plan is in full operation there will no longer be secrets about atomic energy. We believe that this is the firmest basis of security; for in the long term there can be no international control and no international co-operation which does not presuppose an international community of knowledge."

It is to President Truman's credit that when the Acheson-Lilienthal Report finally was prepared and laid before him, he made it his Administration's policy to urge it upon the United Nations. To help make the Baruch Plan a reality, we terminated our wartime agreements to pool atomic knowledge with Britain and Canada. This made sense. Our wartime pacts should not have been allowed to remain as roadblocks to true international co-operation.

But the plan came too late, and there was a basic flaw in the Acheson-Lilienthal Report: It was based on the mistaken belief that we knew everything about atomic power, and Russia knew nothing. Most Americans could not understand why Russia did not snap at the nuclear co-operation offered by the Baruch Plan. The United States thought it was being magnanimous in offering to share with the whole world, including Russia, atomic information that we considered secret and valuable. The joke was on us, and the joke was that Russia already had our valuable secrets. Russia did not need the Baruch Plan. Russia had Klaus Fuchs.

Russia had other spies reporting on the progress of British-American atomic efforts, of course, but Klaus Fuchs certainly was their most valuable agent. He worked at the hard-core center of our atomic effort. The Joint Congressional Committee on Atomic Energy found, after Fuchs' arrest, that he alone had "influenced the safety of more people and accomplished greater damage than any other spy . . . in the history of nations."

Fuchs and a handful of others gave Russia a tremendous advantage. In June of 1944, few Americans outside New Mexico knew what we were doing at Los Alamos. But the Russians knew. In June of 1945, the Russians knew that the world's first atomic explosion was scheduled for the next month. In September of 1945, Russia had a detailed description of the bomb dropped on Nagasaki the month before, and Russia knew it was different from the bomb that had been dropped on Hiroshima. The Russians knew, from Fuchs, essentially everything we were doing at Los

Alamos to develop an atomic bomb from August 1944 until the day the bomb exploded over Hiroshima.

Fuchs gave Russia the advantage of knowing that our impossible project was possible, that an atomic bomb really could be developed.

I knew Fuchs at Los Alamos. He was by no means an introvert, but he was a quiet man. I rather liked him. As a full-fledged member of the British team at Los Alamos, he was entitled to know everything we were doing. He had full access to the laboratory's secret work. He talked with me and others frequently and in depth about our intensive efforts to produce an atomic bomb. It was easy and pleasant to discuss my work with him. He also made impressive contributions, and I learned many technical facts from him.

But none of us penetrated his quiet reserve.

Like so many men who grew up with the political turbulence of the 1920s and the 1930s in Europe, Fuchs thought that he had to make a choice between Nazism and Communism. He chose Communism, deeply convinced that anything else was essentially Nazism or Facism in disguise. Fuchs joined the German Communist Party in 1932, when he was twenty-one years old. The next year he fled to England as a political refugee from Hitler's Nazis. Eventually interned in Canada, he was screened and freed in 1942 to help with Britain's atomic research. Back in England, Fuchs worked with a German physicist, Rudolph Peierls, on isotope separation by the diffusion process, the process that led to construction of our huge facility at Oak Ridge. When Peierls came to Los Alamos in 1944, he brought Fuchs with him.

Fuchs was popular at Los Alamos because he was kind, helpful, and much interested in the work of others. But his exceptional intelligence was combined with excessive reticence. Mrs. Peierls, at Los Alamos parties, called him "Penny-in-the-slot Fuchs," because in order to get a sentence out of him she had to drop a sentence into him. He never talked unless there was a reason for talking. Later, after he was arrested, I understood why.

Fuchs' reserve seldom abandoned him, and he seldom attracted attention in a group. But he drew my notice at a certain Los Alamos dinner party in a way that later seemed significant. The dinner guests' excited conversation concentrated on that day's arrest of Allan Nunn May, a British physicist working in Canada, for giving atomic secrets to the Russians. Some of the dinner guests knew May and liked him. They could not believe he was a spy. Others maintained that we should not have been surprised, that spying had to be expected.

When we left the dinner party, I asked my wife what had been bothering Fuchs. His behavior, although not unusual, seemed to indicate that something was wrong. He had not argued with the others about May, but he never argued. He had remained silent, but he usually was silent. Still, it somehow seemed clear to Mici and me that of all the people at the party, Fuchs had been most deeply affected by May's arrest.

I neither defend nor excuse Fuchs' spying. But I am convinced that he spied because he thought he was doing the right thing for the country and the political philosophy that commanded his allegiance. Russia, however, found it difficult to believe that anyone would undertake the enormous risks of a spy only to satisfy his conscience. Fuchs did what he arrogantly thought was right, but Russia refused to accept this as a contribution to World Communism. Russia insisted on paying for his information. In the sordid story of Fuchs' spying, this payment was the most shameful episode. The Russian payments were trifling. The largest was $400. Fuchs, unmarried, did not need the money, but accepted it "as a symbol of subservience to Russia." The purpose of the Russians in paying anything at all was clear: If he were caught, Fuchs would be treated as a hired spy rather than as a Communist visionary.

When he was arrested in England in 1950, and sentenced to fourteen years in prison for his betrayal, Fuchs offered a coldly analytical explanation of how he had managed to circulate among us without being suspected: "I used my Marxian philosophy to conceal my thoughts in two separate compartments. One side was the man I wanted to be. I could be free and easy and happy with other people without fear of disclosing myself, because I knew the other compartment would step in if I reached the danger point. . . . Looking back on it now, the best way is to call it a controlled schizophrenia."

Many Americans believe that Russia could not have produced an atomic bomb without the information supplied by Fuchs and other spies. This I doubt. From what I have seen of the competence of Russian scientists, I am positive they could have produced an atomic explosion with no outside help. But the knowledge that an atomic bomb actually could be produced, that it was a fact and not a mere theory, was a powerful spur to the Russian achievement. Hiroshima and Fuchs' information prompted the Kremlin to give full governmental support to Russian scientists working in nuclear physics, organizing Russia's atomic efforts to a degree that might not have been attained for years. Fuchs reported and Hiroshima proved to Russia that atomic success was possible.

If the spies did not make a Russian atomic bomb possible, they made it possible a little sooner. They contributed to the disappearance of our advantage. The United States still had some advantage when we proposed the Baruch Plan, but Russia already had the secrets we were proposing to share. This was the most important result of the work of Fuchs and his fellow spies, and this is the saddest part of their story: They effectively doomed the Baruch Plan that would have ensured world peace.

Americans did not seem to care. Thinking they had an atomic monopoly that experts insisted would continue for another twenty years, the American people pushed the problem of international controls aside. We did not bother to reinstate our atomic agreements with wartime allies. Despite the continuing and increasing Russian menace, we allowed nuclear unity between ourselves and other Western nations to disintegrate.

Our advantage began to fade.

Spies, the slowdown of our laboratories, the disintegration of information exchanges with our allies, and Russian stalling on the Baruch Plan—all co-operated to undermine our advantage. So did the exaggerated importance we placed on secrecy in the naïve belief that secrecy would ensure our atomic monopoly.

I vividly recall one postwar conference that I attended during a visit to Los Alamos from Chicago. The conference was with Air Force officials in Albuquerque. The purpose: To find out what kind of nuclear explosives the Air Force wanted us to develop.

We explained that the size of the two bombs already dropped by the Air Force had been influenced by the size of Air Force planes. They had to fit into a B-29. But, we explained, development of a variety of nuclear weapons was possible. They could be bigger, smaller, more or less powerful than the bombs dropped on Hiroshima and Nagasaki. We sought guidance: What were the Air Force requirements?

This conference lasted all of one day. To my astonishment, we could get only one answer: "The bomb we have now is precisely what we need." It became obvious during the day that few of the military men involved in the conference had any notion of how an atomic explosive worked, and even fewer had any concept of what future atomic explosions could accomplish.

What was the reason for this amazing lack of knowledge about atomic explosives and their capabilities? Was it a lack of imagination? A lack of interest? A lack of intelligence? Or was it, perhaps, secrecy?

None of us easily accepts new ideas. Human inertia makes us cling to the old. With secrecy preventing discussion of all new facts, it was only natural that the military men should accept, in our bizarre atomic world, only those changes they had to accept. The "bomb" was an unassailable fact and had to be accepted. But there was no opportunity, because of secrecy, and no incentive, because of inertia, to think further ahead.

I am firmly convinced that in the early postwar years secrecy was a powerful barrier between military men who were clinging to the past and scientists who were turning away from what seemed a frightening future.

Despairing of getting any guidance from the Air Force officials in Albuquerque, we flew back to Los Alamos. On the way, Marshall Holloway, who then was in charge of weapons development at Los Alamos, remarked: "I never knew it was so difficult to find the horse's mouth."

In the summer of 1949, I was given a hint that our advantageous atomic position was about to vanish; but I did not recognize the hint.

I was in England attending a conference as chairman of the Atomic Energy Commission's first reactor safeguard committee. One evening I was invited to dine with the man who had the reputation of being the world's most silent nuclear physicist, Sir James Chadwick. According to his habit, Chadwick did not speak throughout the meal. Lady Chadwick, however, chatted gaily. Near the dinner's end, she inquired about mutual friends the Chadwicks had met at Los Alamos. She asked about General Leslie R. Groves, boss of the Manhattan Project. General Groves was not popular among scientists, and my reference to him was not particularly complimentary. I thought my remark was on safe social grounds, because Groves had been opposed to atomic cooperation with the British.

But my reference to Groves produced a most surprising reaction from Chadwick: He began talking. And he talked for an hour before I could get a word in edgewise. He insisted that Groves was most conscientious, that in high councils it was Groves rather than scientists who pressed for development of the atomic bomb, that it was Groves who had obviated unnecessary delays, that our strong international position was due to the efforts of Groves more than those of any other man, that he had given the United States a tremendous advantage.

Chadwick insisted on walking me to my hotel. He praised

Groves all the way. I protested: "Most scientists just couldn't get along with Groves, and he strongly opposed atomic co-operation with your own country."

Chadwick replied: "Yes, but he was a man of his word. He could be trusted. When he said he would do something, it was done."

I protested no more, but concentrated on Chadwick's unqualified praise of Groves. I knew there was some reason for the unexpected outburst; Chadwick never spoke without a reason. I decided that if a man of Chadwick's stature wanted to tell me something he considered important, I had better listen. At my door he took my hand and looked me squarely and seriously in the eye. He said: "I hope you will remember what I have said tonight."

Chadwick knew something which I did not yet know.

I sailed for the United States, and in a few days arrived for a briefing at the Pentagon.

During the briefing the officer in charge referred to something that everyone else in the room apparently had heard. He said: "Gentlemen, the President's announcement this morning was correct. It has been verified."

After the briefing I went to the front of the room and asked the officer: "What announcement?"

"You didn't hear it?"

"No."

"He said Russia has exploded an atomic bomb."

CHAPTER THREE:

The Hydrogen Bomb

FEW MODERN SCIENTIFIC achievements spring, full of life, from the mind of a single individual. Success demands teamwork. It depends upon hundreds of ideas and thousands of technical skills involved with conception and theory, a mass of detailed calculations and—finally—the actual engineering and construction of the device. Successful development of the hydrogen bomb in the United States was based on this kind of teamwork.

Another story, quite different and quite false, often is presented. A public apparently unprepared to grasp the enormous complexities of modern scientific-technical developments frequently is satisfied with outrageous oversimplifications. Too often only the name of a single individual is mentioned. People are left with the impression that he alone was responsible. This representation is both untrue and unjust. An emphasis on the interaction of many different minds and the contribution of many ideas would come closer to the truth and to the real excitement of modern science.

Inspiration for a hydrogen bomb came from the sun and the stars. A native son of Russia, George Gamow, initiated the theoretical work in the United States that ultimately led to the biggest man-made explosion.

Gamow escaped from Soviet Russia in 1933. The next year he joined the physics department of George Washington University, and on his suggestion I joined him there a year later. He infected me with his curiosity about what keeps the sun shining, and he inspired the first pure research into stellar energy in this country. Our early studies were purely abstract, with no thought of practical application.

Six years before coming to George Washington University, Gamow had reported in the Soviet Academy of Sciences on the work of a British physicist and a German physicist suggesting that the apparently inexhaustible energy of the stars was created by the collision of atomic nuclei. These tiny particles, minute even compared with atoms, contain a million times more energy than that released in a chemical explosion. But this tremendous energy, stored in the nuclei for a billion years, is released only when the nuclei collide; and collision is usually prevented by the electrical repulsion of the nuclei. Exceedingly high temperatures deep in the interiors of stars, Gamow reported, set up a thermal agitation permitting an occasional collision of nuclei. This leads to a coalescence or fusion of small nuclei into larger units, and this process is the very opposite of fission—which still was undiscovered. The energy so released produces the brilliance of the stars and the heat radiated by the sun.

When Gamow finished his lecture, he was approached by a high Soviet official, Bukharin, ousted by Stalin from a pre-eminent position and destined for execution, who then was assigned to monitor scientific developments. Obviously excited, Bukharin asked Gamow whether the nuclear processes of the stars could somehow be simulated by man for a direct application on the earth. Bukharin offered to let Gamow use the Electric Works of Leningrad for a few hours each night to experiment with the possibilities of creating thermonuclear energies. Gamow declined the offer, insisting that thermonuclear reactions—the behavior of atomic nuclei at high temperatures—could not be induced at the earth's relatively low temperatures.

At George Washington University in the late 1930s, thermonuclear problems became for us a kind of game, an intellectual exercise. We decided that the best candidate for any thermonuclear reaction was the lightest of elements, hydrogen. This element seemed most abundant in the stars and the sun, and we knew hydrogen nuclei could approach each other more easily because they carry the lowest electrical charge and repel each other least among all nuclei. In the spring of 1938, Gamow called a conference to consider thermonuclear problems in detail. We accomplished little at the conference except to pose the questions with some clarity. The answers came within a few months. Gamow, with Charles Critchfield and Hans Bethe, succeeded in determining what reactions keep the stars going. They also managed to reconstruct the stars' development, changes in appearance, and the final exhaustion of their energy. Bethe's work was most remarkable: He made a systematic study of every conceivable thermonuclear reaction, catalogued all the meager experimental data of the time, and made some marvelously enlightened guesses about nuclear reactions that had not yet been proved in experiments. His treatment was so complete that nothing useful could be added to his work during the next decade. Bethe proved himself the champion at Gamow's game.

But the research was, in every respect, a game. None of us expected to be able to duplicate the conditions found in the interiors of stars, conditions that we knew would be necessary for a thermonuclear reaction. We knew of nothing on the earth that could deliver the concentrated energy and heat necessary to fuse nuclei. Then, in December of 1938, Otto Hahn and F. Strassman discovered fission. Albert Einstein wrote his famous letter to President Roosevelt the next year, and physics in the United States started toward the grim reality of the atomic bomb.

I moved to Columbia University in 1941 and began devoting my full energies to the atomic bomb project. But thermonuclear questions were not forgotten. Some imaginative scientists, years before a workable atomic bomb was developed, began wondering whether the concentrated energy of a fission explosion could become the trigger for a thermonuclear bomb. In early 1942, I worked with Enrico Fermi on fission problems at Columbia University, and we usually lunched together at the Faculty Club. Walking back to the laboratory after lunch one day, Fermi posed the question: "Now that we have a good prospect of developing an atomic bomb, couldn't such an explosion be used to start something similar to the reactions in the sun?"

The problem interested me, and during the next few weeks I studied the question rather thoroughly. Nuclei of deuterium, or heavy hydrogen, react with each other much more easily than even the nuclei of light hydrogen. And Harold Urey had devised a way to separate deuterium from the much more abundant light hydrogen. The process of separation was not too expensive. Successful substitution of deuterium for light hydrogen, we thought, would represent a long step toward the realization of a comparatively inexpensive thermonuclear reaction. But after a few weeks of concentrated thought I decided that deuterium could not be ignited by atomic bombs. I told Fermi why I thought it could not work, and tried to forget all about the intriguing possibilities.

After my negative report to Fermi, my attention was demanded by some details connected with the perfection of nuclear reactors necessary for the production of atomic bombs. Most of the reactor work was being done at that time at the Metallurgical Laboratory in Chicago, and I made plans to move there from Columbia University. At the last minute the plans were changed. Arthur Compton, the prominent and energetic physicist who led the Chicago effort, explained, tactfully, that I was not needed in Chicago because all theoretical problems connected with nuclear reactors had been solved. Compton was too kind to tell me the real reason why I could not participate in the top-secret reactor effort in Chicago; I had relatives in Nazi-dominated Hungary, and so I could not be cleared for secret work. At about the same time, in the spring of 1942, J. Robert Oppenheimer invited a small group of theoretical physicists to Berkeley, California, for a sum-

THE WORK OF MANY PEOPLE

mer's study of the problems connected with the actual explosion
of an atomic weapon. When the invitations were prepared, it became obvious that the United States already was beginning to
suffer a shortage of qualified, cleared physicists. Oppenheimer
asked that I be given a clearance regardless of my family con-
nections in Hungary, and his request was granted.

As soon as I was cleared, I was invited to both Chicago and
Berkeley. I accepted the Chicago invitation, but agreed to visit
Berkeley and do what I could to further the work there.

At the Metallurgical Laboratory in Chicago, I was assigned to
work with another physicist, Emil Konopinski. We were newcom-
ers in the bustling laboratory, and for a few days we were given
no specific jobs. Both Konopinski and I had been invited by Oppenheimer to the summer session in Berkeley, and I decided that
our best contribution to that study might be a detailed review
of the reasons why deuterium could not be ignited by an atomic
bomb. Konopinski agreed, and we tackled the job of writing a
report to show, once and for all, that it could not be done. We
wanted no one else to waste valuable time investigating Fermi's
curbstone suggestion. But the more we worked on our report,
the more obvious it became that the roadblocks which I had
erected for Fermi's idea were not so high after all. We hurdled
them one by one, and concluded that heavy hydrogen actually
could be ignited by an atomic bomb to produce an explosion of
tremendous magnitude. By the time we were on our way to California, about the first of July, we even thought we knew precisely how to do it.

In Berkeley, Konopinski and I joined Oppenheimer's group just
as it was being formed. Included in the group were J. H. Van
Vleck, Felix Bloch, Stanley Frankel, Hans Bethe, and Robert
Serber. Although we were called together to investigate the properties and behavior of atomic bombs, all of us were soon engaged
in the distant but absorbing question of whether deuterium could
be exploded. I presented a rough proof of what could be done
and how. My theories were strongly criticized by others in the

group, but together with new difficulties, new solutions emerged. The discussions became fascinating and intense. Facts were questioned and the questions were answered by still more facts. As our discussions became more and more detailed, the prospects of success changed almost daily. One day the job would look hopeless; the next day someone would have a bright idea making everything again seem easy. But another member of the group invariably asked a question spotlighting some consideration that had not been included, and the explosion of heavy hydrogen again would appear impossible. A spirit of spontaneity, adventure, and surprise prevailed during those weeks in Berkeley, and each member of the group helped move the discussions toward a positive conclusion. The contributions of Konopinski and Bethe were especially remarkable. Konopinski suggested that, in addition to deuterium, we should investigate the reactions of the heaviest form of hydrogen, tritium. At the time, he was only making a conversational guess. It turned out to be an inspired guess. Bethe subjected all of our ideas to the same kind of exhaustive scrutiny he had used earlier to clarify and systematize our knowledge about thermonuclear reactions in the stars.

We all were convinced, by summer's end, that we could accomplish a thermonuclear explosion—and that it would not be too difficult. Oppenheimer was as interested by the prospect as any of us. He concluded: "Now we really need another laboratory."

So it was, when the Los Alamos Laboratory was established under Oppenheimer's direction the following year, that exploration of thermonuclear problems was one of the laboratory's objectives. One of the first projects undertaken at Los Alamos was a measurement of the properties of tritium, a measurement necessary for the thermonuclear work. One of the first buildings constructed at Los Alamos was designed to handle thermonuclear materials. Several of the gifted scientists recruited to work at the Los Alamos Laboratory signed on only because they were intrigued by the thermonuclear possibilities.

The thermonuclear objectives of Los Alamos, however, were

sidetracked during the laboratory's first year for two compelling reasons: Successful construction of an atomic bomb proved to be somewhat more difficult than anyone had expected, and it became obvious to me that our thermonuclear discussions of the summer before had been incomplete—so incomplete that the new theoretical questions I raised seemed unanswerable, and realization of a thermonuclear explosion seemed most doubtful. The Los Alamos Laboratory, justifiably, gave the highest priority to the field with the greatest promise of early success. Nearly all of the laboratory's theoretical physicists turned their full attention to the atomic bomb project. No matter how difficult it might be, we knew we had to produce an atomic bomb before our enemies could do it. Work on thermonuclear reactions was all but suspended.

Despite the urgency of the situation, Oppenheimer during those years of struggle with atomic questions did not lose sight of the more distant possibilities. He urged me to continue exploring the thermonuclear field, even though it was beyond the immediate aim of the laboratory. This was not easy advice for him to give or for me to take. It is hard to work apart from others in a scientific community, especially when most people are working toward a goal of the highest interest and urgency. Oppenheimer, Fermi, and many of the most prominent men in the laboratory, however, continued to say that the work at Los Alamos would not be complete as long as the feasibility of a thermonuclear bomb remained in doubt. But until atomic success was verified at Alamogordo on July 16, 1945, the thermonuclear program was eclipsed by our country's vital need for an atomic bomb.

After Alamogordo, some of the best scientific minds in the laboratory were applied to thermonuclear problems. Fermi and Bethe were among those who associated themselves with the thermonuclear effort that had been dormant for so long. But their association ended in a few short weeks, before anything could be accomplished. Hiroshima, coming only three weeks after the Alamogordo test, filled many scientists with a moral repugnance for weapons work. Fermi, Bethe, and dozens of others left Los Alamos. Even Oppenheimer, who had supported and urged the thermonuclear effort for years, turned his back on the project. Publicly he announced: "The physicists have known sin." Privately, on the day of Hiroshima, he came to my Los Alamos office for a long talk. He told me that we would not develop a hydrogen bomb. Before Nagasaki, before the war was over, Oppenheimer made it clear to me that he would have nothing further to do with thermonuclear work.

Some members of the small wartime group that had worked on the thermonuclear project at Los Alamos resisted the great exodus of physicists from the laboratory and remained to prepare a summary review of the possibilities of the hydrogen bomb. Stanley Frankel and Nicholas Metropolis worked hardest and longest on this report. They considered the findings we had made in Berkeley in 1942 along with all other relevant data: early measurements made by John Manley, Elisabeth Graves, Marshall Holloway, and Charles Baker; contributions from Fermi and John von Neumann; and the important work of Konopinski who, with Cloyd Marvin, Jr., proved that a thermonuclear reaction—even if initiated on the earth—could under no circumstances spread to ignite the atmosphere or the oceans. The report by Frankel and Metropolis delivered a verdict on the feasibility of a thermonuclear bomb: Difficult, but with hard work and concentrated effort, hopeful.

Neither the hard work nor the concentrated effort was in sight. There was no backing for the thermonuclear work. No one was interested in developing a thermonuclear bomb. No one cared. Even keeping Los Alamos alive was an uphill fight, a crucial battle won by the new director of the laboratory, Norris Bradbury. With the existence of the laboratory itself endangered, all-out support for the development of a weapon as devastating as a thermonuclear bomb could hardly be expected. The exceedingly small group of experts whose thermonuclear skills had been developed during the war disbanded. I, too, left Los Alamos, and

not a single member of the wartime thermonuclear group con-
tinued to devote his full time and energy to advanced weapons.
But the idea of a Super bomb did not die. A very small Los
Alamos group headed by Robert Richtmyer kept the spark alive.
From my base at the University of Chicago, I traveled to Los
Alamos frequently during the years after Hiroshima to confer
with Richtmyer's group. From the beginning, our thermonuclear
work assumed a new direction and acquired a new style.

I am convinced that if, after Hiroshima, men of Oppenheimer's
stature had lent their moral support—not their active participation, but only their moral support—to the thermonuclear effort,
the United States would have shaved four years from the time it
took this country to develop a Super bomb. But the thermonuclear work was given almost no support in the last months of
1945—or in 1946, 1947, or 1948. Many physicists and government
officials were convinced that in the atomic bomb America had
the weapon ideally suited for our policy of massive retaliation.
The people were comforted by published pronouncements that
Soviet Russia could not attain an atomic explosion for at least
twenty years. Some leaders felt that work on advanced weapons
would make the United States appear to be a warmongering nation bent upon a world arms race. Then, in the fall of 1949,
Russia's first atomic explosion made us realize that an arms race
was no longer a possibility to be avoided but a frightening reality
to be faced.

At Los Alamos, the feeling was widespread that this was the
time to pursue development of the hydrogen bomb. A few months
before the Russian explosion, I had returned to Los Alamos on a
year's leave of absence from the University of Chicago. I felt that
the Russians would follow their development of a fission bomb
with a success in fusion. In that case, the Soviet Union would be
far ahead of the United States in the field of nuclear weapons.
When Los Alamos was established in 1943, it was understood that

thermonuclear possibilities were to be thoroughly explored. After Russia's first atomic explosion, most of us at Los Alamos felt that the time finally had arrived.

Our enthusiasm was not shared by the powerful General Advisory Committee of the Atomic Energy Commission, headed by Oppenheimer. This committee often had a determining voice in AEC policies. On October 29, 1949, a month after President Truman's announcement that Russia had achieved an atomic explosion, the General Advisory Committee met in Washington to give the AEC an opinion on the advisability of undertaking development of a thermonuclear bomb. Committee members, after a round-table discussion of the problem, voted unanimously against any H-bomb program. The unanimous report included this statement: "We all hope that by one means or another, the development of these weapons can be avoided. We are all reluctant to see the United States take the initiative in precipitating this development. We are all agreed that it would be wrong at the present moment to commit ourselves to an all-out effort towards its development."

The GAC report carried two supplementary statements that became known as the majority and minority reports, although the controlling recommendation was unanimous. The majority report was signed by Oppenheimer, James B. Conant, Lee DuBridge, Hartley Rowe, Cyril Smith and Oliver E. Buckley. In its final paragraph, the majority report said: "In determining not to proceed to develop the Super bomb, we see a unique opportunity of providing by example some limitations on the totality of war and thus eliminating the fear and arousing the hopes of mankind." The minority report, signed by Fermi and I. I. Rabi, held: "The fact that no limits exist to the destructiveness of this weapon makes its very existence and the knowledge of its construction a danger to humanity as a whole. It is necessarily an evil thing considered in any light. For these reasons, we believe it important for the President of the United States to tell the American public and the world that we think it is wrong on fundamental ethical principles to initiate the development of such a weapon."

The negative recommendation of the General Advisory Committee was not communicated immediately to Los Alamos. An effort was made to keep congressional leaders from knowing that scientists close to the problem might disagree with the GAC report.

A few days after the GAC meeting, I was on my way from Los Alamos to Washington to keep an appointment with Senator Brien McMahon, chairman of the Joint Congressional Committee for Atomic Energy. I stopped to see Fermi in Chicago. Despite our very close personal relationship and his knowledge of my almost desperate interest in the thermonuclear effort, he insisted that he could not even give me an indication of the GAC decision. But it was clear from the tenor of his remarks that certainly Fermi and possibly the entire GAC did not favor an all-out crash program. While I was in Fermi's office, I received a telephone call from John Manley, secretary of the General Advisory Committee who also was associate director of Los Alamos. Manley asked me not to see Senator McMahon. I asked why I should not. He replied that it would be unfortunate if congressional leaders thought that scientists had a divided opinion on the thermonuclear question. I told Manley that I had an appointment with Senator McMahon and intended to see him. Manley insisted that I should not. I offered to telephone Senator McMahon and tell him that I was canceling my trip to Washington because I had been asked not to see him. Then Manley gave up, saying: "All right. You better go and see him."

I still did not know the contents of the GAC report when I saw Senator McMahon, and he did not reveal them to me. He did, however, use strong words in reference to the report even before I had an opportunity to ask about it. He said: "I read this report, and it just makes me sick." Still a little mystified about the actual recommendation of the GAC, I told Senator McMahon that I considered it vital to the nation's defense that we proceed with the thermonuclear work. He assured me that he would do everything in his power to make the thermonuclear bomb a reality.

Almost two weeks passed before I had certain knowledge of the GAC recommendation. Manley, back in Los Alamos, asked me into his office and showed me both the minority and majority reports. I could see little difference between them, and I was certain that the thermonuclear effort had been effectively killed.

I was, however, completely mistaken. The report produced precisely the opposite effect among the Los Alamos scientists. Immediately, of course, the GAC report did stop work on the thermonuclear bomb, because it was tantamount to an explicit instruction to that effect. After a few days, however, the implications of the report began to sink in. It seemed to restrict the Los Alamos scientists to minor improvements in the old field of fission. But many of the scientists, especially the younger men, found it difficult to control an adventurous spirit urging them to get into the newer field of thermonuclear reactions. The GAC report seemed to state the conflict rather bluntly: As long as you people work very hard and diligently to make a better atomic bomb, you are doing a fine job; but if you succeed in making real progress toward another kind of nuclear explosion, you are doing something immoral. To this, the scientists reacted psychologically. They got mad. And their attention was turned toward the thermonuclear bomb, not away from it.

This psychological reaction to the GAC report, this scientific anger, certainly could not have produced a hydrogen bomb by itself alone. Solution of the theoretical and engineering problems involved in the thermonuclear program required an intensive effort, a concerted action impossible to achieve in a laboratory instructed not to work on the problem. Without a clear go-ahead, Los Alamos could not have produced a hydrogen bomb. Empty anger was not enough. A decision was needed. And President Truman was urged to make that decision by AEC Commissioner Strauss, Senator McMahon, and other members of the Joint Congressional Committee for Atomic Energy.

Ironically the man who gave our atomic secrets to Russia also had an important influence on the decision to proceed with the hydrogen bomb. Klaus Fuchs, who was at Los Alamos when we reviewed all we knew about thermonuclear reactions after Hiroshima, confessed in late January 1950 that he had passed secrets to Communist agents. Four days after Fuchs' confession, President Truman overrode the recommendation of the GAC and directed the Atomic Energy Commission to go ahead with the hydrogen bomb.

The presidential directive was not a complete surprise to me. A few days before President Truman's decision was announced, I met Oppenheimer at a conference on atomic energy. He made it clear that a top-level decision was being made, and that it probably would direct development of a hydrogen bomb. Recalling his effective leadership of the laboratory during the war, I asked Oppenheimer whether he would really go to work on the hydrogen bomb if President Truman did authorize an all-out thermonuclear program. His reply was negative.

Although I was prepared for the presidential decision of January 29, 1950, I was not prepared for the language of the decision. President Truman directed the AEC to *continue* its thermonuclear program, giving the impression that we could produce a hydrogen bomb simply by tightening a few last screws. People understood from his announcement that the job was almost done. Actually, work had not begun. We had eight years of thermonuclear fantasies, theories, and calculations behind us; but we had established no connection between theory and reality. We needed a thermonuclear test.

I still was associated with the Los Alamos Scientific Laboratory when President Truman announced his decision. But, distressed by the opposition of the GAC, I had accepted an appointment as professor of physics at the University of California in Los Angeles and planned to begin teaching in the fall of 1950.

President Truman's decision changed my plans. I had suggested the thermonuclear approach then being pursued at Los Alamos. Naturally, when our efforts were given the presidential go-ahead, I wanted to see the work through to completion and find out whether my ideas were right or wrong. Having argued strongly for an all-out thermonuclear program, I felt that I had no choice but to attempt to do a job that appeared as difficult as development of the atomic bomb itself—but which was to be undertaken without the constellation of world-renowned physicists that had been involved in the wartime atomic effort. I stayed on at Los Alamos.

Immediately and almost simultaneously we tackled two vital problems. Both were mathematical. The problems: A detailed review of the favored design of the hydrogen bomb, and preparations for the world's first thermonuclear test.

I was vitally interested in the review of the favored hydrogen bomb design. That design was based upon one of my ideas. The detailed reconsideration of the most likely H-bomb design was started on two fronts, and it soon began to resemble the classic race between the tortoise and the hare. On one front, instructions and information were prepared for what then was the fastest electronic computer. On the other front, an ingenious mathematician, Stanislaw Ulam, and his hard-working friend, Cornelius Everett, undertook the same computational task by straightforward hand execution. Mathematical ingenuity and hard work won the race. Ulam's results were available even before completion of the lengthy instructions for the electronic brain.

Ulam's first partial results were disquieting. His more complete answers were most discouraging. I could hardly believe them. Ulam's findings seemed to conflict with earlier machine-made calculations. Ulam's work indicated that we were on the wrong track, that the hydrogen bomb design we thought would work best would not work at all.

I decided to wait, before becoming too upset, for the more detailed and accurate results from the electronic computer. When these results were in a few weeks later Ulam's work was verified. It was completely clear that the plans we had considered most hopeful had to be revised. Our theories of thermonuclear principles seemed to be on safe ground; we knew what had to be done. But we no longer could point to a particular device and say: "This is how to do it."

Ulam's proof that our ideas about bomb design were wrong made it absolutely necessary to confirm our other thermonuclear theories. None of our assumptions or general ideas had any actual connection with reality. If we were to proceed toward development of a practical hydrogen bomb, we knew that we must proceed in confidence with ideas that were solid and sure. We had to establish a connection between theory and practice. We needed a significant test.

Bomb design was given a low priority while we turned our most intense efforts toward preparations for a test that would establish beyond all doubt that a thermonuclear explosion was possible.

Our first job was to make detailed calculations anticipating the results of the first thermonuclear test. Because of the shortage of high-speed electronic computers, much of this arduous work also had to be done by hand. Under the supervision of John Wheeler, Rolf Landshoff and Robert Richtmyer, an incredible amount of numerical data was turned out by the people in the Los Alamos computing division. The data were needed to compare the test's results with our theory of thermonuclear burning.

During the last half of 1950 and the early months of 1951, we built the most complex kind of apparatus to record the results of the test explosion, a blast expected to last for only a small fraction of a second. The delicate observation equipment had to be very sensitive and very fast. It would be vaporized by the explosion, but had to record and transmit the blast's effects before being destroyed. Under the direction of Alvin Graves, Frederick Reines, Jack Clark, and William Ogle, crews from Los Alamos as well as the Naval Research Laboratory and the University of California's Radiation Laboratory installed this mass of intricate equipment on the Pacific island of Eniwetok.

Meticulous, systematic Hans Bethe was drafted to review our theoretical calculations and measurements. He okayed our work, and we won AEC approval for the first thermonuclear tests. The first test was included in a series of operations code-named Greenhouse.

During the months between approval of our calculations and the Greenhouse explosion in May 1951, I was able to concentrate on the problems of constructing an actual hydrogen bomb. The contraption that we built for the Greenhouse explosion was not a bomb, but a purely experimental device designed to establish a scientific principle.

Carson Mark, chief of the Los Alamos theoretical division, during those months before Greenhouse recited some of the difficulties of practical bomb design for a visiting admiral. Mark, who delighted in his contempt for the military mind, paraphrased the admiral's reply and later told me: "He behaved like any other admiral. His reaction was, 'Damn the difficulties. Full speed ahead.'"

Carson's story irritated me. Then I began to wonder whether we could find detours around the difficulties. The detours eventually led to a new approach.

I was guided by two convictions: Ulam had shown that our original ideas about the construction of a practical bomb were unworkable. I was equally certain in my own mind that if we failed in our first attempt to build a practical hydrogen bomb, the General Advisory Committee would recommend abandonment of the entire thermonuclear program. Initial success was imperative. There might be no second chance.

I approached the problem by attempting to free myself entirely of our original concept. That done, it soon became obvious that the job could be done in other ways. During the urgent computations for Greenhouse, many of the hard-working physicists had participated in offhand discussions about the bomb's final design. Some of these ideas were fantastic. Some were practical. None were fully examined. They had been shoved aside by the vital need to complete the calculations for the test. With the theoretical work on Greenhouse finished, these weapons ideas could be examined in detail. Eager and anxious to come to grips with the real problem, our group at Los Alamos devoted its full attention to ways of constructing an actual bomb.

About February 1, 1951, I suggested a possible approach to the problem. Frederic de Hoffmann, acting on the suggestion, made a fine calculation and projection of the idea. The results, showing how a thermonuclear bomb could be constructed, were contained in a report that I thought would be signed jointly. De Hoffmann, however, had other plans. He signed the report with only my name, arguing that the suggestion counted for everything and the execution for nothing. I still feel ashamed that I consented.

To some who were not closely connected with the Los Alamos effort, our report may have appeared as unexpected and ingenious. Actually, it was the result of hard work and hard thought by many people. The thoughts were incomplete, but all the fruitful elements were present, and the various ideas and suggestions would undoubtedly have been crystallized within a short time into something concrete and provable. If the Los Alamos Laboratory had continued to function after Hiroshima with a full complement of such brilliant people as Oppenheimer, Fermi, and Bethe, I am convinced that someone would have had the same idea much sooner—and we would have had the hydrogen bomb in 1947 rather than in 1952. I am just as certain that if we had not proved the practicality of the hydrogen bomb in our report of March 1951, America's thermonuclear effort would have been junked and construction of a successful hydrogen bomb would have been delayed by even more years.

During March and April of 1951, I urged the feasibility of constructing a hydrogen bomb upon anyone who would listen. Early in March, I discussed the report in detail with Norris Bradbury, the director of the Los Alamos Laboratory, Mark, head of our theoretical division, and others at the laboratory. In April, I explained my ideas to Gordon Dean, chairman of the Atomic Energy Commission. Dean seemed interested, but somehow distracted. After leaving his office, I discovered the reason for the distraction: The zipper on my trousers had failed, and my fly was open. Dean remembered my open fly, but not my ideas. Two months later, during another presentation, he seemed to be hearing the ideas for the first time. But in the meantime he had told a magazine reporter that I was a "brilliant if somewhat disarrayed scientist."

Our proof that a practical hydrogen bomb could be economically constructed was based, of course, on theoretical calculations that had not been verified experimentally. That verification, the basic proof needed before making a real H-bomb, came with Greenhouse. Few scientific experiments have been conducted under conditions as exotic or in a place as beautiful as the Pacific setting for the first thermonuclear explosion. Rising early that May morning, we walked through the tropical heat to the beach of Eniwetok's placid lagoon. Again, we put on dark glasses. Again, we saw the brilliance of another nuclear explosion. Again, we felt the heat of the blast on our faces. But still, we did not know whether the experiment had been a success. We did not know whether the heavy hydrogen had been ignited. We did not know whether we had merely seen the explosion of the triggering atomic bomb or actually had witnessed the world's first thermonuclear explosion. The mushroom cloud we saw rising beyond the lagoon showed only that we had been successful in asking a question. The answer had to come from the reports of the recording instruments.

Time was required to gather and interpret those reports, and the twenty-four hours following the test were filled with anxiety.

That afternoon, to break the tension, Ernest Lawrence invited me to swim with him in the lagoon. When I came out of the water to stand on the white sands of the beach, I told Lawrence that I thought the experiment had been a failure. He thought otherwise, and bet me five dollars that we had been successful in igniting heavy hydrogen and producing a thermonuclear reaction.

I was hardly awake the next morning when Louis Rosen burst into my quarters to announce: "I have the evidence! Only one piece, but I have evidence that the test was a success. Please, please tell no one until it is verified." I promised. But Lawrence was leaving the island that morning before additional readings could be made. I kept my promise to Rosen. I told no one, and I waited as long as I could for final verification. But when Lawrence left for the air strip, I could wait no longer. I ran after his jeep and silently handed him five dollars. It was worth it. I knew that success at Greenhouse ensured the successful construction of a hydrogen bomb along the lines detailed in the report to which De Hoffmann had signed my name two months earlier.

A month after Greenhouse, the Atomic Energy Commission called a significant round-table conference to determine the best way to build a hydrogen bomb. The meeting was held June 19 and 20 at the Institute for Advanced Study at Princeton. Oppenheimer, as chairman of the Weapons Committee of the GAC, presided. Members of both the AEC and the GAC attended, along with Los Alamos scientists.

I was amazed when Carson Mark, in his presentation, did not mention the hydrogen bomb report that I had handed him three months before. My amazement multiplied when Gordon Dean, still chairman of the AEC, spoke without mentioning the same report, which I had explained to him two months earlier. My amazement approached anger as other scientists and officials who knew of the report spoke without referring to it. Finally, I could contain myself no longer. I insisted on being heard. My demand was met by a spirited debate, but it was decided that I should be allowed to speak. I walked to the blackboard and again went through the theory and calculations that already were familiar to half the men in the room.

Response to the theory, now supported by the experimental evidence of Greenhouse, was enthusiastic and unanimous. Gordon Dean, who apparently had found my sloppy dress an insurmountable distraction two months before, later testified: "Out of the meeting came something which Edward Teller brought into the meeting within his own head, which was an entirely new way of approaching a nuclear weapon. I would like to be able to describe that but it is one of the most sensitive things we have left in the atomic energy program. . . . At the end of those two days we were all convinced, everyone in the room, that at least we had something for the first time that looked feasible in the way of an idea. . . . I remember leaving that meeting impressed with this fact, that everyone around that table without exception, and this included Dr. Oppenheimer, was enthusiastic. . . ."

During the months preceding and following the Princeton meeting, ingenious and reliable calculations were carried out in connection with this new kind of nuclear explosion. Marshall Rosenbluth, Conrad Longmire, Lothar Nordheim, and many others made accurate predictions about details of the way our new device would function.

Under the leadership of Marshall Holloway, a new test was prepared on one of the islets of the Eniwetok chain, Elugelab. On November 1, 1952, this islet was wiped off the face of the earth by the first full-scale thermonuclear explosion.

I was not on hand for the explosion of the first hydrogen bomb. I left Los Alamos exactly one year before that momentous event. The battle for the thermonuclear bomb had been won at the Princeton conference, and I was drawn to the fight for establish-

ment of a second weapons laboratory. On November 1, 1951, I
left Los Alamos and took a last look at the gold-lettered poem
framed on my office wall, a prayer fondly quoted by Lewis
Strauss:

> Providence, who watches over children and drunkards and fools
> With silent miracles and other esoterica,
> Continue to suspend the customary rules
> And protect the United States of America.

My inability to see development of the thermonuclear bomb
through to a final, successful conclusion was a great disappointment. But there were good reasons for my leaving Los Alamos.

It was an open secret, among scientists and government officials, that I did not agree with Norris Bradbury's administration
of the thermonuclear program at Los Alamos. Bradbury and I
remained friends, but we differed sharply on the most effective
ways to produce a hydrogen bomb at the earliest possible date.
We even disagreed on the earliest possible date itself, on the
timing of our first hydrogen bomb test. The dissension with Bradbury crystallized in my mind the urgent need for more than one
nuclear weapons laboratory.

I knew that science thrives on friendly competition, on the
fostering of different points of view, and on the exchange of
ideas developed in different surroundings. I knew, too, that a
single group of scientists working together can easily become fascinated by special aspects of a development—to the neglect of
other hopeful approaches. My conviction grew that the safety of
our country could not be entrusted to a single nuclear weapons
laboratory, even though that laboratory were as excellent as Los
Alamos. This conviction was hardened by a growing awareness,
as our work progressed at Los Alamos and our thermonuclear
knowledge increased, that we were pioneering a big new field of
weapons development. I began to doubt that one laboratory
would be physically capable of handling all the work that had to

be done. Weighing all of these ideas and circumstances, I came to the inescapable conclusion that at least two weapons laboratories, working in co-operation but also in the traditional American spirit of competition toward the mutual goal of adequate national defense, were vital to the future of the United States.

I also concluded that I could advocate establishment of a second weapons laboratory most effectively if I were not associated with the existing Los Alamos Laboratory. So, regretfully, I left Los Alamos in November 1951, and returned to the University of Chicago.

During the following year, the first hydrogen bomb was developed and perfected at Los Alamos. My work, during that year, took me from the University of Chicago to the University of California. In October of 1952, while in California, I was invited to the South Pacific to watch the explosion of "Mike," the world's first hydrogen bomb. I very much wanted to see the explosion of the device that had consumed my energies and that had dragged me into so many arguments. But I knew that I really was not needed at Eniwetok. So I compromised with my desire. I attended the first hydrogen bomb explosion by watching the sensitive seismograph at the University of California in Berkeley.

On the morning of November 1, 1952, I was escorted into the dark basement room where the seismograph was writing its tremulous record on a photographic film with a fine beam of light. The spot of light seemed unsteady. It moved more than it should to record the continuous minute trembling of the earth or the pounding of ocean waves on our shores. The light's jumpiness, I learned, was due to the movements of my own eyes; in the darkness my eyes were not steadied by the surrounding picture of solid objects. I braced a pencil and held it close to the luminous point. Now the point seemed steady. The earth was quiet. This was about the time of the shot at Eniwetok. Nothing happened on the seismograph, and nothing could have happened.

About fifteen minutes were required for the shock of the explosion to travel, deep under the Pacific Basin, to the California coast.

I waited impatiently, and watched the seismograph make a time signal each minute. At last the time signal came that had to be followed by the explosion's shock, and there it seemed to be: The spot of light danced wildly and irregularly.

But I almost convinced myself that what I had seen was the motion of my own hand and the pencil it was holding rather than the signal from the first hydrogen bomb. The film was taken from the seismograph and developed, and the tracing appeared on the photographic plate. It was clear and big and unmistakable. It had been made by a wave of compression traveling thousands of miles and bringing positive assurance that our first hydrogen bomb had been a success.

I believe that everyone who worked on the hydrogen bomb was appalled by its success and by its possible consequences. I also believe that everyone who was closely or distantly connected with the effort—along with those who have made subsequent contributions—was driven by the knowledge that the work was necessary for the safety of our country.

We would be unfaithful to the tradition of Western civilization if we shied away from exploring what man can accomplish, if we failed to increase man's control over nature. The duty of scientists, specifically, is to explore and to explain. This duty led to the invention of the principles that made the hydrogen bomb a practical reality. In the whole development I claim credit in one respect only: I believed and continued to believe in the possibility and the necessity of developing the thermonuclear bomb. My scientific duty demanded exploration of that possibility.

Beyond the scientific responsibility to search the horizons of human knowledge, the responsibilities of scientists cannot be any greater than those of any other citizen in our democratic society.

The consequences of scientific discoveries are the responsibilities of the people. Every citizen, whether he is a politician or a farmer, a businessman or a scientist, has to carry his share of the greater responsibility that comes with greater power over nature. But a scientist has done his job as a scientist when that power has been demonstrated.

CHAPTER FOUR:

A Laboratory in the Cold War

MY DECISION TO LEAVE Los Alamos even before the final development of the hydrogen bomb in order to argue more effectively for establishment of a second weapons laboratory apparently was well timed. Others had been considering a second laboratory, and my departure from Los Alamos seemed to emphasize the need.

I moved from Los Alamos to the University of Chicago in November of 1951. In my campaign for a second laboratory, I first tried to approach the Atomic Energy Commission. Oppenheimer still was chairman of the General Advisory Committee of the AEC. Shortly after leaving Los Alamos, I met Oppenheimer at a scientific conference, and I made a request: "Look! You never did give me a chance to talk to the GAC when it was deciding whether to go ahead with the hydrogen bomb. Please let me talk to the GAC now about setting up a second laboratory." He consented, and a meeting was scheduled for mid-December.

Just before the GAC meeting in Washington, Chairman Oppenheimer suggested that perhaps I would prefer addressing a closed session of the committee, a meeting from which AEC officials would be barred even though they held security clearances. I decided not to waste my ammunition. I replied: "No, the more people from the AEC who hear what I have to say, the better I'll like it."

So I was given a full chance to talk about the second laboratory. Everyone in the room knew of the continued and accelerated work on the hydrogen bomb. Here was an example of unexpected progress. I tried to predict the future, although it could not be predicted, and argued that new scientific problems would keep two laboratories more than busy. I appealed to the scientific spirit of curiosity and adventure, and I pointed to the value of friendly competition. I realize, in retrospect, that my projections fell far short of the real progress that was to come. But at the time members of the committee seemed to be interested, listening and at least partially convinced.

I came out of the meeting confident that my presentation had been a success, certain that I had made my point: A strong second laboratory was needed to provide healthy competition in the thermonuclear field.

But weeks passed and nothing happened. The AEC made no effort to find a location for a second laboratory, no effort to recruit scientists to work in a second laboratory. I learned later that the AEC was afraid that establishment of another laboratory might lower the morale of the men working at Los Alamos, that a new laboratory, instead of accelerating progress, might slow future developments.

I took my recommendation that a second laboratory be established to David Griggs, chief scientist for the Air Force. I recited my reasons for thinking that a second laboratory was essential to the nation's security, and told Griggs that I was afraid my arguments had made no impression upon either the GAC or the Atomic Energy Commission itself. He said nothing. But a short time later, during a Florida meeting of the Scientific Advisory Board of the Air Force, Griggs arranged for me to meet General James A. Doolittle, who usually was introduced in the scientific meetings as Dr. Doolittle. It was my first meeting with the famous flyer. He listened with a smile to my arguments for building an arsenal of varied thermonuclear weapons instead of concentrating on a single, big hydrogen bomb. At first, I did not know whether the smile indicated interest or skepticism. When I later asked, Griggs told me: "He *said* he was interested, didn't he?"

The campaign for a second laboratory was interrupted, after a fashion, for a trip to California to visit Ernest O. Lawrence in Berkeley. I arrived on ground-hog day, 1952, and the weather was beautiful. Lawrence, who had staunchly supported the thermonuclear program, now was interested in establishment of a second laboratory. He was a remarkable man—practical, enthusiastic for scientific progress, and a generous backer of everyone who had the ability and determination to make a step forward.

During my visit, Lawrence and I drove to Livermore, a quiet community about an hour's drive east of Berkeley, located in a valley known for good wines and fields of roses. The Navy, during World War II, had used a square mile of the Livermore Valley as a training camp. The University of California's Radiation Laboratory in 1950 had opened a branch on the former Navy base and had started work on a big accelerator.

After returning from Livermore, Lawrence took me to dinner and asked me to move from Chicago to the University of California. I said I would come on one condition: That I could work in a laboratory devoted to the development of thermonuclear weapons. Lawrence said he wanted to establish just such a laboratory, and suggested that I go to Washington and secure authorization. I told him that I was discouraged. I had tried to convince both the General Advisory Committee and the Atomic Energy Commission, and I had not been successful. I had no reason to hope that anyone would listen to me.

But within days I received a telephone call from Griggs' office in Washington. The Air Force really was interested in a second weapons laboratory and wanted more details about the possibilities. General Doolittle had taken the ball and carried it to the highest officials of the Air Force. I rushed to Washington and presented my case to Secretary of the Air Force Thomas K. Finletter. At first, he listened in icy silence. But he soon warmed to the theoretical possibilities and military practicalities of thermonuclear weapons. Finletter flew to Los Alamos and verified for himself the importance of developing hydrogen bombs and my assessment of the areas in which more work could be done. Then he asked me to state my case before Secretary of Defense Robert A. Lovett.

I do not know what brought about the final decision to establish a second weapons laboratory. Lewis Strauss had argued the case effectively. Willard Libby, an excellent chemist who made some of the greatest contributions to the uses of radioactivity, lent his consistent support. Ernest Lawrence and others whose opinions were highly respected were on record as favoring establishment of a second laboratory. Defense Secretary Lovett listened to the problem and made a farsighted statement; he maintained that a second laboratory was, indeed, necessary to our security. The Air Force laid plans for a laboratory under its own jurisdiction and even began negotiating for a site. Then the Atomic Energy Commission, at last, became interested and began investigating possible locations for a second laboratory of its own.

I wanted the new laboratory to be established at the University of Chicago, but many of my colleagues there had no appetite for work on weapons. Lawrence, in California, was more hospitable. And, most important, he was confident that enough scientific manpower could be recruited to staff another laboratory. At a time when many scientists were repelled by the memory of our surprise atomic attacks on Hiroshima and Nagasaki, when many of the men who had helped develop the atomic bomb had returned to their classrooms and university laboratories, when few felt inclined to subject themselves again to the circumscribed and regulated life demanded by governmental secrecy, at such a time Lawrence undertook the task of recruiting talent for a new laboratory.

Our nation's second weapons laboratory was established at Livermore during the summer of 1952. I arrived from Chicago on July 14 and settled into the job of helping to convert the former Navy training base into a laboratory that would look for new approaches toward releasing the power of the nucleus.

The University of California's Radiation Laboratory was the creation of Ernest Lawrence. For many years it has been the outstanding laboratory in experimental physics. During World War II, it served national defense in a most effective way. As director for this laboratory's new branch at Livermore, Lawrence selected a young physicist who was full of vitality, good humor, and common sense, Dr. Herbert F. York.

Space travel was York's secret love. In his home he had a beautiful picture of the moon and its craters. On the wall next to it there was an empty frame reserved for a picture of the back side of the moon. This was for the future. As for the past, York had worked with a lusty group of young experimentalists to complete a difficult series of measurements on the 1951 thermonuclear experiment in Eniwetok. As for the present, York in 1952 had a most practical idea that thermonuclear reactions might be controlled by sealing hot hydrogen gas into a magnetic bottle.

To develop nuclear explosives, it is necessary to perform tests. The Livermore Laboratory was barely established when we began preparing for a series of tests that we expected to point the way to the most effective development of new weapons. The next test series, to be conducted in Nevada, was scheduled for the spring of 1953. During his earliest days at Livermore, Herbert York wrote a different figure on the blackboard in his office each day. One day it would be 217; the next day it would be 216; then 215, 214, 213. I asked what these figures meant. "Of course," he replied, "they are the number of days we have left to prepare for our first test."

During those early months, the Livermore Laboratory did not have an electronic computer. And such a computer always had been considered essential in our planning. We wanted to know as accurately as possible what to expect from our tests. Nuclear testing is an intricate art. In a tiny fraction of a second a great amount of decisive information is available. Making successful observations and capturing the most essential information are the purposes of nuclear tests and the bases of any future progress. It also is important, however, to anticipate a test's results, to attempt a rather precise prediction of what will happen during a nuclear test, and then to compare what happened with what we thought would happen. It is necessary to check theory against reality.

We needed a computer to help us formulate our prognosis of the Livermore Laboratory's first test series. Although the laboratory had no computer, one was available to us in Philadelphia. In the fall of 1952, I went to Philadelphia with a small group to get our calculational methods straightened out with this computer.

The first steps in such a process are always the same. Instructions are given to the machine. The computer then starts to give back some answers—and the answers make no sense. Mistakes—small or large, few or numerous—have crept into the many sheets of instructions. One by one, the instructional mistakes are eliminated, and only then can the computer begin to function effectively.

We worked, ate, and slept on the Philadelphia computer during the short time that it was available to us. We gave the machine its instructions and went through the painstaking and sometimes agonizing job of finding and correcting the errors that obviously had been included in our instructions. The problem finally was running. Then, quite near the end, the computer broke down. It did not matter. We could calculate the last few steps with the slide rule. And, much more important, we knew that we could handle this part of our job.

Sidney Fernbach, who was with us in Philadelphia, today runs one of the nation's best computing laboratories in Livermore. As in many similar laboratories, Fernbach has hung an abacus in a glass case over Livermore's best computer. The case's inscription reads: "In case of emergency, break glass."

Problems of computation are close to my own interests. But they are, in fact, only a small fraction of the great task of preparing for a nuclear test. Thousands of individual problems must be solved in areas as different as nuclear physics, engineering, and common labor, and the efforts of many people specializing in many fields of endeavor must be co-ordinated. But our fledgling laboratory was up to the job. When the day of the test finally arrived, when the chalked figure on York's blackboard was a zero, we were ready.

The experiment succeeded, but it brought an unwelcome answer: No. The piece of progress we had hoped for was no progress at all. We had enough data to understand in detail what had happened, and new knowledge in the life of a laboratory—even if that knowledge is disappointing—is most important. But we would have been happier if our first experiment had produced something of immediate value.

The initial difficulties of the Livermore Laboratory were far from ended. In a field that was new to most of us, we tried to look for essential progress along lines quite different from those that were rightly pursued by the excellent and expert workers of Los Alamos. Our early failures and their continued successes produced an unavoidable and expected result: We were subjected to a heavy dose of ribbing from our colleagues at the original weapons laboratory. These gibes had an effect that was to endure and was for the best. The young scientists of Livermore developed an ambition for excellence, an appetite that was hard to satisfy, an overwhelming desire for progress that was to keep us going.

We learned, during the summer of 1953, that excellent progress on our part would, indeed, be necessary. The new leader of the Soviet Union announced that Russian scientists had developed a hydrogen bomb.

The United States within a short time gathered radioactive explosion products that showed the Russian statement was not an empty boast. Precise information cannot be obtained easily from such long-distance observations; this is like trying to judge the cooking abilities of a neighbor by smelling his smoke. But this much was clear to us: Only a few months after our first successful thermonuclear test, the Soviet Union had produced a powerful explosion based on the same general principles.

Disappointed by the outcome of our first tests in 1953, the men at Livermore under the direction of Herbert York undertook difficult and ambitious preparations for a big 1954 test series in the South Pacific.

Los Alamos scientists fired the first shot of the series on March 1. It was successful beyond expectation. but this explosion also released radioactivity into a wind that suddenly changed direction. There was suffering and the beginning of an alarm over fallout that was to grow beyond all expectation and beyond all reason.

With great caution, the series continued with Los Alamos shots. Their success was undiminished. Then came the first big attempt of the Livermore Laboratory. Again, it was a disappointment.

Although I had visited the Pacific Proving Grounds, I saw none of the 1954 experimental shots. I never have seen a full-scale hydrogen explosion. But when the Livermore Laboratory's experiment proved disappointing and questions arose, I took a plane out to Eniwetok.

On the morning after my arrival I received a teletyped message from one of our excellent theorists in Livermore, Dr. Montgomery Johnson. From the early results of our experiment, he had deduced the reason for our difficulties. His teletype was short but convincing. I had urged an ambitious program, and we had been anything but successful. We had tried to do too much, and we had tried to do it in the wrong way.

Much as I disliked the chore, I had to persuade my friends to halt Livermore's participation in the 1954 test series. The disappointing results of our first shot made it abundantly clear that we were wasting our efforts on a bad plan. After a day of discussion, all of us in the Pacific from Livermore were agreed: If you have made a mistake in buttoning your coat, you must undo all the buttons and start again.

Back at Livermore, we started again. But our efforts this time were led by a group of real experts. An expert, according to a favorite definition of Niels Bohr, is a man who by his own painful experience has learned all the mistakes that can be committed within a narrow field. We at Livermore had made all the mistakes that seemed possible. We now were experts, and each year from 1955 to 1958 the laboratory brought in a rich harvest of unexpected and practical results.

Development of fusion bombs was placed under the direction of Harold Brown, a theoretical physicist who had developed an unusually sharp eye for facts, for hardware, and for people. He did much to transform the hydrogen bomb from a clumsy contraption into a handy instrument.

Development of fission bombs was entrusted to John Foster, a young man of incredible energy and unbounded enthusiasm, who drove his collaborators hard, made them like it, and had a knack of getting from every man more than anyone suspected possible. His work turned toward tactical nuclear weapons. In a few years long strides were made toward bombs of low yield that can be used in a flexible and effective manner.

But perhaps most was accomplished at Livermore during those years by a quiet, unassuming, pleasant man who abandoned an interest in rockets and turned to nuclear explosives, Mark Mills.

The theoretical supervision of all our projects became Mills' responsibility. Taking his cue from the sad post-mortem sessions that had followed our early failures, Mills launched the exceedingly useful pre-mortem discussions that preceded our later successes. Before any new device was tested, it was reviewed and discussed by some of our experienced scientists who had nothing to do with its development. Mills' pre-mortem discussions of each new device provided valuable independent criticism while welding the laboratory into a single, purposeful unit. The pre-mortem sessions helped us to avoid becoming a collection of specialists who had only a nodding acquaintance with each other's difficulties and accomplishments.

Even while the Livermore Laboratory was making rapid and valuable progress in weapons development, Ernest Lawrence was participating in a serious and determined attempt to ease cold-war tensions by finding a way toward effective and verifiable disarmament. Harold Stassen, leader of the Eisenhower administration's disarmament effort, organized an advisory group of experts. As a member of this group, Lawrence was responsible for all aspects of disarmament connected with nuclear energy. He asked several of us at Livermore to help him in this work. Foremost in our group was Mark Mills.

These disarmament efforts, like all others, eventually were blocked by the stone wall of Communist intransigence. But during the discussions we did make a simple and practical proposal: Nuclear arms are small, powerful, relatively inexpensive, and easily hidden. Disarmament, therefore, should not begin with nuclear disarmament. The first steps toward disarmament, instead, should be taken in fields where the cost of weapons is higher and where armament is more conspicuous and more easily checked. Only after international tensions are relaxed and mutual confidence established by measures of conventional disarmament should we tackle the infinitely more difficult task of nuclear disarmament.

In the meantime, we thought an important concession could be made to public opinion. The dangers of radioactive fallout in the atmosphere had been exaggerated out of all proportion. Millions of people were worried about fallout. Although the danger was purely imaginary, the worries were real. We proposed that the amount of radioactivity released into the atmosphere should be limited to a small amount that could be proved harmless in a completely convincing way. This simple and moderate proposal, unfortunately, was neither pressed upon the Administration nor explained to the public.

As the fear of fallout mounted, the clamor increased in this country for a halt of all nuclear tests. The emotional appeal of such a radical demand was all too clear: The root of all the fears, troubles, and anxieties of the atomic age was the atomic bomb. Stop development of such monstrous weapons, and all the world's difficulties will vanish. Let us set the clock back beyond Hiroshima. Or, if we can't do that, let us at least stop the clock now.

Clocks can be turned back or stopped, but time cannot. I felt that we could not stop progress, that advances certainly would be made in the nuclear field by Russia if not by the United States.

Early in the summer of 1957, Lewis Strauss took Ernest Lawrence, Mark Mills, and me to see President Eisenhower. We described to the President some of the probable future developments in the field of nuclear explosives. One point was raised in the discussion which was and still is of great importance: We can perfect "clean" nuclear explosives. These can be used in war to destroy an intended target without releasing radioactivity to be carried by the winds to do damage indiscriminately where no damage was intended. These "clean" explosives can also be used in peace as a powerful workhorse in mammoth construction jobs.

President Eisenhower listened to our arguments. And, for the time being, we obtained permission to proceed with our work.

Within months I became deeply worried about the future of the Livermore Laboratory. In the fall of 1957, Russia's Sputnik flashed through the skies, and the people of the United States suddenly were engrossed in the space age.

The time of Sputnik was the time for us to redouble our efforts to ensure the safety of the free world. But we did little. We did increase our work in rocketry and we did, at last, establish a sizable space program of our own. Some defense funds, cut in an "economy" move, were restored to the budget. But in the development of nuclear weapons, there were signs of a coming slowdown.

That the nation should do more about exploring space for our peace and security was necessary. With the Soviet Union the first into space, establishment of an effective United States space program was mandatory. But to neglect the fast-growing field of atomic energy and particularly to neglect development of nuclear explosives seemed to me to be ill-considered and dangerous.

Still, the national neglect of nuclear programs that followed Sputnik could be understood. We faced a new challenge in space, and the challenge captured the public imagination. To think of man soaring to the moon was something new and exciting. To think of nuclear explosives suddenly was old hat. People were fascinated by the glamour of space. Nuclear explosives seemed unfashionable and repulsive.

Herbert York, whose work as director of the Livermore Laboratory had been excellent, went to Washington to devote himself to his original ambition: Space exploration. Before long, he was named Assistant Secretary of Defense for Research and Development. I asked Ernest Lawrence, as over-all director of the University of California's Radiation Laboratory, to give me the responsibility for the Livermore branch. A few months earlier, I had expected to work only on purely technical projects. But under Lawrence's direction I felt that I could make an important administrative contribution at Livermore during the dangerous

period when public interest in nuclear projects and support for
our work were waning.

Lawrence promised me his full support, and so I began an
unusual, difficult, and important job. I hoped to work as director
of the Livermore Laboratory for only one year, a year that I felt
would be crucial in the continuing development of our nation's
defense. Then I expected that Mark Mills would assume direction
of the laboratory, allowing me to return to science. But this was
not to be.

Mills, in April of 1958, was working in the Pacific Proving
Grounds. A new series of tests was approaching, and Mills was
involved in some important preparations. On the evening of
April 7, he found it necessary to move from one island to another in the Eniwetok chain, and he requested a helicopter. The
weather was threatening, but no one was aware of a real danger.
The helicopter was considered safe.

A young physicist, Dr. Harry Keller, and an Air Force medical
officer, Col. Ernest A. Pinson, flew with Mills in the helicopter's
cabin. Two pilots occupied the cockpit. Flying low near the edge
of the lagoon, the helicopter was caught in a squall. It crashed
into eight feet of water.

The two pilots got out safely. The passengers were trapped in
the cabin.

Colonel Pinson was able to float and breathe from the air bub-
ble that formed above the water in the cabin. Then he kicked out
a cabin window, escaped and joined the pilots. Right after this
harrowing experience, he returned with the pilots to rescue his
friends from the cabin.

They found Harry Keller unconscious. They dragged him from
the cabin and in the darkness, on top of the helicopter, started
artificial respiration. Keller escaped with a case of pneumonia,
and after several weeks he recovered.

Colonel Pinson and the two pilots searched in vain for Mark

Mills. Hours later, when the rescue team arrived, he was found, still strapped in his seat, dead.

Mark Mills' death was a dreadful blow. On the following day I assumed the directorship of the Livermore Laboratory. I felt lonely and lost. I had thought that Mills and I would undertake the job jointly, and that within a short time he would assume the full responsibility.

But Mark Mills even in death was a potent influence for a unified effort, friendly spirit, and good humor in the Livermore Laboratory. Mills was gifted with a very pleasant and even temper. After his death, the scientists of Livermore seemed to enter a silent conspiracy: The right way to keep the memory of Mark Mills among us was to imitate him.

It became increasingly clear that the tests of 1958 would be the last—at least for a long time. The Soviet Union stepped up its propaganda for a cessation of nuclear tests. The Eisenhower administration seemed to become more and more interested in nuclear disarmament. Herbert York told me, quite explicitly, that the test series of 1958 would be our final chance to make experimental progress. I was deeply grateful to him for this warning. At the same time, it was one of my greatest disappointments to find that he did not help us in our fight for continued development of nuclear explosives. This was a great change from his earlier words and actions. I never was able to understand his reasons.

The Livermore Laboratory made a superb effort to realize the most from this last opportunity for experimental advances. During the hectic months before a test cessation finally became effective that fall, we had many surprises. Some were disappointments. Some were successes surpassing our most optimistic expectations. We had to make last-minute adjustments. We sometimes had to act on guesses.

The planners of our nuclear devices—John Foster, Carl Haussmann, and others—pressed to include as many experiments as possible in the 1958 series. The laboratory's deputy director, Kenneth Street, worked feverishly with Duane Sewell, who represented common sense in our midst, to schedule everything possible and then just a little more on the test program. And finally it was Gerald Johnson's job, first in the Pacific and later in Nevada, to convert these test plans into realities.

When it was all over, when the series of experiments was finished, when the test moratorium became effective on the last day of October, there was no one in the Livermore Laboratory who could have continued the killing pace. Many on the staff had been working twelve hours a day, steadily, for weeks. Families had been separated for months. But the operation was completed without mishap, and the total results added up to the proper continuation of the increasingly successful program of Livermore.

The efforts of the people at Livermore during the critical summer and fall of 1958 were incredible. The result of their dedicated labor is that our nation today is stronger, and we have a little more time in which to prepare for a difficult future.

While the pitch of activity rose in Livermore during the summer of 1958, an international Conference of Experts convened in Geneva to consider the technical feasibility of policing a test moratorium. Ernest Lawrence was asked to participate. His health was not good, and he knew that the exertion and excitement of Geneva could be dangerous. But he accepted the difficult assignment without hesitation. Lawrence took Harold Brown with him to Geneva. We missed Brown at Livermore during this decisive period, but the need for his quick and thorough understanding was even greater at Geneva.

After participating in the Geneva talks for only two weeks, Lawrence became seriously ill. He tried to stay, but his health did not improve. He came home in a dangerous condition.

I was most anxious to see him, but it was important that he should not be disturbed. At last I was permitted a brief visit, but I was warned that all serious conversation was to be avoided. Lawrence was cheerful when I saw him in the Palo Alto hospital, and it was almost easy to follow the doctors' orders and talk with him pleasantly about pleasant subjects. But at one point he changed his tone. It was clear that he wanted to say something important.

Defying his physicians' explicit orders, Lawrence spoke to me briefly about business. He talked about Harold Brown. The work Brown had done in Geneva, he said, had been splendid. Brown had been able to respond with whatever attitude was demanded by the difficult talks. Displaying a magnificently shrewd sense of diplomacy, he had at various times been moderate, sharp, or determined. He had been the best defender of our cause. Lawrence knew that I was looking for someone to succeed me as director of the Livermore Laboratory. He urged me to stay on the job as long as I could. But he also told me that when I did want someone else to assume the responsibility, I could find no one better than Harold Brown.

A few weeks after this discussion, Lawrence was dead. He had used himself beyond endurance. He had opened a broad field of science, had built a splendid laboratory, and had helped others so they could carry on his work. And he had sacrificed his life for science and for his country.

I spent more than two years as director of the Livermore Laboratory. They were the busiest years of my life. In many respects they were the most satisfying, and the satisfaction came from the human success and the human growth of the young people around me.

The laboratory itself grew. The staff came to number nearly four thousand, and the spheres of scientific interest broadened. In addition to development of nuclear weapons, large sections of

the laboratory became engaged in attempts to control thermonuclear reactions, in work on nuclear rockets, in plans for peaceful applications of nuclear energy, and other projects.

But although the Livermore Laboratory became large, it did
not become unwieldy. Its organization remained close-knit, and
this was largely to the credit of Kenneth Street, a deeply conscientious man of enormous vitality who was a fighter pilot during the war, a professor of chemistry after the war, and later
deputy director of the Livermore Laboratory. He longed to return to his students and to his research. But he first wanted to see
the organization of the Livermore Laboratory on a solid foundation. At Street's suggestion, we placed the laboratory under the responsibility of a half-dozen associate directors. Each had charge
of certain areas of activity. The associate directors met weekly to
make over-all decisions jointly. This prevented the laboratory's
administration from becoming cumbersome, and at the same
time maintained Livermore as a living, unified organization—
much more than a sum of its parts.

Fears that establishment of a second weapons laboratory would
demoralize the scientists of Los Alamos and perhaps actually slow
our nuclear progress never did materialize.

The first hydrogen bomb was developed and perfected at Los
Alamos. It was tested successfully just as the new Livermore
Laboratory was being organized. And within three years of the
founding of the weapons laboratory at Livermore, the young
physicists gathered in California began making substantial and
important contributions toward the development of lightweight
nuclear weapons.

The laboratories at both Los Alamos and Livermore are today
operated by the University of California under contracts with
the Atomic Energy Commission. While the two laboratories constantly aid each other by pooling information, the men of each
laboratory are prodded and goaded into doing their very best

work by a spirit of friendly competition. It is a competition for ideas, not for glory. It makes no real difference which of the two laboratories is credited with great accomplishments. The only important thing is that each laboratory does the very best that it can—and that together they do what is enough.

With two great laboratories engaged in a competition for ideas to keep the United States strong, I became more and more certain that the time had come when I could relinquish my post at Livermore. The very excellence of my associates at the Livermore Laboratory convinced me that my work as director was not essential. For decades I had considered myself primarily as a scientist and as a teacher—not as an administrator. I decided, almost twenty years after becoming an American citizen, that I could best serve my country by returning to the classroom and the laboratory.

But there was another more urgent and more compelling reason for the decision to leave my job. As director of the Livermore Laboratory, I had to be most careful in making any public statement. And if one is too careful, one cannot really be convincing.

Care was essential. As director of a weapons laboratory operated for the Atomic Energy Commission, my personal and private views and recommendations on our nation's course in the nuclear age could be interpreted as reflections of official AEC policy. John McCone, chairman of the AEC, treated me as a real friend and gave me every possible latitude to express my own ideas publicly. But the very fact of his friendship increased my responsibilities and my caution.

The drift toward appeasement, toward making some accommodation with the Soviet Union, on the part of both the American people and American officials made me more uneasy with each passing month. In 1949 and 1950 a group of influential scientists argued against the development of the hydrogen bomb. They said—at various times—that the effort was immoral, that further progress was impossible, and that if we stopped in our dangerous course the Russians would do likewise. Now, a decade later, many of the same scientists argued against further work on nuclear weapons. Their arguments were the same: The work is immoral, it is useless, and in any case the Russians will cooperate. In 1949 these arguments did not prevail. Ten years later they seemed to find general acceptance. But as long as I was director of the Livermore Laboratory, I felt that I could not speak out in a strong voice.

Because I had been involved in a number of significant developments and discussions, I had an opportunity to be heard in a debate likely to determine the future of the United States. This opportunity appeared to me as a duty. There were many things I wanted to say, things that I was convinced needed saying, that could be said effectively only if I were free of any official restraints. They could be said only if I divorced myself from government work.

So on July 1, 1960, I resigned as director of the Livermore Laboratory and asked Harold Brown to take that post. My immediate purpose was to write the book you hold in your hand.

PART TWO:
Science in the World

CHAPTER FIVE

How to Be an Optimist in the Nuclear Age

THE FREE WORLD IS LOSING the cold war. On our rapidly contracting globe, peace has become precarious while war has become sudden, frightening, and devastating. To be a pessimist today requires courage, the courage to realize that we are on the road leading to the end of freedom. To be an optimist also requires courage, but to be an optimist in the nuclear age demands even more: It demands imagination.

Recent history has proved that imaginative optimism can work wonders. At the end of World War II, Europe seemed doomed. The cities were ruins; the people were starving; neighbor hated neighbor. Europe today is rebuilt. In a new prosperity, Europeans live better than ever before. And the hatreds of centuries have been buried and forgotten. The United States helped to achieve all this with the Marshall Plan and other measures of foreign aid, but the rebirth actually was accomplished by the Europeans themselves. Tackling the tremendous task of reconstruction with optimism and with imagination, they have done a job that the pessimists said could not be done.

The pessimist of the nuclear age is terribly concerned about the arms build-up between nations. He is convinced that man during the next few decades will destroy either his liberty or himself. The optimist of the nuclear age, on the other hand, believes military preparedness is the price we must pay for something we desperately need: Time.

There is a special urgency about being an optimist in the nuclear age. If we do not prepare to defend ourselves, we will be defenseless. If we do not make ourselves safe from attack, we will be attacked. If we are not strong, we cannot hope for peace. And peace, even if uneasy, is necessary if we are to have the time to meet one of the greatest challenges of this or any other age. This challenge is not a part of the uncertain future. It is with us now. It demands recognition and must be faced. It has been called the Revolution of Rising Expectations.

Millions of the world's peoples are emerging from primitive poverty, from tribal traditions, from oppressive serfdom. They are clamoring for political equality, for a decent standard of living, for the things they know can be achieved and which they have come to expect because of the example of the United States. And they want these things not in the next generation, not in the next century—but right now.

This Revolution of Rising Expectations is the completion and culmination of the Industrial Revolution. Eighty per cent of all human beings today live in want and misery. Progress in other parts of the world has made them realize that a better life is possible. They want to participate in that better life.

The United States set in motion the developments that led to this present situation. Our government's basic document declares that "all men are created equal." In making this Declaration, we signed a blank check. This check now is being presented for payment, and the sum appearing on it is much greater than all the gold, all the wealth in the world. It reads: The welfare of all mankind.

This is more than anyone can pay. Yet the United States is deeply committed to make the payment. If we fail, our form of society and our way of life cannot survive.

And there does exist a way in which we can pay.

Modern science has created many of our present dangers, and even more dangers will surround us in the future. But modern science also promises the realization of our hopes. We can be pessimistic about science and imagine that it will lead to our destruction. Or we can be optimistic and believe that science will be a boon to all mankind, an instrument that will raise the standard of living throughout the world, an influence that will help create true peace and universal freedom.

These different attitudes toward modern science are reflected by the authors of science fiction.

As a boy, I enjoyed science fiction. I read Jules Verne. His words carried me into an exciting world. The possibilities for man's improvement seemed unlimited. The achievements of science were fantastic, and they were good.

Today I do not read science fiction. My tastes did not change. Science fiction did. Reflecting the general attitude, the stories used to say, "How wonderful!" Now they say, "How horrible!"

Still, it is through science and science alone that we can satisfy the urgent and justified demands of the world's needy billions.

Precisely how science will enable us to meet the Revolution of Rising Expectations, I do not know. My imagination is limited, and even my guesses probably will fall short of the developments that actually will occur during this century. But there can be no doubt that the demands of the world's needy must be met and can be met, and they will be met through science.

Obvious and practical uses of atomic energy in the cause of world peace and for the benefit of the world's needy were proposed as early as 1957. These proposals have yet to become realities because we have been blinded by our fears and prejudices.

Harold Brown and Gerald Johnson, in February of 1957, called a conference at the Livermore Laboratory to sift fact from fancy in the new field of using nuclear explosives for peaceful and beneficial purposes.

Most people responded to such ideas with a shrug and with an incredulous smile. But, after a short time, many of us at the Livermore Laboratory were convinced that nuclear explosions could be thoroughly useful.

During the same summer, Brown mentioned the idea to Dr. I. I. Rabi, a famous physicist with a quick wit. Rabi responded to Brown's enthusiasm with a dry remark: "So you want to beat your old atomic bombs into plowshares."

Brown had no reply, but he now had a name for his special interest: Project Plowshare.

Fortunately, there was an early opportunity to get started with Plowshare. David Griggs, who had effectively aided establishment of a second weapons laboratory, suggested in 1956 that we explore the effects of an explosion deep underground. Griggs, by profession, was concerned with the physics of the earth, and thought that an underground explosion might produce information about the processes occurring in the earth's crust. He pointed out that all the radioactivity produced by an underground explosion would be imprisoned. Necessary safety measures could be simplified, and we no longer would need to mobilize an army of meteorologists to predict wind directions for a test. We could gain flexibility by preparing appropriate locations for underground testing, and we then could proceed with a nuclear experiment whenever we were ready.

Gerald Johnson, who was in charge of Livermore's nuclear tests, recognized these advantages. He also realized that an underground experiment could have an important bearing on our plans for Project Plowshare. The experiment was scheduled for September 1957.

An explosive equivalent to 1700 tons of TNT was placed in a mesa in the Nevada desert. From an observation post a few miles away, a small group from Livermore watched the explosion. They saw much less than they would have seen in an atmospheric test.

The mesa shivered and appeared to lighten in color. The top

of it jumped upward nine inches, throwing up some sand that cascaded down the slopes. Then the earth fell back into place, apparently unchanged except for a few fissures. A slight shock was felt at the observation post. No trace of radioactivity escaped. The experiment was complete.

Then the real work started. The Livermore team had to discover what had happened inside the mountain. The radioactive deposit had to be found. It took weeks to locate the radioactivity, months to piece together details of the underground drama.

The explosion, 797 feet from the mesa's nearest surface and 900 feet from its top, vaporized rock to blow a hole 110 feet in diameter. This hole was lined with four inches of molten rock which contained much of the radioactivity produced by the explosion. Icicles of rock formed in this molten layer and dripped. Then the entire cavity collapsed. Forming a cup beneath the point of explosion, the molten layer congealed into a glassy substance imprisoning much of the radioactivity in an all but insoluble form.

The porous, water-saturated rock around the original hollow sphere was crushed and lost much of its water. When the hollow sphere collapsed, a chimney of rubble 400 feet high and weighing more than 100,000 tons was formed above it. Unlike nearby material, the rubble in this chimney was water-permeable. Some radioactivity had escaped into it. All this radioactivity was watched for years. It moved inches, feet. Long before it could reach any living thing, it would decay. After more than a year the loose material in the chimney again solidified, and it no longer was permeable to water.

All this was highly interesting, and it was most important to Project Plowshare. Our experiment had confirmed that we could break up large quantities of rock and make it permeable to water. And other nuclear explosions had taught us that we could greatly reduce the total radioactive output of a bomb. In time, we could make our Plowshare tools "clean."

Many of Plowshare's potentialities are thoroughly understood today. Others are only dreams for the future. The most important and effective applications may have occurred to no one.

If anyone wants a hole in the ground, nuclear explosives can make big holes. We know how to make holes of a thousand-yard diameter for a small fraction of the cost of traditional excavation methods. The ability of nuclear explosions to move vast quantities of earth and rock—and to move them cheaply—opens a new and important discipline: Geographical engineering. We will change the earth's surface to suit us. We can place appropriate nuclear explosives in such a way that craters resulting from their detonation will overlap, creating man-made harbors, digging deep and rather smooth canals for seagoing vessels, opening shallow and rock-filled rivers to navigation. The cost of moving a cubic yard of material today is one or two dollars. Plowshare can do it for a few cents.

The world needs more harbors and canals. There is much too little protection for big ocean-going vessels along the western shores of South America and Africa. More water transportation, because it is the cheapest form of transportation, would speed the development of backward countries, would increase trade, and would strengthen ties between peoples. But Plowshare should be demonstrated at home before it is exported to others.

Where can the United States make a beginning? Where large populations have settled, we do not want to dig harbors and canals with nuclear explosions. In areas where there are few people, there is no immediate need for harbors or canals. So Plowshare planners have selected as possible sites for artificial harbors areas that are not yet heavily populated but where we expect great developments in the future. There are many areas in which rich ore deposits remain untouched because there is no nearby harbor for economical transportation of the resources.

Such a site has been found in Alaska, where coal deposits near the Pacific coast and our Navy's valuable oil reserves on the inland Arctic slope south of Point Barrow remain virtually unreachable. Ogoturuk, Alaska, south of Point Hope on the Arctic Ocean, is being given careful consideration as the site of our first Plowshare harbor. The harbor basin and the canal connecting it to the ocean would cost less than 10 million dollars. Only four nuclear explosions, each with a yield of 20 kilotons, would be needed to dig a deep-water canal with a width of 250 to 300 yards. A turn-around harbor basin 600 yards in diameter could be dug at the end of the canal with a 200-kiloton nuclear explosion. It would not be difficult to use somewhat bigger yields and create a harbor-canal structure of really respectable dimensions.

We ship coal from Pennsylvania to Japan today through the Panama Canal, and such shipments are made at considerable expense. Appropriate harbors in Alaska would be an economic boon to our forty-ninth State and would benefit the Japanese people by giving them cheaper fuel. It would be wonderful if the nation that has been exposed to the destructive power of atomic explosions would be the first to benefit from the peaceful uses of the same instrument.

Radioactive fallout resulting from such a peaceful series of explosions would be negligible. The huge holes needed for harbors and canals would be created with nuclear devices buried rather deep underground. They would raise vast quantities of earth and rock into the air to be blown away from the site by the wind, and they would push some dirt outward to form the lips of the canal and harbor. But most of the explosion's radioactivity would be trapped deep underground. No more than fifteen per cent could escape as gaseous radioactivity. Some of this could turn into dangerous Strontium 90, but if we are careful in the selection of sites for Plowshare explosions and if we take the necessary precautions, we can be sure that no person will be exposed to radiation effects greater than everyone receives from natural sources.

Furthermore, we have had some success in the development of "clean" nuclear explosives that create little or no radioactive fallout. These "clean" explosives, used for the excavation of Plowshare harbors and canals, would eliminate all concern about resulting fallout. They would make all of our operations simpler, and they would ensure safety without additional expense. Development of "clean" nuclear devices, in fact, is important to many Plowshare applications.

Another facet of Plowshare, one in which the use of "clean" nuclear explosives would be mandatory, would be the exposure of huge deposits of minerals for economical mining. Many mineral deposits are only 300 to 400 feet below the earth's surface. Nuclear explosives, used in a technique which the Russians call "diffusion blasting," can remove up to 1000 feet of the earth's crust, uncovering valuable deposits simply by blowing away the dirt that covers them. The ores then would be exposed for economical open-pit mining, or strip mining, such as that conducted at the huge Mesabi Range in Minnesota. This would eliminate the need for costly dig-and-tunnel mining operations. This aspect of Plowshare could multiply the mineral resources available to the peoples of the world.

"Right now, we are utilizing atomic energy for our economic needs in our own economic interest. We are razing mountains. We are irrigating deserts. We are cutting through the jungle and the tundra. We are spreading life, happiness, prosperity and welfare in places wherein human footsteps have not been seen for a thousand years."

I wish that this statement described our Plowshare program. Unfortunately, the statement was made by Andrei Vishinsky shortly after the Russian nuclear explosion in 1949.

Since that time, the Communists have conducted several large explosions for peaceful purposes. Three explosions in the Lan'chou area of China uncovered deep-lying mineral deposits in 1956. Three other explosions were used in Russia in 1957 and 1958 to make a canal that diverts the Kolonga River. The

Communists say that these explosions have been conventional rather than nuclear. But they have refused to show us their important results, so we do not know whether nuclear explosives were used.

The Communists might develop Plowshare before we do. The time may be near when the Russians will announce that they stand ready to help their friends with gigantic nuclear projects. The consequences of such aid would be an economic penetration a hundred times more extensive than those following the Soviet offer to help Egypt construct the Aswan Dam. Use of nuclear explosives can accomplish feats which billions of dollars cannot. Cheap, safe, and "clean" nuclear explosives in Communist hands also would carry a most important implication: If the Soviet Union has surpassed America in the peaceful uses of the greatest force on the earth, Russia certainly must be ahead of the United States in military applications. As a propaganda weapon, Plowshare could finish the work begun with the launching of Sputnik.

Digging waterways and uncovering minerals are jobs that our nuclear explosives surely can perform. There are many other hopeful and exciting Plowshare possibilities. Some of these, at present, are only dreams. But dreams do come true.

With the help of Plowshare we might extract oil or minerals from rocks. We learned during the Nevada test of September 1957 that even a small underground blast can cause the break-up of large amounts of consolidated volcanic ash. Before the experiment, water could not be pumped through the volcanic rock at the test site. But after the blast, water could be pumped through the column of rubble that caved into the hollow sphere created by the explosion. Different kinds of rocks behave differently, but we hope that a thermonuclear explosion in rocky formations containing oils and minerals will make it possible to obtain the valuable deposits by pumping hot water or a chemical leaching fluid through the blast's rubble. The run-off water, or fluid, then could be processed and the oils or minerals could be gotten much as hot water now is used to bring sulphur from the earth.

Using atomic energy to obtain conventional fuels may seem ironic, but we use both electricity and natural gas to start wood burning in our fireplaces. Even if nuclear reactors can be developed to provide our electrical power needs, conventional oils still will be needed for many years as fuel for automobiles and airplanes and as the foundation of our chemical industries, for the production of plastics and paints. And the untapped oil reserves locked in rocks and sands are enormous. In our own country some 700 billion barrels of oil are imprisoned in shale rock formations in the Green River region of Colorado, Utah, and Wyoming. These rich deposits are solid. But once the rock is broken up, air can be forced underground, a fire started, and the resulting heat can liquefy and drive out as much oil as can be found in all of Arabia.

Additional billions of barrels of oil are contained in tar sands of the Athabaska Lake district near Fort McMurray in northern Canada. The rich Athabaska oil reservoir could produce 100 million dollars' worth of oil from each square mile.

If we employ hydrogen blasts to free these oil reserves and make their products usable, we would have an important political advantage: The West no longer would have to depend on the oil of the Middle East.

Another dream inspired by Plowshare is the possibility of actually changing the compositions of substances underground. In some instances we might eliminate the necessity for expensive blast furnaces and reduction plants. This process—using the earth itself as a retort and a nuclear explosion as the heat source— might turn iron- and oil-containing shales into valuable minerals. In the heat of the explosion, metallic iron would be produced. The iron could be separated easily at the mine. Transportation costs would be lowered drastically, and many conventional steps in the production of iron would become unnecessary. This would mean a great deal to the economy of many backward nations. With proper technical assistance, they could profitably exploit low-yield ore deposits without having to build expensive reduction plants. To turn these present fancies into future facts, repeated experiments will have to be performed using the high temperatures which even small nuclear explosions can yield.

One possible Plowshare product is the hardest, rarest, and most beautiful material on the earth: Diamonds. High pressures near a nuclear explosion could be used to compress some pure carbon until its atoms arranged themselves into this unique substance. We already know that compression can accomplish this aim. With proper arrangement of materials underground, diamonds could be mass-produced.

But what would this accomplish? Produced by the bushel, the stones would have no value. Actually, no large crystals would be obtained, so ladies need not sell their jewelry right away. In order to grow big crystals, long periods of high pressures would be necessary, and nuclear devices could create these only for an instant. But the diamond powder that we could make would be of the greatest importance. These hard-edged pieces are used in machine tools. Their universal availability would provide better tools for many industries, and Plowshare could be the source of a newly common material that would enhance the world's welfare.

Still another Plowshare dream, on which work is in progress, is to deposit and contain the heat of a nuclear explosion deep underground. We hope that the contained heat, replenished by periodic new explosions, can be carried to the surface by water, air, or nitrogen, and used to turn the turbine of an electrical generator much as volcanic heat is now used in Italy and New Zealand to produce power. The cost of the thermonuclear fuel would be negligible. But the maintenance and repair of the pipes that would be damaged by each explosion might well be prohibitive. Perhaps this particular dream should be called a pipe dream.

There probably is no substance more important than water. Its conservation and judicious distribution loom as urgent peacetime problems in the world's immediate future, and the best answers might be provided by Plowshare. We are just beginning to know how to use nuclear explosions to increase the usable supply of water.

Surface reservoirs could be created in certain areas by using Plowshare techniques to collapse mountains at the mouths of river canyons. Nuclear explosions, properly placed, could push mountains into a canyon, providing the earth fill for a reservoir lake in much the same manner that a natural upheaval recently created Earthquake Lake in Yellowstone National Park. Northwest of Fairbanks, Alaska, for example, mountains near Rampart could be pushed into the Yukon River, creating a huge reservoir that would improve the climate of the entire area and would power a larger electrical plant than that operated at Grand Coulee Dam in Washington. Alaska does not need this much power now. But in the decade needed for the reservoir to fill, Alaska will grow. Decades should not be wasted in hesitation. We should begin now to make the best use of nature's gifts.

Some Australians already have been attracted by the idea of using Plowshare techniques to provide more water for agriculture. In Australia, too much water runs the wrong way. Most rivers run down the eastern slope of the mountains near the Pacific, ending their short courses in the ocean and leaving Australia's western reaches a desert. The streams could be diverted to irrigate the desert. We can pierce the mountain ranges and excavate a system of necessary reservoirs most easily and most efficiently with nuclear explosives. The savings over conventional methods of moving large quantities of earth would be enormous. This project is a dream only because it is so great. Courage and enterprise could make it a reality.

Some of our own rivers flow through desert regions on beds of water-impervious rock. Waters of these rivers cannot penetrate the bedrock to raise the underground water levels in the desert regions, so it flows unused to the sea. Plowshare gives us the hope of planting nuclear explosions beneath these rivers, cracking the bedrock so some water would flow underground into the soil. We could, in this way, raise the water table to feed plants in desert regions.

Quite a few of these Plowshare projects would be not only economical but highly profitable. Used for peaceful purposes, nuclear explosives can bring the dreams of truly massive engineering feats into the realm of economic reality. Used to increase, conserve, and distribute the world's supply of water, nuclear explosives can make deserts bloom and help stave off the threat of large-scale hunger posed by the world's exploding population. Day by day, the need for some Plowshare applications is becoming more obvious. And development of "clean" nuclear explosives could make our nuclear tools safe and available for widespread uses.

Explosives using the fusion principle are particularly adapted to the purposes of Plowshare. These are the instruments that can give us the cheapest and cleanest power. When the hydrogen bomb first was discussed, its potential destructive effects occupied the minds of most people. It is difficult to foresee the ultimate consequences of any scientific achievement. It would be inhuman if the scientist should not care how the fruits of his labor are used. It would be presumptuous if he were to abstain from possible developments because he feared the ultimate consequences of his work. He cannot know these consequences. That hydrogen explosions have caused great alarm, we know. That they may cause great damage in the future, we cannot deny. That they may be of almost unlimited benefit to future generations, we have every reason to hope.

But, although we could start on this great peaceful undertaking today, the work remains undone. Plowshare has not been allowed to make its potentially magnificent contributions to the comfort and economic security of men. Plowshare has been held back by a refusal to accept the idea that nuclear explosives might be used for anything other than destruction. The tendency of most Americans to see only evil in the atom, to equate atomic power with the suffering and devastation of Hiroshima, has thwarted Plowshare. Hopes for disarmament and discussions of a test moratorium again and again have postponed needed experiments.

Plowshare may well become the first large-scale, thoroughly economical use of atomic power for peace. But beyond our present atomic horizon, there loom even greater possibilities: Control of the oceans of air and water that carry the life-giving elements.

I doubt that we ever will produce and expend enough energy to control the weather directly. Weather derives its changing properties of calm and violence from the sun, and the solar energy reaching the earth in a single second is more than the energy created by the explosion of our largest thermonuclear device. But someday we might influence the weather indirectly.

Before anything can be controlled, it first must be understood. We are just beginning to approach an understanding of weather. We know that very small causes can grow into very big effects. A slight disturbance of the air masses on the front separating the calm air of the poles from the steady westerly winds encircling the globe in temperate latitudes can trigger a whirlpool a thousand miles wide and can affect the weather over the United States for an entire week. We can and we should increase the number and range of our weather observations. We will use satellites and other means to keep track of clouds and winds. Then, using improved electronic computers, we shall be able to predict weather and trace the origin of each development back to its original trigger.

When this high degree of meteorological understanding has been attained, we might be able to create triggers of our own and realize the age-old dream of actually doing something about the weather. We might spread a cloud of dust over a strategic location or find some other way to upset the temperature balance between air masses. We might break droughts. We might regulate the precise location and time where a hurricane arises, thus predetermining the place where the destructive winds would dissipate.

Such new command over nature will give us responsibilities beyond our present ability to imagine. When rain will be the servant of man, man must be master of himself. Control of clouds will bring either conflict or co-operation between nations. The prospect may seem terrifying, but in the long run this situation or one similar to it will surely arise. Science brings progress; progress creates power; power is coupled with responsibility. This responsibility we shall not escape.

Our greatest undeveloped source of food is the ancient womb of all life and the present home of most of the earth's organic materials: The oceans. Although there are millions of hungry peoples in the world today and although the oceans produce and contain vast amounts of food, we continue to go after that badly needed food with Stone Age methods. On land we no longer are hunters. We have cultivated continents to grow the kinds of food we want and need, and we have developed agriculture as an art that has multiplied the yield of food from each acre. But at sea we continue to use the methods of our Stone Age ancestors by going out with the same kinds of nets and hooks to pull in the same kinds of fish in the same old ways.

From a present so primitive, we surely will progress. We already are beginning to understand the biology of the sea, the limitations of growth in the oceans. We can dream of growing fish in the oceans. We can dream more fantastically of growing only the fish we want, killing the parasites as we have learned to destroy weeds among food-producing plants. The time may not be so distant when we shall know enough to induce mutations and produce genetic changes in fish, creating new breeds of higher food value that would behave in some respects like the salmon which return from the Pacific and swim up the Columbia River to spawn. We might create a new species of fish that would graze on fields of algae we have grown and that would swim into appropriate nets and enclosures when the time came for our ocean crop to be harvested. This may sound fantastic. But the accomplishments of today's farmers would have sounded just as impossible to the Stone Age hunter.

The oceans embrace all continents. They belong to all nations. No individual, no company, no single nation can embark successfully on the global task of oceanic cultivation. The oceans can nourish all humanity only after all humanity has learned, somehow, to act together.

After Hiroshima, it became easy to say that all of us must live in a community of fear. We also could talk of a community of need—of a community of hope.

The position of the pessimist was firmly established at the end of the eighteenth century by an English political economist, Thomas Robert Malthus. His publication was epoch-making, not because he was correct but because he was believed. He stated what was evident: that populations tend to increase in geometric proportion. Logic seemed to force the conclusion that hunger, pestilence, or war were necessary to prevent overcrowding of our planet.

Malthus' predictions have not been substantiated by historical fact in countries of Western civilization. Births have accelerated and lives have been lengthened by medical science. But, at the same time, standards of living have become more decent for a greater proportion of the world's peoples. Human fertility, as Malthus envisioned, has been great. But, so far, human ingenuity has been greater.

As the industrial revolution extends over the rest of the world, there is hope that the gloomy predictions of Malthus will not be realized. There are projects for the future that would multiply the wealth of the world and continue to support an increasing population. Our growth probably will not be limited by our inability to obtain food, raw materials for our industries, or energy. All these are likely to be supplied in abundance during the age of science. The growth and prosperity of the world's population faces only one limitation: Our inability to get along with each other.

Science and technology have grown up inside narrow national boundaries. They are continuing to grow within these same compartments. The problems of our day—such as the construction of nuclear reactors, exploration of space, and the education of future scientific pioneers—are still considered particular to each specific country. But the time is near when necessity and opportunity will conspire to render boundaries between neighbors less meaningful.

The spirit in which we approach these difficult problems may determine whether we can succeed in carrying on the tradition of the American Revolution and our belief in the freedom and equality of men. The choice that lies before us can be stated by a pair of definitions:

A pessimist is a person who is right, but gets no satisfaction from it.

An optimist is a person who chooses to believe that the future is uncertain, and that it is his duty to do something about it.

CHAPTER SIX:

The Renaissance of Alchemy

ONCE UPON A TIME, an alchemist discovered the philosopher's stone. He went to his prince and said: "Sire, what many have sought has been found. I have discovered the substance. One cubic inch of it would weigh billions of tons. But with the help of a tiny speck of this substance, I can make gold and many unheard-of materials. I can make a machine that will keep running on almost no fuel at all. And I can give you power beyond the imagination of man. But the gold will be more expensive than any in your treasury. Whoever touches the machine will die. And God may guide the hand wielding the power that will be placed in it."

The prince had wisdom and courage and faith. He understood the warning, but he also knew that what God placed in the hands of man, man could not refuse.

This was the beginning of modern alchemy. Our philosopher's stone was the atomic nucleus, and the prince was Roosevelt.

Surprising similarities exist between the alchemist of medieval times and the atomic scientist of today. The alchemist tried to transmute base metals into gold; scientists have made materials that have not been on the earth since the Day of Creation. Alchemists strived to build a perpetual motion machine that would require no fuel; scientists have developed nuclear reactors that feed on almost nothing but which are, unfortunately, expensive to run because the machines are intricate and require careful and delicate handling.

Even during World War II, the weapons work conducted at the Los Alamos Laboratory was a relatively small and isolated part of our tremendous nuclear undertaking. Most of the people associated with atomic energy had only vague notions about an atomic bomb. Then, as now, scientists were attracted more to peaceful work than to weapons development, and the most intensive efforts were made toward such peaceful goals as the separation of isotopes and the construction of nuclear reactors for atomic energy.

Our first successes with nuclear reactors came easily, and the ease was deceptive. The amazing discovery that an atom could be split was made by Otto Hahn and F. Strassman in December 1938. During the next eight months, we indulged in a little calculation, a lot of speculation, and even a few laboratory experiments with the kind of chain reactions that would be necessary for the operation of a nuclear reactor. Then, in August of 1939, Leo Szilard prompted Albert Einstein's letter to the White House, and President Roosevelt decided to build the machine.

After the historic decision had been made, government officials tackled the problem of costs. The Bureau of Standards invited several scientists to Washington in November 1939 to discuss this problem. I never will forget that conference, nor will some of my good friends allow me to forget it. Enrico Fermi, whose requests for funds had been refused in the past, would not attend the 1939 meeting. Instead, he asked me to carry his best estimate of reactor costs to Washington. We knew that a nuclear reactor would not work unless the production of neutrons in the chain reaction could be slowed down and controlled. We thought this might be accomplished with pure graphite, a material that was not exactly inexpensive. I reported that because costly materials were needed, a rather large sum of money would be required for our nation's reactor work. I asked for an amount that seemed to me to be large indeed: $6000. It was appropriated, and that was about what this country spent on reactor development in 1940. Important advances were made that year, and scientists became more courageous in requesting funds. Millions of dollars were spent in 1941, and by 1945 our spending on atomic projects totaled two billion dollars.

Our first nuclear reactors were built faster than any have been built since. The famous first reactor located beneath the squash court of the University of Chicago took only one year of intensive effort to construct. Four years usually are required today to build a reactor, but our first was in operation only four years after the principle of fission was discovered. From this speedy and comparatively easy effort, the nuclear reactor emerged as the work horse of the atomic age. It produces vast amounts of energy from small amounts of matter. It is less difficult to understand than the operation of an automobile engine.

Consider the atom. At its center is a grouping of particles called protons and neutrons. Taken together, these protons and neutrons are known as the atom's nucleus. Strong forces are required to hold the protons and neutrons together. When we begin to split, or fission, a nucleus, we must first work against these strong forces. But the direction of these forces soon is reversed. The products of the fission are pushed apart with the release of a million times more energy than that obtained in the chemical rearrangement of groups of atoms known as molecules.

Each element has a distinctive number of protons in its nucleus. The heaviest natural element, uranium, has 92 protons in the nucleus of each atom. Because of the repulsion of this great number of protons, fission fragments are pushed apart with particularly great energy when the uranium atom is split. Just one pound of fissioned uranium would produce the same amount of energy as the burning of almost three million pounds of coal.

Although the number of protons in the nucleus of any atom of any one element is always the same, the number of neutrons may vary. In common uranium, for example, about 139 atoms out of every 140 will have 146 neutrons, giving a grand total of 238 protons and neutrons. So this common form of uranium is known as U-238. But the 140th atom lacks three neutrons, so it is known as U-235.

In a reactor, an additional neutron is fired into a mass of both kinds of uranium nuclei. Under proper conditions, chances are good that this neutron will be captured by one of the U-235 nuclei, because these nuclei are hungry for neutrons. When the additional neutron is attached to the U-235 nucleus, a considerable amount of energy is released, causing a violent motion within the nucleus. This motion has the effect of splitting, or fissioning, the nucleus into two charged portions. These fly apart under the force of their mutual electrical repulsion, releasing even more energy than was obtained when the additional neutron first was attached to the U-235 nucleus. As the two charged portions of the nucleus fly apart, additional neutrons—one, two, three, or more—are shot out at terrific speeds, velocities of about 10,000 miles a second. Some of these are captured by other atoms of U-235, split them, and cause even more neutrons to be shot out to split more U-235 atoms. This chain reaction creates a "population explosion" of neutrons. At the same time, a tremendous amount of energy is released as heat and radiation.

In an atomic bomb the energy produced by the original fission and resulting chain reaction is not controlled. When one neutron splits the nucleus of a U-235 atom, the fragments throw off an average of two neutrons. These two strike two other nuclei, producing four neutrons which find and fission four more U-235 nuclei, shooting out eight neutrons. After the number of energy-loaded neutrons ejected from split atoms is doubled eighty times, the whole material is involved in an almost instantaneous transformation producing tremendous energy—enough to devastate a city like Hiroshima.

In a nuclear reactor, on the other hand, the neutron economy is very carefully controlled. The chain reaction is not allowed to build up speedily, and when energy is produced at precisely the desired rate, a balance is struck. Materials are inserted into the reactor to absorb the excess neutrons in each step of the chain reaction, so the production of new neutrons is exactly equal to the number of neutrons lost or captured by the inserted materials.

Before the end of World War II, even before we had tested our first atomic bomb, a group of scientists at the reactor laboratory in Chicago, that was code-named the Metallurgical Laboratory, made plans for future reactor uses. The group included Fermi, Szilard, Wigner, Arthur Compton, Walter Zinn, Sam Allison and Alvin Weinberg. They aimed high. They foresaw that our future energy needs could be obtained from nuclear sources. Their brilliantly conceived program has influenced the thinking of scientists and industrialists ever since.

But when peace came, the momentum of the early development was lost. Many excellent scientists abandoned reactor projects. Some who returned to their university laboratories at the end of the war were convinced that all reactor problems had been solved. Others left because, even after the war, reactor research continued to be shrouded in secrecy. Scientists who had considered it their patriotic duty to live under security regulations during the war found the same regulations grating in times of peace.

There were some good reasons for keeping our reactor work secret after the war. The chief difficulty, then as now, in manufacturing nuclear weapons was the production of fissionable material for those weapons; reactors can be adapted for the production of plutonium, the material in the atomic bomb that was dropped over Nagasaki. Shortly after the war, the United States nevertheless offered to give the world our basic reactor secrets.

But the Russians, who had their own ways of learning our secrets and enough scientific talent to capitalize on them, rejected the nuclear collaboration offered by our Baruch Plan. So our nuclear reactor program continued to be a secret program.

There can be no doubt that this secrecy harmed our reactor development. Science thrives upon freedom of discussion, and scientists—given a choice—almost always prefer to work on open rather than secret projects. When it became clear that reactor work was to be conducted in strict secrecy, so many scientists returned to the freedom of university laboratories that the Atomic Energy Commission decided to close one of its two reactor laboratories. The AEC believed there was not enough interested scientific talent to keep the reactor program operating at Oak Ridge. Many Oak Ridge scientists lost confidence in the AEC and left government work altogether. A few others moved to the Argonne Laboratory, the new home of Chicago's former Metallurgical Laboratory. But a few stubborn, dedicated men insisted on continuing their work at Oak Ridge.

Eugene Wigner stayed long enough at Oak Ridge to found a reactor school whose graduates were called Doctors of Pile Engineering—DOPE, for short. One DOPE was an unknown Navy captain who put his education to good use, developed the nuclear submarine, and became an admiral: Hyman Rickover.

Wigner eventually left Oak Ridge to return to Princeton University. But a small group of reactor experts headed by Alvin Weinberg stayed on at Oak Ridge, working under terrible handicaps, although they were pressed by the AEC to go elsewhere. Their work slowly gained recruits and recognition, and it is to their credit that the United States Government today has two excellent laboratories—Oak Ridge and Argonne—working primarily on reactors. But it had taken years to recover from the decline after World War II. This decline is one of the reasons why our leadership in atomic energy disappeared so soon.

The small scientific force that gathered around Wigner and Weinberg at Oak Ridge and Zinn at Argonne tackled many difficult long-range problems: What materials might be used most effectively in reactors? How might the best fuels be produced most economically? Can reactors be operated in competition with the most effective conventional producers of power? This was a tough assignment, and it was undertaken with a lot of sweat, an occasional tear, and the hope that the effort would cost no blood.

Responding to the hope that our reactor progress would be bloodless—and recognizing the dangers of reactors and the resulting need for high safety standards—the Atomic Energy Commission in 1947 established its Committee for Reactor Safeguards.

I was the committee's first chairman. During those early years, the committee was about as popular—and also as necessary—as a traffic cop. Some of my friends, anxious for reactor progress, referred to the group as the Committee for Reactor Prevention, and I was kidded about being assigned to the AEC's Brake Department.

The committee's stated function was to pass on the safety features of planned reactors. But the committee also undertook an unassigned and unstated role: We attempted to help various groups working on reactors to share their knowledge. The committee was successful in both important efforts. Thanks to a good deal of care and a great deal of luck, there was not a single fatal reactor accident in the committee's jurisdiction during those early years. And, by acting as a clearinghouse for reactor information, the committee was successful in breaking down the compartmentalization of reactor technology. This compartmentalization had forced many reactor developers to work in the dark, not knowing what other scientists were doing or had done in the same field. The committee made the experiences of all useful to all.

From the beginning, our committee knew that the dangers of nuclear reactors probably would be overrated. To the uninitiated, we knew, reactors would seem frighteningly similar to atomic bombs.

Actually, there is no danger that a reactor might be converted into an atomic bomb. This could not happen. Bombs are carefully constructed to attain a very fast multiplication of neutrons in the fissionable material. The specific goal in bomb construction is the sudden, explosive release of vast amounts of energy. In a reactor, on the other hand, neutron-absorbing materials maintain an exact and precise control of the nuclear chain reaction, making any kind of explosion improbable and an explosion of atomic force impossible. Even if an error in the handling of a reactor's neutron-absorbing materials should allow the nuclear chain reaction to run out of control, the multiplication of neutrons would be relatively slow. This slower generation of neutrons in a runaway reactor would produce heat. The heat, in the worst case, would cause an explosion. But an explosion created by the heat of such a runaway chain reaction would be no more violent than familiar chemical explosions.

Although there is no chance that a reactor could explode with the force of a nuclear weapon, reactors present an even more serious and insidious threat: The possibility of contaminating the atmosphere with radioactivity. An operating reactor is loaded with radioactive particles. The longer a reactor is run, the greater is the accumulation in the reactor of fission products that have comparatively long radioactive lives—and these longer-lived products are dangerous to humans.

Released accidentally and gently from a powerful reactor, these radioactive atoms would be more deadly than the same kinds of atoms released explosively from a hydrogen bomb. The intense heat of a hydrogen bomb explosion drives radioactive particles high into the atmosphere, and they are dissipated and diluted before they finally fall back to the earth. There is no clear-cut evidence that radioactivity so greatly diluted is a real danger to human beings. But radioactivity escaping from a large nuclear reactor would not be so diluted. It could expose people in an area of a hundred square miles to full-force, dangerous contamination. The day an accident in a powerful reactor released radioactive poisons near one of our large cities would be a black day in history.

To avoid the very real and very great danger of an accidental release of radioactivity from a reactor, our committee established a simple procedure: We asked the planner of each reactor to imagine the worst possible accident and to design safety apparatus guaranteeing that it could not happen. The committee reviewed each reactor plan, trying to imagine an accident even worse than that conceived by the planner. If we could think of a plausible mishap worse than any discussed by the planner, his analysis of the potential dangers was considered inadequate. In most cases, the required discussion of potential accidents created a reasonable spirit of caution, and we could advise the Atomic Energy Commission that the reactor would be sufficiently safe.

In assessing reactor designs, we could not follow the usual method of trial and error. This method was an integral part of American industrial progress before the nuclear age, but in the nuclear age it presented intolerable risks. An error in the manufacture of an automobile, for instance, might kill one to ten people. An error in planning safety devices for an airplane might cost the lives of 150 people. But an error allowing the release of a reactor's load of radioactive particles in a strategic location could endanger the population of an entire city. In developing reactor safety, the trials had to be on paper because actual errors could be catastrophic.

Although intolerable, we knew that errors were unavoidable. We could insist on installation of complicated and thoroughly efficient reactor safety equipment, apparatus practically foolproof. But the operators of this equipment necessarily would be human. To err is human, and in anything foolproof the fool can undo the proof. The most dangerous factor in the operation of a nuclear reactor is man. We only could hope that unavoidable human errors in reactor operations would not be made at a tragic cost.

We had historical evidence that the most stringent safety regulations would not necessarily guarantee safety. Our atomic development, despite the greatest precaution, already had cost the lives of a few unintended victims.

The first radiation fatality in this nation's atomic advance occurred at Los Alamos. Oppenheimer, as director of that busy laboratory, used every possible occasion to warn his personnel about the dangers of radiation. He established strict codes of safe conduct that seemed to leave no margin for a radiation accident. After the surrender of Japan, Oppenheimer sent his congratulations to the personnel at Los Alamos, praising and thanking them for exercising extreme caution and developing the atomic bomb without radiation accidents.

That same evening, a young scientist named Henry Daghlian returned to the laboratory alone to complete an experiment. There was a rule that no one should work alone on the assembly of a critical mass of radioactive material—that is, a mass big enough to maintain a chain reaction. But Daghlian ignored the rule.

Daghlian's experiment was almost complete. He started to insert the last piece of material, the piece that would push the mass to a critical stage. Had he followed standard safety practice, had he inserted the piece from below, he would have retained complete control. He could have withdrawn the dangerous piece when the counters showed a high acceleration of disintegrations. But he tried to insert the last piece at the top of the assembly. His fingers slipped, and the last piece fell into the assembly uncontrolled. There was a sudden, bluish glow. Daghlian knew what had happened, and he reacted with great courage. He hit the assembly, and it flew apart. Actually, the reaction probably had stopped before he hit the assembly. But Daghlian had been exposed to an excessive dose of radiation, and in a few days he died.

Such accidents are tragic. Fortunately, they are exceedingly rare. But because they are tragic, each is carefully analyzed so we can learn lessons necessary to avoid similar mistakes in the future. The analysis of these unintentional and dreadful experiments has guided us to greater safety.

Complete safety does not exist. But the probability of human errors in reactor operation can be decreased by using completely automatic devices. In addition, one must recognize which types of reactors can be constructed with the greatest safety.

Stationary reactors are the safest. When a reactor, large or small, is built in one place to be operated in one place, it can be equipped with ingenious safety equipment, mechanically interrelated, that all but eliminates the hazard imposed by the presence of human beings. Furthermore, our committee's specifications demanded that big stationary reactors be enclosed by a roomy gas-tight shell with walls strong enough to withstand any explosion that could possibly be expected, thus ensuring containment of radioactive poisons even in the improbable off-chance that the reactor's safety devices should fail and allow an explosion to occur. This containment, especially of big reactors near centers of population, is essential. To people downwind from the reactor, it conceivably could be a matter of life or death.

Mobile reactors designed to provide power for the vehicles carrying them are not as safe. The vehicle's space limitations may preclude installation of some safety devices used to guard against accidents in stationary reactors. And mobile reactors aboard moving vehicles are exposed to a hazard unknown in the operation of a stationary reactor: the threat of a collision that might release a mobile reactor's radioactive contamination into the atmosphere.

Operation of a mobile reactor is always risky. But some risks cannot be avoided. Our nuclear-powered submarines, for example, are capable of going anywhere in the world and returning any attack made upon our nation. They are most important to our national strength, essential to our nation's defense, and are becoming a decisive element of our retaliatory force. Our nation would risk a great deal more by not operating these nuclear submarines than we risk by operating them. The nuclear power plant of these submarines has been built as carefully and as safely as possible. They are as well equipped with automatic safety devices and are as well contained as any stationary reactor. We need not worry about them.

The mobile reactor used to power a ship is, by all odds, the most reasonable. There is space on a vessel for all kinds of safety apparatus. But the value of commercially operated nuclear surface ships to our economy is, to my mind, doubtful. And the risk presented by a nuclear-powered commercial ship is much greater than the acceptable risk of a nuclear submarine. Operated under the strictest military discipline, a nuclear submarine is not likely to be involved in a collision.

Nuclear airplanes certainly are more dangerous than nuclear ships. There is a great probability that radioactive contamination would be released from a nuclear-powered plane's reactor if it should crash on land. I do not believe that nuclear-powered commercial planes, flying passengers and freight across our nation, can be justified in the foreseeable future—even if it were possible to build such airplanes.

After having spent close to one billion dollars for development of a nuclear-powered airplane, our government decided that the success of this undertaking was more doubtful than ever; it was abandoned, at least for the time being, during the early months of the Kennedy administration. It is possible that some kind of nuclear planes might someday be needed for our defense. If that day should come, we should guarantee our own safety by insisting that the nuclear planes give our cities a wide berth. I should prefer that a nuclear plane would fly only over the oceans so its reactor would sink harmlessly into the sea in case of a crash. If a nuclear plane crashed on land, its reactor probably would crack and stop operating. But the heat in the reactor would force great amounts of radioactivity into the atmosphere, poisoning the air for many miles in a downwind direction.

Some other suggested uses of mobile reactors involve monumental risks and infinitesimal justifications. In the operation of these mobile reactors, the dangerous human factor would be determining, and reactor safety would be impossible. Included in this category of high-risk reactors would be those suggested as power plants for automobiles and locomotives. They would carry a constant threat of heavy radioactive contamination to every part of our nation. There is no reason to believe that the number of collisions involving nuclear-powered automobiles would be any less than today's staggering number of collisions between gasoline-powered automobiles. But in a collision of nuclear-powered cars, the escape of radioactivity could hardly be avoided. Such a calamity is dreadful to contemplate, and certainly too terrifying to risk.

The peaceful atom in 1953 was given a great new impetus when the Eisenhower administration, in a courageous about-face after years of secrecy, decided to relax controls and encourage private enterprise to enter the field of reactor development.

AEC Chairman Lewis Strauss, finding private industry interested in reactors, urged President Eisenhower to adopt a position that would open reactor research to the public and put the powerhouse of the nuclear age to work for mankind. President Eisenhower heeded the advice and on December 8, 1953, delivered his famous Atoms for Peace address before the United Nations.

President Eisenhower discussed the "many difficult problems that must be solved in both private and public conversations if the world is to shake off the inertia imposed by fear and is to make positive progress toward peace." Then he laid before the United Nations a broad plan for the organization of an international agency to conduct reactor research with materials contributed by individual nations, and he said:

"The more important responsibility of this Atomic Energy Agency would be to devise methods whereby this fissionable material would be allocated to pursue the peaceful pursuits of mankind. Experts would be mobilized to apply atomic energy to the needs of agriculture, medicine, and other peaceful activities. A special purpose would be to provide abundant electrical energy in the power-starved areas of the world. Thus the contributing powers would be dedicating some of their strength to serve the needs rather than the fears of mankind."

A most important outgrowth of President Eisenhower's address was the 1955 Conference on the Peaceful Uses of Atomic Energy held in Geneva. The Russians initially declined to attend. But when it was perfectly clear that there would be a party, Russia decided to come. It was the first large confrontation of the scientists of the East and West.

The conference was a great success. The United States finally stripped the cloak of secrecy from its nuclear reactor program. This, of course, brought the day closer when other nations would be able to develop reactors, produce plutonium, and eventually construct nuclear weapons. But we knew that progress could not be delayed. We knew that if we did not share our knowledge of reactors, other nations eventually would develop their own reactors—but in secret.

Russian scientists, who had been isolated and who were eager for recognition and exchange, were anxious to show off their remarkable accomplishments, and they made effective contributions to the conference. They raised the Iron Curtain on extensive areas of Russian science, and delegates from the United States for the first time glimpsed the amazingly rapid progress of the Soviet scientific effort. We realized, finally, just how much the Russians knew and what they were able to do with what they knew. This realization forced many United States delegates to conclude that science was moving ahead faster in Russia than in America.

After the Geneva conference, many large corporations in this country took advantage of the opportunity to develop and build their own nuclear power plants. The widespread interest in nuclear power was caused in part by the 1956 nationalization of the Suez Canal and the resulting question of whether large quantities of conventional fuels would remain easily available.

Private industry plunged into the design and construction of nuclear power plants with considerable optimism. Many people thought the golden age of really abundant fuels and universally inexpensive electrical power might be just around the corner. Interest in this bright future of nuclear-produced electricity was keen, and companies were anxious to participate. Since private industry first was permitted to build and operate nuclear reactors under AEC licenses, more than 130 utility companies in every part of our nation have undertaken some kind of atomic program.

The early experiences of these companies and other firms abroad clouded the future of nuclear-produced electricity, but left the cloud with a silver lining. As more became known of the difficulties of producing electricity in nuclear-powered plants, the optimists were forced to become realists. Some even became pessimists.

No one in 1955 and 1956 knew the economics of nuclear-produced power. No one really knows today. Government bookkeeping is necessarily arbitrary and frequently does not reflect an accurate picture of costs. Private industry has been unable to make a completely accurate assessment of the cost of nuclear-produced electricity because nuclear power plants have been operating for so short a time and the uranium cores for those plants are purchased from the government at a government-fixed price that may not represent actual cost.

We do know today that nuclear power is expensive. The dangers of radioactivity inherent in the operation of nuclear reactors add to the costs of operation. Necessary safety devices make reactor construction expensive. Operators must be expensively trained. The reactor must be run by remote controls which must be thoroughly reliable, and this increases the cost of power production. The reactor's waste products, contaminated with radioactivity, now are buried deep underground at considerable expense. Such extraordinary, costly safety precautions are not required in the operation of a conventional power plant.

Reactor fuel, U-235, is rather cheap. Separation of U-235 from common uranium, U-238, by the diffusion process is surprisingly economical. Neither is the fuel scarce at the present time. Stimulated by the AEC's policy of purchasing uranium, Americans have gone prospecting for the mineral. In a modern "gold rush," we have discovered that uranium, even in concentrated ores, is not too rare.

The cost of fuel for electrical power plants, whether nuclear or conventional, is about the same. The big cost differences are in the capital and operating expenses due to the novelty and the need for extreme safety in nuclear-powered generating plants. These high capital and operating costs make the production of electricity in nuclear plants substantially more expensive than in conventional plants.

The present high costs of nuclear-produced electricity almost certainly will be lowered in the years ahead. Experience in this new field will cut costs, but until this experience is obtained, nuclear-produced electricity probably will be economical only in areas where conventional fuel is expensive. It is as cheap or cheaper than conventionally produced electricity in some out-of-the-way places today because nuclear fuels are much less bulky than conventional fuels and therefore cheaper to transport. Nuclear power plants offer another distinct advantage, they do not pollute the atmosphere with smoke and fly ash.

In the long run, we face a serious problem: Availability of fuels. If we continue to use present reactor designs and exploit only rich ores, the energy that is available in nuclear fuels is considerably less than the energy available in conventional fuels. And some scientists predict that we will have exhausted all available conventional fuels within the next century. This does not mean, however, that we face a bleak and fuel-starved future. Nor does it mean that nuclear reactors will continue to be used only for specialized purposes, never seeing really widespread use as power producers. In a progressive and orderly manner we are learning more and more about how to extract needed uranium economically from poor, low-grade ores that really are abundant.

But the best answer to the problem of fuel availability appears to be the development of a new kind of nuclear reactor which is more difficult to build but which offers radical help: The breeder reactor.

Most reactors today are burner reactors using U-235 as fuel. In natural uranium only one out of 140 atoms is fissionable U-235, and even this fraction of the total energy content of uranium is not utilized completely by today's burner reactors. Breeder reactors, on the other hand, could convert virtually all of the natural uranium into readily fissionable plutonium. This conversion, called breeding, theoretically would provide about 140 times more energy from a given amount of common uranium than is obtained today in burner reactors. Actually, energy losses would occur in the operation of breeder reactors, but such reactors nevertheless would produce at least twenty times more energy from a given amount of uranium than we can get from today's burner reactors.

An element somewhat more abundant than uranium can also be used. This element is thorium. The breeding process can convert thorium into an active variety of uranium, and its energy can be utilized in reactors.

Many ordinary rocks contain a few parts per million of common uranium or thorium. This is a small fraction, but if breeder reactors can be made to convert natural uranium and thorium into practical fuels for nuclear reactors, common rocks would yield more energy than their weight in coal—and the world would have a practically inexhaustible supply of energy: We could burn rocks.

I believe that some of the vexing problems that have plagued reactor development will disappear. An increasingly difficult problem is the necessary disposal of radioactive wastes. These waste products might become useful by-products of our reactor program. Instead of being buried, radioactive wastes might be processed and put to work as radioisotopes. We might convert these radioactive liabilities into assets.

Many radioisotopes are produced by the fission process itself. Others are made by exposing an element to neutrons in a nuclear reactor. The element absorbs a neutron and becomes radioactive. Atoms of the activated element are called radioisotopes, and each looks and acts the same as any other atom of that particular element—except that it is radioactive and gives off atomic particles or waves of radiation of its own. It sends out signals that say: "Here I am." These signals can be detected and followed with special instruments.

Radioisotopes are being used in hundreds of ways in hospitals, in factories, and on farms. They already constitute a big and expanding industry now surpassing 100 million dollars a year.

All over the United States, manufacturers are using radioisotopes to make products that work better or last longer. Radioisotopes can both standardize and improve manufactured products. Soaps have been improved, for example, by using them to wash clothes soiled with dirt containing radioisotopes—and then checking both the clothes and the laundry water to detect the radioisotopes in each as a measure of how much dirt the soap actually removed. Radioisotope tracers are used in much the same way in studies of wear on tires, pistons, gears, cutting tools, floor waxes, paints, furniture finishes, plastic counter tops, and hundreds of other products.

A simple property of radiation is used to measure thickness and density. This has helped to standardize the manufacture of products as diverse as automobile tire fabrics, cigarettes, and sheets of paper, glass, or metals.

Used daily in many hospitals, radioisotopes have become tremendously important in medical research, diagnosis, and healing. Radioactive tracers tell medical men exactly how, when, and where various minerals, salts, and other substances are absorbed by the body. Disorders of the thyroid gland, for example, often are diagnosed by having the patient drink a weak solution of radioactive iodine. By measuring the accumulation of radioisotopes deposited by the iodine in the thyroid gland, doctors can tell how quickly it is absorbed and determine whether the thyroid is behaving normally. Just as medical science has used familiar radium for years, radioisotopes today are being used as a source of radiation to destroy harmful tissue growths.

By watching the movements of radioisotopes through plants, agricultural specialists have learned that nutrients are absorbed through leaves as well as roots. We used to believe that minerals could be taken up only by the roots of plants. Now we can spray these minerals from airplanes flying over large fields. Radioisotopes also are being used in studies of animal nutrition. Added to various diet supplements fed to farm animals, the radioisotope tracers can be followed through the animal's digestive system, and the particular value of an individual diet supplement can be measured accurately.

Much more research is necessary before radioisotopes even begin to approach their potential usefulness in agriculture. The need for this research is vital. The world's exploding population demands that we obtain maximum food value from each acre, plant, and animal. Radioisotope tracers can show us the way to this maximum food production.

More radioactive isotopes could be used in crop conservation and in food sterilization. We might control infestation of our storehouses by rodents and insects with a limited amount of radiation. Much more radiation is needed to sterilize canned food. No radioactivity would enter the food, but at these high levels of irradiation undesirable chemical side effects appear. But sterilization by heat or conservation by freezing also produces some changes that we do not like. Each type of food must be investigated to find out how it can best be preserved. These applications might require great amounts of radioactivity. The time may come when we will need more radioisotopes than we can produce.

Even more varied applications of radioactivity would be involved in the production of new species of farm products, vegetable or animal, with the help of mutations. Most research in this field now is done in the laboratories of universities and research institutes.

Mutations produce new properties which will be inherited. In most cases, the new properties are harmful. In fact, they usually are lethal. But in a few lucky instances, they create a superior agricultural product. In finding this better product, we have to use the hit-and-miss method, and an important part of the work is to recognize the superior product whenever it happens to occur.

This research method demands a great number of experiments. I can find no good reason why tests in this field should not be made more plentiful, more inexpensive, and more effective by having them done on farms by farmers.

Radioisotopes are not too dangerous to be placed in the hands of the nation's farmers. Successful farmers in the United States are, by and large, intelligent men; many successful farmers are graduates of colleges or universities and have been educated in the intricacies of plant and animal life. I think we should permit and urge these farmers to conduct experiments with radioisotopes on their farms. We do permit educated and responsible druggists to handle deadly poisons and urge educated and responsible doctors to experiment with dangerous microbes. Both poisons and microbes are more dangerous in some ways than radioisotopes. Microbes multiply; isotopes do not. When a poison is misplaced, it might be difficult to find; isotopes can be located with a simple Geiger counter.

With more extensive research, I am positive that hundreds of new uses will be found for radioisotopes. They are being widely used today. But this is only a beginning. We have in our hands a new and simple tool. Scientists already have used this tool to determine the age of a Pharaoh's tomb. In what ingenious ways this tool will be used in the future, no one can guess.

Our success in exploding a hydrogen bomb led to an effort to develop a new kind of nuclear reactor. This consequence of our thermonuclear success was both logical and inevitable. Since a fusion bomb had been proved many times more powerful than a fission bomb, it seemed to follow that a fusion reactor would produce much more energy than a fission reactor. Government officials, in effect, turned to scientists who had developed the thermonuclear bomb and said: "All right! You have succeeded in unleashing the destructive power of fusion. Now try to tame and control this power for peace."

Unfortunately, this was easier said than done. Fusion proved much more difficult to control than the chain reaction of fission. To tame fission, we needed only to balance the production and loss of neutrons. This slowed the production of energy, giving us time to carry it away. A fusion reaction also can be slowed by using a highly diluted gas for fuel, sharply reducing the rate of fusion. The interior of a fusion reactor, in fact, should contain so few atoms that it could qualify as a fairly good vacuum.

An ingredient in addition to atomic fuel is necessary for the functioning of any reactor. In a fission reactor, this added ingredient is the population of neutrons that strikes and splits atoms. In a fusion reactor, the required added ingredient is an extremely high temperature that will agitate particles so that they will approach each other close enough to start the fusion process in spite of their great mutual electrical repulsion. The temperature needed is much higher even than the extreme temperatures existing in the center of the sun and stars. Such exceedingly high temperatures might be expected to destroy any vessel used to contain a fusion reaction. But this is not the case. Since the particles in the interior of a fusion reactor would be so few, the container itself would not be destroyed. Rather, these few particles would strike the walls of any container and lose their energy long before they could find each other and fuse. Thus the process would be quenched even before it was begun.

For a long time it has been clear that there is a way to avoid these difficulties of containment. When exposed to extremely high temperatures, the particles from which atoms are made do not stay together. The atoms of hydrogen used in fusion reactions are torn apart into particles carrying positive and negative electrical charges. In a magnetic field, these charged particles do not move along a straight line, but spiral around the magnetic lines of force. In this way, magnetism can confine the particles. To construct a fusion reactor, we first must try to make a strange container called a magnetic bottle.

Careful experiments had shown that high-energy particles could be contained in a magnetic bottle for reasonably long periods of time. But once this was understood, we began to encounter real difficulties. If the bottle's reactor fuel was too highly diluted, fusion was improbable because the few particles in the bottle seldom were able to find each other. When we tried to increase the number of particles, they acted upon the magnetic fields and shoved them aside. The bottle, in other words, leaked. So it became obvious that the primary difficulties of controlling thermonuclear reactions have little to do with the kinds of problems we solved during development of the thermonuclear bomb. The questions involved in thermonuclear control are more closely related to those of a quite different field: A study of the motion of gases.

During the last century, when an increasing number of people became interested in the possibility of flying, their main difficulty was that they did not understand the laws governing currents of air. Gentle motion of air occurs in simple, regular patterns. But at an increased speed, an entirely new type of behavior begins; this is called turbulence. The question of when and how turbulence arises is crucial when trying to understand how the wings of a bird or an airplane are supported by air.

The problem of confining hot fusion gases is similar but more involved. In addition to the motion of gases, we must consider the interaction of particles with magnetic and electrical forces. In most cases, complicated and rapidly changing patterns result which correspond to turbulence and in which the magnetic lines can be shoved aside—and the heat of the gas is lost. We are looking, hopefully, for the exceptional cases in which the motion of the gas is simple and the magnetic bottle is leakproof.

When people tried to build the first flying machines, quite a few scientists produced gloomy proofs that no one ever would be able to fly. But the flight pioneers were able to disregard these learned arguments, because they knew that flight was possible. They had the example of the birds. And they had conducted experiments with man-made kites. Studies of kites had a great deal to do with the art of flying and demonstrated beyond all doubt that some solution to the problems of flight did exist.

In our efforts to build a fusion reactor, we are not as fortunate as the builders of flying machines. We have no birds to encourage us. We do have the shining examples of the sun and stars, but they accomplish confinement by the enormous weight of the outer layers of the hot gases of which stars consist. Nothing of the kind can be reproduced in a laboratory.

But laboratory experiments with magnetic bottles can be conducted, and they can be compared with last century's game of flying kites. I believe our progress in the United States toward controlling thermonuclear reactions has been effective and fast. We did not rush prematurely into construction of big machines, but concentrated from the very beginning on the investigation of small kites. Some of our kites now are beginning to flutter in a promising manner.

Time has verified our early suspicion that fusion is more difficult to control than fission. Just four years after the discovery of the principle of fission, our first controlled fission reactor was functioning. After ten years of intensive effort on the control of fusion, we still have no proof that practical control is feasible. I have little doubt that someday we will control fusion. Some of my friends are less optimistic. The effort to control fusion is called, in our strange language, Project Sherwood. And one of my friends has explained the project's name by saying: "It sure would be nice if it worked; it sher wood."

Optimistic as I am, I do not believe that cheap energy from controlled thermonuclear reactions will be available in the years immediately ahead. When we talk about economical fusion reactions, we probably are behaving like cave men crouching around their newly discovered miracle, man-made fire, and predicting that the day would come when fire would carry their burdens and do their chores with an unbelievable speed and efficiency.

We are living in a scientific age. Developments that used to take thousands of years now may be crowded into decades. I would guess that our children will obtain energy from controlled thermonuclear reactions, but the results of this accomplishment may not be guessed much more effectively than cave men could speculate on the future role of fire. It is possible, nevertheless, to venture a few simple guesses.

Fuel for thermonuclear reactions can be obtained abundantly from the hydrogen in the waters of the oceans. In fact, one in every 6000 atoms of hydrogen is good fuel for a fusion reactor. With the help of fission, we may burn rocks; fusion may burn water. In either case, the people of the world would have a practically inexhaustible supply of energy.

The most convenient energy, however, may be produced by fusion reactors. Like fission reactors, fusion reactors will produce radioactivity. But in the operation of fusion reactors, we can greatly reduce the amount of radioactivity and we can eliminate all but relatively harmless radioactive products.

Fusion reactors, furthermore, might produce electrical energy directly. Today we use the indirect method: The burning fuel turns water into steam; the steam pushes a piston; the piston turns a wheel; the wheel carries coils past other coils; and in the moving coils—at long last—an electric current is generated. Electrical plants powered by today's fission reactors use this clumsy and expensive generating equipment operated by steam heated by the reactor. Fusion reactors hold the promise of producing electricity directly by the interaction of hot gases and magnetic lines of force. The hot gas can act upon the elastic walls of the magnetic bottle as steam acts upon pistons, and the lines of magnetic force set into motion by the hot gas can induce useful currents in appropriately placed coils. In the entire apparatus there would be no moving mechanical parts. The only movement would be in the hot gas, the magnetic lines of force, and the resulting flow of current through the coils.

These are distant possibilities; we hope they will be realized. We hope they will be economical by the end of this century. But there may be somewhat unexpected, earlier developments. Even today a serious effort is being made to produce electricity by the interaction of magnetic fields and hot gases—heated not with fusion but with conventional fuels.

Energy production is not the only useful result which we may expect from thermonuclear reactions. Fusion reactors might provide new and better methods of space propulsion, and they may generate powerful electromagnetic waves that could carry signals of great strength. These may be most useful in communications. We might increase the intensity of these electromagnetic signals sufficiently to transmit energy to be used as power for space stations or satellites.

There can be no guess, question, or doubt about one result of our efforts to control the thermonuclear reaction: We understand much more about a number of remarkable phenomena that take place within the bowels of the earth, in the stars and in interstellar space. The interaction of magnetic fields with moving fluids near the core of our planet has explained the existence and the slow variations of the earth's magnetism. We receive electromagnetic signals from distant stars, and cosmic radiation is raining down upon us from the depths of our own Milky Way system. We are beginning to understand in some detail that these signals and rays are produced in the interplay between magnetic fields and the exceedingly dilute gases near stars and in the huge, almost empty spaces of our galaxy. All this is similar to the processes in our magnetic bottles. Project Sherwood's most valuable contribution, eventually, may not be an inexhaustible supply of energy—but an increased knowledge of the secrets of our vast universe.

CHAPTER SEVEN

The Lure of Infinity

INFINITY HAS A STRANGE and powerful appeal for men. We have known two visible symbols of infinity: The oceans and the heavens. But the oceans proved to be finite. Thousands of years ago, Greek scientists calculated the size of our globe, and many centuries later the disciples of Prince Henry the Navigator conquered the earth's watery expanses. Today we stand on the threshold of infinity's other symbol: Space. The human mind has grappled with the enormity of space, but we do not know whether space is truly infinite or whether it, too, is finite. This we do know: Modern explorers in the coming years will look back and see our earth as the small object it really is. And when they do so, these explorers will have penetrated much less than a billionth part of the universe that is our home.

I do not know, and I think no one really knows, what inspired the brave men who explored the Atlantic Ocean five centuries ago. Most historians say the inspiration was a search for commerce and power. That may be. It also may have been a lure less practical and rational or an overwhelming curiosity that demanded an answer to the question of whether the earth was round or flat. Columbus' confessed goal, we know, was trade with the Far East. In this, he failed. But he accomplished much more —even though he did not expect it and never fully realized it.

I believe we should undertake our space explorations with an open mind, without rigid goals, without preconceived objectives. We have only vague notions of what we will find in space, and we still cannot realize which of the things we find will be really important. Columbus' example has taught us, however, that if we fix our eyes on a predetermined purpose, we may be blind to discoveries of greater significance.

When Jules Verne described the first voyage to the moon, he had no doubt about the place from which space explorers should be launched: It was the United States of America. But we, the practical-minded successors of Jules Verne's contemporaries, left the initiative to others. On October 4, 1957, the first man-made satellite was thrust into space. It circled the earth 1400 times before it was slowed down in the fringes of our atmosphere and disintegrated like a falling meteor. It was a product of Russian technology. It was called Sputnik, the Companion.

Whatever else we are politically or philosophically, in the first place we are men. In 1957, men embarked on a great adventure. Everyone participated, in spirit, when Sputnik was launched on its journey. Every scientist had an even more specific reason to welcome the beginning of space exploration. Science is the spearhead of the great adventure that has multiplied our understanding, our power, and our responsibilities a thousandfold. The rise of Sputnik was an inspiration to all of us. At the same time, it was a cause for worry.

Before Sputnik, the United States was the acknowledged world leader in all matters of massive technology. The superiority of American know-how, the excellence of American industrial and technical methods, was unquestioned. Most Americans considered it axiomatic that in these areas the United States always would remain in first place. Then, in the sky at night, we could see Sputnik as incontrovertible evidence that someone else had been able to do something that we did not have the vision or the initiative to do. Sputnik, suddenly, put us in second place.

Sputnik caused fear. It was painfully apparent that Russia, capable of throwing a satellite around the earth, also could launch a device armed with an atomic bomb or a hydrogen bomb. Watching Sputnik flash overhead in the night, Americans realized as never before that our nation was in the range of Russian rockets—rockets that could carry the terrible destructiveness of nuclear weapons from launching pad to target, from continent to continent, from hemisphere to hemisphere in twenty minutes.

Sputnik shrank the world and canceled the guarantee of safe isolation that had been provided us by the great oceans. Sputnik made it obvious and essential that we revise our preparations for national security, overhaul our plans for civilian defense, abandon concepts that suddenly were obsolete, and concentrate on a new kind of technological exploration.

In the range of Russian rockets, we could not hope to evacuate our cities and prime target areas in case of attack. Our fighter planes, designed to meet approaching bombers, could not be used to protect us against missiles. Wartime attack by long marches of weary men had been a matter of months. Bombing tactics perfected during World War II made conflict a matter of hours. Sputnik made destruction a matter of minutes.

The Russian achievement was a surprise. Actually, it should have been expected. Long before Sputnik, we had persistent reports and published evidence of a great Soviet effort in space technology. In Geneva during the 1955 Conference on the Peaceful Uses of Atomic Energy, our scientists were impressed by Russian interest and achievements in space projects. Our military experts were aware that Russian rocketry had played a great part in repulsing German forces at Stalingrad, and we were equally aware that after World War II some of the most accomplished German rocket technicians and space scientists had disappeared behind the Iron Curtain.

Russia had good reason to be interested in rocket development, and good reason to be content with the step-by-step progress from short-range to long-range rocketry. Concerned about the behavior of nations near her borders, Russia had a potential use for short-range rockets.

The United States, on the other hand, was only mildly interested in rocket development after World War II. Our military strategists believed that rockets would be useful to the United States only if they could span the oceans and hit a target with an accuracy that would destroy that target. We did not believe that this high degree of accuracy would be possible, considering the probability of error posed by thousands of miles of delivery. While Russia was pushing rocket development, our military leaders felt that delivery of a long-range rocket would be so inaccurate that even with an atomic bomb as a pay load, a long-range rocket would not destroy an intended target. So, instead of developing rockets as carriers for atomic weapons, the United States concentrated on refinements of bombers.

This was a grave error of judgment. No single political administration can be blamed for it. It was a military decision that neglected the rule that a person must learn to walk before he can run. The Wright Brothers had to fly their clumsy airplane a few hundred feet at Kitty Hawk before we could develop modern jet planes. The atomic bomb had to be developed and tested before we could construct a practical thermonuclear bomb. The short-range rocket should not have been given a low priority by our military experts, but should have been recognized as a forerunner of the intercontinental ballistics missile and of the vehicles that were to reach out into space. Our experts' erroneous judgment gave Russia a head start in rocketry. It opened the missile gap.

This dangerous error involves a bitter lesson that we have not yet learned. Military planners in the United States depend too much on their crystal balls. They attempt to look into the scientific future, and try to make precise predictions of military requirements for many years to come. They try to order keys for specific locks they have not even seen. They try to guess what weapons our potential enemies might develop in the decades ahead, and then formulate plans of defense against those weapons. But the future always is uncertain and unpredictable. We know, from the past, that the course of progress can be accelerated or diverted by a single unexpected idea. The weapons which our military strategists think a potential enemy will develop years from now might, indeed, be developed much sooner —or not at all. A Russian scientist's inspiration might provide a break-through to speedy progress, or it might set the development of Russian weapons careening down an entirely new track.

Our best scientific defense against this uncertain future is to make progress where progress can be made. That most marvelous of human instincts, curiosity, if permitted literally to reach for the stars, would pay much higher dividends than any closely motivated, narrow plan. We do have the capacity for mobilizing considerable resources once we have a firmly established purpose. But we often are not doing enough exploratory work. Only after such work can long-range goals be established with real hopes of success. If we had been allowed the free exercise of our scientific curiosity and had been more inspired by an extension of human knowledge—then the United States would be stronger today.

The United States, fortunately, did not altogether neglect rocketry. Despite the judgment of our military strategists that rockets and missiles had little value in our weapons arsenal, the United States immediately after World War II made a start on rocket projects. The program remained modest indeed until we proved the capabilities of the hydrogen bomb. Then such farsighted men as John von Neumann and Trevor Gardner realized that missiles tipped with thermonuclear bombs would be decisive weapons. Military planners who had discounted missiles as carriers for atomic bombs, impressed by the greatly increased destructive powers of thermonuclear bombs, reconsidered the practical value of rockets and missiles to our national defense. A step-up was ordered, belatedly, in our missile program. It was not until 1953 and 1954 that rocket development in the United States ✓ finally began to gain momentum.

This is the historical reason for Russia's being ahead of the United States in rocketry in 1957, when the first Sputnik was launched. Russia has been ahead of us ever since. Their rockets are bigger and more powerful. They can carry heavier weapons or more equipment. So they can be used in a more flexible manner. And, as far as we can guess, the Russians have more rockets than we. In 1962, the missile gap continues to be a harsh reality.

Even though we have not yet closed the missile gap, even though we have not caught up with Russia in missile performance, even though we should do a great deal more toward building a retaliatory force of poised missiles that cannot be destroyed by an initial enemy attack, our advances have been many and excellent.

We have succeeded in constructing intercontinental missiles that can carry hydrogen bombs. We have produced effective rockets of increasing reliability. We have made a good start toward development of mobile rockets that can be shifted around on land or on sea. In a remarkably short time we have perfected a rocket that can be launched beneath the surface of the ocean. This mobile missile has been named, strangely enough, after the only stationary star in the firmament: Polaris.

Carried aboard nuclear submarines far from prime targets in the United States, the Polaris is an integral part of the kind of retaliatory force upon which the survival of our nation depends. Our nuclear submarines are reliable because they need not surface, have long endurance, and are hard to detect—especially when they are beneath the polar icecap, where they can be attacked only with extreme difficulty. Unfortunately, our nuclear submarines are big, expensive, and few. Today they serve their purpose well. Tomorrow better, faster, and more numerous units will be needed to ensure us against nuclear blackmail.

A retaliatory force is important. A truly effective active defense system would be even more desirable. It would be wonderful if we could shoot down approaching missiles before they could destroy a target in the United States.

An ICBM headed for a target in the United States would move with great speed, much faster than a jet airplane or a bullet. Our reaction time would be necessarily short. The answer to the speed of an ICBM attack is automatic equipment that would locate enemy missiles and release our anti-missile missiles to carry nuclear explosives toward their targets in space. Plans for our missile defense are aided by the circumstance that we would be shooting at a target following a predictable course. We could observe the orbit of the approaching missile, and we could determine the remainder of its orbit with the precise methods of astronomy.

Unfortunately, the defense can be frustrated by simple countermeasures. An incoming ICBM could be accompanied by a swarm of decoys, difficult to distinguish from real missiles. The decoys would draw the fire of our anti-missile missiles. Furthermore, there are ways of deflecting the course of a missile after it has been launched, so its path would not be predictable and it would not be such an easy target for an anti-missile missile.

Any problem of defense, including a defense against missiles, obviously must be considered from both sides. A defense is really good only if it is not much more expensive than the offense. And a defense is good only if it cannot be outwitted with ease. The process of offense and defense is a deadly game, the systematic development of answers to answers. If it is found in this process of move and countermove that the aggressor has the easier and less expensive task, there is something basically wrong with the defense.

Establishment of anti-missile defenses today seems difficult and costly. Outwitting and defeating those defenses might be relatively easy and cheap. If this proves correct, it would be a mistake for the United States to build an anti-missile defense system at a huge cost. But we certainly must continue to look for a satisfactory missile defense system. Once it is found, we should try it out, and we also should develop methods to defeat the defense. We can be guided only by the results of this exploratory work. We cannot establish technical goals to correspond to our wishes. We must, instead, find out what is feasible by exploring the possibilities on a moderate scale. If we find that we can build an adequate anti-missile defense, we certainly should.

But if our anti-missile defense can be foiled, we should at least make sure that our retaliatory force can reach targets in Russia. Russia has the biggest rockets. She may well have the best nuclear explosives. It may be difficult to penetrate her rocket defenses. If the Communists should become certain that their defenses are reliable and at the same time know that ours are insufficient, Soviet conquest of the world would be inevitable.

In the past, we allowed guesses rather than hard exploratory work to guide our technical developments. This led to the missile gap. If we repeat this mistake, it may well lead to defeat.

The dangers of the missile age are great, and they are real. But there is one popular worry that is not so serious. It is not probable that satellites carrying hydrogen bombs will hang over our heads. This modern sword of Damocles, unlike the original, is not suspended; it does not remain in one place, but it travels. And it remains in orbit unless it is stopped. It is just as hard to stop a satellite as it is to get it started. To bring a satellite back to a precisely defined target would require a considerable load of fuel, a load weighing more than the bomb itself. To place both the bomb and the additional load of fuel into orbit would require a much greater original amount of fuel. These considerations make attacks from satellites rather impractical. Why launch a missile from a satellite when it can be launched more easily and more effectively from the earth? A big, globe-circling launching pad, furthermore, could hardly be hidden. It would move fast, but as a rule it would be easy to predict its path.

Once a man-made object has started a long journey around the earth, it can be used more easily and more effectively as an instrument of peace than as a weapon of war. And in this peaceful field we have worked with diligence and with success.

Earth's atmosphere gets thinner at high altitudes. The last remnants of oxygen and nitrogen in the uppermost layers of air are exposed to those potent rays from the sun which never reach the earth's surface. The most energy-rich rays beyond the violet color of the rainbow tear the molecules of these gases into their electrically charged components, the electrons and the ions. At the very top of our air-cover, the atmosphere is replaced by the ionosphere.

All of this has great practical importance and has been known for quite a few decades. The electrons of the ionosphere reflect long radio waves and guide broadcast signals on their curved paths around the world. We are most acutely aware of this whenever radiation from the sun disturbs the ionosphere and radio signals fade.

Although we have known about the ionosphere for years, what was beyond we did not know. When our first satellites soared, we found out. James A. Van Allen and other American physicists discovered and studied great radiation belts surrounding our earth. In these belts the simplest charged particles, electrons and protons, spiral around the magnetic lines of the earth. These magnetic lines form a giant magnetic bottle, somewhat similar to the little laboratory bottles in which we trap hot gases and try to control fusion.

The Van Allen belts worried us for a while. The fast electrons and protons have the same effects as the rays from radioactive materials. They can interfere with sensitive apparatus, and they can injure people. Fortunately, the walls of a satellite stop most of the electrons, and the rest of the radiation could be tolerated by a space traveler for a few hours. Effects of the Van Allen radiation, furthermore, are quite weak below an altitude of one tenth of the earth's radius and above the altitude of one earth radius; the space traveler could cross the danger zone in a short time.

The great radiation belts bulge out near the equator, but they are anchored in the ionosphere near the earth's two poles. They influence the polar lights and they have an effect on the manner in which the ionosphere guides the waves of radio broadcasts.

Our space explorations have helped us to understand the paths of radio waves. Now it is possible to do something about them. Shorter electromagnetic waves, like those carrying radar or television signals, are not naturally reflected back to the earth; they go right through the ionosphere. They do not follow the curvature of the earth. This is why coaxial cables or microwave towers are needed for coast-to-coast transmission of live television shows.

In the summer of 1960, we launched into orbit a light package which was inflated into an exceedingly thin-walled, 10-story-high silvery balloon. This was the Echo satellite. Bouncing back the rays of the sun, it shone like a bright star. But, more usefully, it also could bounce short electromagnetic waves back to the earth. Since an amazing amount of information can be transmitted by these shorter electromagnetic waves—more than enough information to affect the behavior of each luminous point on a television screen—satellites like our Echo can be expected to show the way to vast improvements in the world's communications systems. Such satellites probably will make world-wide transmission of live television a reality. And if we put power stations into orbit, we could do more than merely reflect shortwave signals. We could amplify them. This could become important for long-range telephonic communications. The time may come when one can talk with anyone on the earth for an hour at the cost of one dollar. For better or for worse, all men will be neighbors.

Satellites may enable us to do something about the weather. Until quite recently, men had only an isolated worm's-eye view of the weather. They could look up at the sky and see whether the sun was shining, whether it was raining, and how fast the wind was driving the clouds at various altitudes. The first major advance in meteorology came with the telegraph, which permitted a speedy compilation of various worm's-eye views and the beginning of a systematized kind of weather prediction. During the last few decades, the air age has provided a bird's-eye view of the weather. This new dimension has given us a much better picture of the behavior of air masses, at least over the restricted parts of the world densely criss-crossed by airplanes. But aerial observations are infrequent over parts of the world where a great many weather changes originate. Our knowledge of the weather, as a result, is still sketchy and primitive. Satellites, for the first time, offer us an angel's-eye view of the weather. Proper instrumentation of a satellite will let us study the formation and movement of air masses simultaneously in the earth's entire atmosphere. This knowledge certainly will lead to much better weather prediction. It can be expected to lead to a better understanding and perhaps even control of weather.

The facts we have learned with the help of our weather satellite, along with all other scientific data gathered by our other space vehicles, have been made available. It is a striking fact that most of the original work in space research has been published by Americans. We can be justly proud of this. But mere publication of facts does not necessarily mean that we have discovered more facts than the Russians. It may mean only that we are not as enamored of secrecy as they.

A satellite might be loaded with cameras and transmission equipment, implementing the "Open Sky" plan long proposed by the United States. This kind of inspection satellite could provide us with instant information about visible activities anywhere in the world. In an age in which a nuclear attack might begin and end within half an hour, immediate knowledge of world events surely is vital.

No matter how peaceful or beneficial their intended uses, all satellites would have important military applications. An Echo satellite could be used for much more effective military communications. Knowledge and prediction of weather could be used in limited warfare to determine the best times to drop men and supplies. An inspection satellite loaded with cameras and transmission equipment probably would be regarded by a nation objecting to aerial observation as a mechanical spy.

Because any satellite has military usefulness, I am afraid the day might come when the Communists would attempt to raise the Iron Curtain into the sky and shoot down our satellites. If that day does come, it will be necessary to fight for the freedom of space—just as it was necessary in the past to fight for the freedom of the seas. The United States must be prepared to fight this space war. If it comes, I expect it will be a limited war in the best possible sense. It will be limited in its objective: Freedom of space. It will be limited in its area: Space itself. And, best of all, it may be limited as no other war in history has been limited: There need be no deaths and certainly no mass destruction. The war for space will be a war of equipment and apparatus, of satellite and anti-satellite, of remote-controlled machine against machine. The lives of millions of people and the destinies of cities will not be involved in the war itself, but only in the consequences of a defeat that would leave space as the province of an enemy.

Impractical space projects have always fired the public imagination and inspired man's sense of the romantic.

Some people, concerned about the population explosion on our crowded earth, look into the vast expanse of space and dream of colonization and interplanetary trade. Will this be the ultimate value of our space exploration? Will our children or their children become space pioneers and move their families to the moon or Mars or Venus? Will the people of the earth establish a long-distance commerce with space colonists, exchanging our manufactured goods for their valuable minerals? I think not.

Even if space colonization should one day be possible, it would be quite disagreeable. Mars would be the most likely location for the first space colony. It has a surface area about one fourth that of the earth and, more important, it seems to have a limited water supply that would be necessary for human habitation. The atmosphere of Mars includes a little oxygen—probably not enough for comfort but possibly enough to sustain human life. Colonists probably would have to master the art of shallow breathing. They also might change their way of walking; since Mars has less gravitational pull than the earth, colonists might find it easier to get around by leaping like kangaroos. One overriding disadvantage probably will keep humans from settling on Mars: It is cold. Humans could carry nuclear reactors to Mars as a source of energy and heat, but for comfort I definitely would prefer Antarctica.

I doubt that interplanetary trade ever will become a reality. Any mineral found in space, even gold or uranium discovered in the purest state, would not be valuable enough to justify the fantastic expense of shipping it back to the earth on freight missiles. But there is something that we can bring back from space, a commodity well suited for long-distance transportation because it has no weight: Knowledge.

Until very recently the earth's atmosphere prevented us from seeing the universe in any wave length other than the limited spectrum between violet and red, which we call visible light. After World War II, an additional window on the universe was opened by radio telescopes. This new way of looking at the universe already has led to remarkable discoveries. It has enabled us to reach farther into the universe with instruments than we can see with the most powerful telescopes. In the depths of space, it has shown us the slow, gigantic drama of colliding galaxies.

Our space effort almost certainly will lead to establishment of astronomical observatories on satellite stations and on the moon. Once outside our murky atmosphere, powerful telescopes and radar equipment should be able to offer a clear picture of the universe, giving us more facts about the history and structure of stars and galaxies than we have ever known or imagined. We shall be able to look at the world in all wave lengths, from radio waves that are miles long to X rays that have wave lengths smaller than the nucleus of an atom. With this equipment operating in space beyond our atmosphere, we may even be able to determine whether heaven really is infinite or whether the universe, like the earth, is finite.

Our government has decided to put a man on the moon and to bring him back. President Kennedy hopes this can be accomplished "before this decade is out." We are racing the Russians to the first foothold outside the earth. We are planning to spend billions of dollars, and many people are asking: Will this money be wasted?

It is my firm belief that man will get to the moon and that he should get there. The moon will be only the first stepping-stone in an inspiring adventure that will take us to every corner of our planetary system. The fascination that these plans have for our children is the most obvious and not the least important reason for this great adventure.

But there are additional, more concrete reasons for spending the large amounts of money required for this fantastic undertaking. A man in space can gather much more information than can mere apparatus. He can react to surprises in an intelligent way. He can handle unexpected situations. On the moon, he will be able to observe and ask questions that never would have been asked if human hands had not dug into the moon's dust.

The space astronomer, furthermore, will be able to work more efficiently on the moon than on a space platform. Wherever he happens to be in space, he will need energy. Atomic energy will be available to him. But atomic reactors need shielding, and shielding is heavy. To place one pound of material into orbit today costs $10,000. Even improved techniques will not cut the cost much below $1000 a pound. The heavy shielding required for an atomic reactor on a satellite would vastly increase launching costs. But an economical reactor shield already is available on the moon, for dirt on the moon will continue to be dirt cheap.

Astronomers on a space platform would require food, water, and oxygen. Everything needed would have to be sent up to them. A different situation would prevail on the moon. With energy from a dirt-shielded reactor, men on the moon probably could boil out from the materials of the moon all the water required. With the help of the same energy source, men could derive oxygen from moon materials and probably could produce carbon dioxide. With these ingredients and with sunlight, food could be grown. Men on the moon would be almost self-supporting. They would need the means for a return to the earth, some apparatus for explorations and self-support, a few vitamins and luxuries. But their sustenance would be moon-bound.

The moon could become a springboard for further space exploration. Water produced on the moon could be electrolyzed to produce hydrogen and oxygen that could fill the tanks of a rocket for travel over greater distances. Space vehicles, whether they run on chemical or nuclear energy, need such refueling. The slight gravitational pull of the moon would make it easy for a space ship to pull out of this space-refueling station.

Unfortunately, it is probable that Russians will be the first men on the moon. But the extension of man's knowledge to the planetary system will be a great event, and we must participate.

In exploring space, we will try to answer a question that is more interesting to us, as living beings, than any other: Is there other life in the universe?

There seems to be no life on the moon, where there is neither air nor water in the free state. We don't know about Venus, because its surface is hidden by the veil of an opaque atmosphere surrounding that planet. The existence of life on Mars is a distinct possibility. Looking at Mars with a spectroscope, scientists have found intriguing lines characteristic of the carbon-hydrogen bond—a bond that is found on the earth wherever there is life and in some substances such as petroleum that are remnants of ancient life. The existence of this combination of carbon and hydrogen atoms on Mars suggests the existence of life on Mars. But life on Mars may be so strange and so unusual in appearance that our first space explorers may not recognize it as life at all.

All living things on the earth—man, monkey, fish, amoeba, and even virus (which may not be alive)—are first cousins in the eyes of chemists; precisely the same complicated groupings of atoms are repeated in each one of them. We do not know what this complicated structure signifies. But we can put our limited understanding of life into a small capsule: Life is a little matter and a great deal of purposeful complication. I would like to know whether the Martian complication is similar to the terrestrial complication. If it is similar, we may have a common origin. If it is different, our origins may be independent.

A search for any kind of life on Mars might prove disappointing. That particular planet might have no life at all. Even so, I am confident that the universe is teeming with life. Our sun is but one of a hundred billion stars in our galaxy. Many of these suns, surely, have planets. And some of these planets, like the earth, should be inhabited. Beyond our galaxy of a hundred billion suns, there are billions of other galaxies. Considering the immensity and age of space, I cannot believe that we are the only living beings. It would be very strange to believe that. It seems most unlikely that we are the only intelligent beings. It would be presumptous to believe that. The universe is probably ten billion years old, and life on earth has existed for only the last half-billion years or so. There must be others living and thinking.

Enrico Fermi, about ten years ago, changed the course of a luncheon discussion in Los Alamos with a sudden, simple question: "Where are all the people?"

Because his question had no connection with our previous discussion and because space exploration even then was on our minds, I guessed Fermi's meaning: There must be other beings beyond our planet with civilizations older than ours. Why hasn't their superior knowledge led to their exploration of our planetary system? Why have we been neglected by explorers from other galaxies? Why hasn't the earth been visited?

The answer to all these questions is distance. Our sun is in an isolated arm of our Milky Way, and it is quite easy to understand that no one has yet happened to come by this godforsaken neck of the woods. Distances from sun to sun immediately outside our planetary system are so vast that star-hopping may remain forever an impossible dream for man. Traveling at 186,000 miles a second, light requires four years to get from our sun to the nearest known star, Proxima Centauri. I doubt that man ever will travel to this star. According to Einstein, no one can travel faster than the speed of light. No one can go even as fast as light unless he is divested of all weight and mass. But men are clever: We someday might build a lightweight rocket powered by nuclear fusion that could carry a man at one twentieth the speed of light. Even then, a traveler would take eighty years to get to Proxima Centauri, and, considering man's life span, this is a discouragingly long time.

But I would expect that men someday will be able to send some very light apparatus to Proxima Centauri. Light equipment would need proportionately less fuel to get it there. The rocket would not be as heavy as a man-carrying vehicle; it would not have to return to the earth; and the undertaking would not be as gigantic. Still, three generations of scientists would have to wait on the earth for the equipment's first reports.

Interstellar traffic is not nearly as difficult in other parts of the universe. In the core of our own galaxy, 30,000 light-years away, the stars are much closer together. In that core, it is quite possible that people from different stars already are exchanging information and even colonizing other planets. From our suburban isolation we can hardly expect to reach the metropolitan center of our galaxy, but we might be able to launch radio equipment into space—beyond our reception-blurring atmosphere —where we could listen on all wave lengths. Then, if there are intelligent beings at the core of our galaxy, we would have a chance of listening in on their radio broadcasts. We might hear and decipher interesting interstellar discussions or receive disturbing news about interstellar wars. But the news, of course, would be 30,000 years old.

As distances are measured in space, the center of our own galaxy is relatively close to the earth. The closest galaxy similar to our own, Andromeda, is much farther away—almost two million light-years from the earth. And beyond Andromeda, galaxy follows galaxy at similarly great intervals to distances of billions of light-years from the earth. Light just now reaching us from some distant galaxies may have started its long journey when the world was quite new. The human race will be excluded forever from even the nearest galaxy.

Forever, though, is a long time. I have no realistic hope that we can reach Andromeda, but men 500 years ago had no realistic hope that they could hurl rockets around the world. And since progress breeds accelerated progress, the wildest dreams of today might be realized within only a few centuries.

There is a faint and fantastic hope of being able to develop the kind of powerful, long-lasting source of energy needed to propel a capsule far into space. We might use anti-matter. Each particle of matter has its opposite in anti-matter, and we know we can make anti-particles of all kinds. When matter and anti-matter meet, they consume each other and transform themselves into pure energy. Because it is so extremely efficient, this technique of producing energy is the best source of power for interstellar travel.

But the use of anti-matter also presents an obvious problem. There may be no way of containing anti-matter, since any vessel necessarily would be constructed of matter and would disappear as soon as it was touched by anti-matter. The problem of containment, however, might be answered by the magnetic bottle since magnetism and anti-magnetism are the same. The lines of force of a magnetic bottle could contain anti-matter as well as matter. The idea of filling a magnetic bottle with matter and anti-matter and using it as a spaceship's source of power may appear harebrained. But at least it does not contradict the laws of nature, so who can say that it never will be feasible?

Suppose it can be done, and suppose that we try to get to Andromeda. Let us say that light requires two million years to travel from here to Andromeda and, although Einstein proved that we cannot do it any faster, Einstein's theory of relativity allows some hope that someone, someday, might get to Andromeda without having his life span prolonged almost indefinitely.

Scientists and engineers working very hard for a few hundred years could conceivably develop a vehicle and a means of propulsion that would allow man to go almost as fast as light. Suppose we put an astronaut in this vehicle and shoot him off toward Andromeda. The time required for him to get there would be relative; it would have one duration for him and a different duration for the people he left behind on the earth. This difference, to a space traveler, would be most important. And it can be determined in advance.

Einstein showed that although the time difference does not remain the same for all observers—and this is a most surprising but true statement—another quantity does remain the same for all. This quantity can be called Q, and it can be calculated with the help of a simple formula. Take the distance (ct) that light moving with the speed c could have covered during the observed time difference t between take-off and landing; multiply this length by itself, giving $(ct)^2$. Then take the distance between take-off and landing, call it R, and multiply that by itself, giving R^2. Subtract one from the other for the quantity: $Q = (ct)^2 - R^2$.

This Q remains the same for all observers, and this proven rule of Einstein's is important.

Observers on the earth would see the rocket heading toward Andromeda almost as fast as light. The rocket would appear to take just a little more time than light would have taken to reach the distant galaxy—slightly more than two million years. The distance actually traveled between the earth and Andromeda would be, let us say, precisely two million light-years. So the difference —Q—between the two huge quantities—$(ct)^2$ and R^2—would seem quite small to people on the earth, since the astronaut's rocket traveled the distance almost as fast as light.

The difference—Q—will be the same for the astronaut. But he will have to use different figures in the rest of his formula. His world will be his rocket. In this world he will remain stationary.

He will depart from the earth and arrive at Andromeda in the same position: at the controls of his spaceship. He will have to say that he did not move, but that the universe moved past him. He must say, therefore, that the distance he actually covered between his departure and arrival—*R*—is zero. This will be fully valid and justified, and this is an important point in Einstein's work. The astronaut will feel the same as you feel on our whirling planet: The sun rises and sets and the universe moves around you, but if you are sitting still you do not move.

The difference—*Q*—must be the same for the astronaut as for the earth-bound observers. Since *Q* appeared small for the people on the earth, *Q* also must be small for the astronaut. But since the distance covered by the astronaut between take-off and landing—*R*—seems to him to be zero, the time required for the flight will seem much shorter to him than to people on the earth.

To the astronaut, the rocket flight from the earth to Andromeda might seem to have taken perhaps only twenty years. To observers on the earth, the same flight will seem to have taken a little more than two million years.

Suppose the astronaut spent ten years exploring the galaxy of Andromeda and then returned to the earth. He would expect a hero's welcome, a ticker-tape reception in New York, and a high decoration from Congress. Far from it. He would be only fifty years older than when he began his historic flight, but the earth would have aged more than four million years. All his friends and relatives would be dead. No one would speak his language. He would find the world inhabited by a strange race that would consider horribly deformed, but which in reality would be far superior to his own both in understanding and in intelligence. They would undertake the scholarly task of deciphering his notes. And when his wild tale of a space flight begun four million years before had been confirmed by archaeological investigations, this new arrival, this astronaut, this specimen of an ancient and extinct race would be put in a zoo.

Space has its dangers. Even fantasies about space seem to end tragically. But fact and fiction about space do remain interesting and inspiring. For our children, no topic holds a greater fascination. And the kindling of young curiosities may well be the most important consequence of our adventuring into space.

CHAPTER EIGHT:

Seeds of Tomorrow

AT THE END OF WORLD WAR II, the leadership of the United States in technology and science was unquestioned. America's daring and practical spirit of enterprise was legendary. To bigger and better engineering, we had recently added brilliant and fantastic scientific discoveries. We excelled all others in the quality and quantity of our scientific research and in our technical ability to utilize new scientific facts. Never before in the history of the world had the men of one nation assumed such power over nature. The scientific leadership of the United States was universally recognized and admired.

That leadership today is in doubt. We have been challenged by a formidable competitor: The Soviet Union.

In 1945, many thought of Russia as a country inhabited by backward peasants. Russia's progress in many fields of science and technology during the last decade has changed that image. In the spectacular fields of aviation, atomic energy, and space exploration, the Soviet successes have been particularly great. The dramatic swiftness of Russia's rise in the practical sciences has had an immeasurable effect upon the world's opinion of Communism. Applause for Communist science in many parts of the world is applause for Communism itself. Russia's progress has created an admiration for the Communist method, especially in the world's backward countries that aspire to the same swift progress.

Bootstrap progress that carries a nation from a low level of scientific accomplishment to a position of scientific challenge or dominance is most difficult to achieve. When such progress is achieved, it demands respect. It could not have been achieved in the Soviet Union if the Russian leaders and people, after their revolution against czarist rule, had not been motivated by an overriding ambition. And the strong motivation would have gone for nothing without tremendous improvements in Russian education.

Soviet scientific successes are recent. But the arduous work leading to those successes has been going on for decades. The fountainhead of Russia's impressive technical strides has been the incredibly rapid improvement of technical schooling. All the amazing Soviet scientific-technological advances have stemmed from the Russians' post-revolution determination to achieve better education. The accomplishment of Russian teachers probably has been the most impressive feat performed behind the Iron Curtain.

A great battle has been won by the Soviet Union in the schoolroom. We now are becoming aware of the consequences of this victory. But what we have seen so far is only a beginning. We had less foresight than the Russians in improving important segments of education, and the consequences will be increasingly advantageous to the Communists for years to come.

The education of a scientist takes many years, and the best scientific minds are the youngest minds. The majority of scientists do their most important work and make their most valuable contributions before they are thirty. Scientists who will have reached this age of greatest productivity in a decade are students today, and more students today are being given a better scientific education in the Soviet Union than in the United States. I think that in ten years Russia will be the world's recognized scientific leader.

Although we cannot hope to retain our scientific leadership, we can hope to regain it. We shall be able to catch up with the Soviet Union and once again establish our scientific leadership only if we begin now to improve the education of our children. If we are to have a plan, a purpose, and a hope for tomorrow, we must plant the seeds in the schoolrooms today.

The importance of improving both the quantity and quality of scientific education in this country cannot be overemphasized. Progress in science is exciting and admirable no matter where or how it occurs, but in these fateful years Soviet advances must be matched. Today's science is tomorrow's technology. Science is needed for a better and a more abundant life, but it also is the foundation of modern military strength. Science can help the Soviet Union win the world either directly, by giving the Communists supremacy in weapons, or indirectly, by producing the tools for economic penetration and by commanding admiration for Communist know-how and for Communist methods from the world's uncommitted nations. If we do not act now to educate our children and prepare them for the task of reclaiming scientific leadership for the United States, there is no doubt in my mind that before the end of this century the world will be modeled after the Communist plan and not after our own ideals of liberty and respect for the individual.

Our preschool children today are ready and eager for a scientific renaissance. Their young imaginations and curiosities are soaring into space. They see the results of science everywhere; they are fed, clothed, moved, and amused by technology. American children are more interested in science today than ever before. It is vital that we nurture and encourage this interest. If we allow it to die, our way of life will die.

The Soviet Union is winning on the battlefield of the schoolroom for two primary reasons: Russian children are more anxious than American children to become scientists, and the Soviet government has simplified education.

Russian children know, as soon as they are old enough to learn anything about their society, that a scientist in the Soviet Union is a privileged person. Scientists in Russia have all the honors, all the comforts, all the security that the country can offer. This means a great deal in Russia, where so many have so little. A Russian child realizes, early in life, that he will be comfortable only if he becomes a politician—and a successful politician, at that—or a scientist. And he can be secure only if he becomes a scientist. Ambitious youngsters work hard to become scientists, because only in science can they hope to achieve acclaim, comfort, and security.

Children in the United States are not attracted to science for these reasons, because scientists in America do not occupy such a privileged position. They are, in fact, considered outside the society.

The United States is the most complete democracy the world has known. Our nation is much more than a political democracy. We also are democratic economically and intellectually. Our industrial production is for the masses. Books are written for the masses. Magazines are circulated among the masses. Movies are produced for the masses. Radio and television programs are beamed toward the masses. Politicians appeal to the masses. Baseball games, football games, basketball games, wrestling and boxing matches, horse races, and all other sports events are staged to delight the masses. The crowd decides what is good, and the crowd's value judgments—expressed in sales or box-office receipts, measured by pollsters, revealed in voting booths—control every segment of American life.

This is as it should be. But the very virtues of democracy create some American shortcomings. Science, music, art, or any other intellectual achievement requires certain habits and tastes that are not inborn, but acquired. The best student, the young poet, the budding engineer, the person inclined toward serious theater or classical dance—all acquire value judgments different from those of the majority; so they are not as popular as the football player or the movie starlet. If, after some years, the intellectual in America achieves an outstanding success, if his accomplishments are spectacular and well publicized, he may find himself on a pedestal. But he never is accepted by the crowd, and he never is understood. He is called a highbrow, an American epithet that defies translation into English or any other language, connoting a peculiar authority and gentle ridicule.

The people seem to say to the intellectual and especially to the scientist: "Go ahead and play, but please leave us alone." Now a good scientist is in love with his work. He could not otherwise continue to make the long and difficult effort needed to bring order to an unexplored patch of the intellectual wilderness. So, as he sees the common man turn his back, the scientist also withdraws. He seems to say: "All right! You call me a highbrow, so this is precisely what I shall be. I am interested only in my intellectual associates, and we will talk to each other in scientific polysyllables which only we understand. Sometimes I wonder whether anyone understands them but myself."

A chasm separates the common man from the intellectual in our country. It has impaired our strength and it has fragmented our science. The intellectual, deprived of an audience, has lost the knack of talking to intellectuals in fields other than his own. Our intellectual community has been split into many highly expert cliques. Our leaders in science, art, and literature indeed have been turned into highbrows. They have gathered on mountain peaks of specialized interests. They have lost contact not only with the common crowd but also with each other.

I was painfully reminded of the isolation of scientists by a politician whom I saw during the campaign of 1956 on a television program. He was a good politician, running for office, and he knew enough to say nothing that was not popular. He was asked a question about radioactive fallout. I do not remember his reply, but I do recall his first words: "Of course, I know nothing about nuclear physics, but . . ." Had he been asked about legislation to prevent the bribery of athletes, I cannot imagine that he would have prefaced his reply by saying: "Of course, I know nothing about baseball, but . . ."

This situation saddles the United States with a dangerous disadvantage in the education of future scientists. Children in the Soviet Union know that if they become scientists they will become privileged and secure individuals in Russian society. Children in the United States know that if they become scientists they will be called "squares," "double-domes," and "eggheads"; they will place themselves outside society. Rather than travel the hard road of the nonconformist, our children are more inclined to seek society's acceptance as businessmen or as members of the established professions of law, medicine, or clergy. Our really ambitious children might seek the fame and fortune that the crowd heaps upon such national heroes as television actors and rock 'n' roll singers.

In addition to making science attractive as a vocation, the Soviet government has simplified education.

A few months after the Bolshevik Revolution in Russia, the Commissar for Education, Lunacharsky, issued an order that abolished three letters from the Russian alphabet. Before that time, Russian words were spelled almost—but not quite—phonetically. Three sounds of the language could be written in either of two ways. Lunacharsky decided it was confusing to have alternative ways of spelling these three sounds, so he eliminated the need for selection by abolishing the three superfluous letters. Only one way to spell the three sounds remained, and the Russian language became completely phonetic.

A very few weeks after a Russian child enters school, the world of books begins to open up for him. This is a wonderful experience, and the wonder is lasting. Hungarian spelling, like the original Russian system, is largely phonetic. I had no difficulty in learning to read. I still remember, as a matter of fact, the thrilling experience of reading my first book; it was the story of two Hungarian puppies. Few Americans, I have found, remember reading their first book. This is natural, because students learning to read in the United States hardly experience a thrill of accomplishment. Learning to read words that have groupings of letters unconnected to the sounds those letters would make if pronounced is a formidable task—a chore better forgotten than remembered.

The Soviet government in 1927 did for arithmetic what Lunacharsky had done for the alphabet. Russia abolished the last remnants of historic but absurd measurements and completely adopted the metric system, a method of measuring everything in simple multiples of ten.

The metric system is not a Russian product. It was created by an earlier revolution and was adopted in France in 1791. But Soviet leaders were wise enough to see the advantages of the metric system and foresighted enough to put those advantages to use.

Metric measurement is based upon the meter, representing one ten-millionth of the distance between the earth's equator and pole. No other system of measurement is so simple, so clear, and so universal. Two lengths multiplied give an area. An area multiplied by a third length gives a volume. For students using the metric system, a start in geometry is easy and progress in physics is not made unnecessarily difficult.

The metric system is the arithmetic language of the scientific laboratory. Young Russian students who understand and use this system from the time they first learn to count have an obvious advantage in their education as scientists. Metric arithmetic is a window through which Russian students get their first glimpse of the simple orderliness of the world. They are stimulated to look further. Their interest in science is aroused, and they soon are prepared to get acquainted with the puzzles of the universe in which we live.

American students, by comparison, have a difficult time. From their early struggles with reading and spelling, our youngsters get the impression that education is arbitrary, difficult, and boring. This impression frequently hardens into a real dislike for learning by the time a child suffers a head-on collision with our confusing and forbidding method of measuring length, volume, and weight. He is told to measure length by miles, area by acres, and volume by gallons. There is no logical connection between these units. The words we use to describe length and area do not suggest to a child the simple truth that by multiplying two lengths he can get an area. Before he can begin to measure length, area, and volume, the American student must learn by rote that there are twelve inches in a foot, three feet in a yard, five and one-half yards in a rod, 5280 feet in a mile, 640 acres in a square mile, and either two pints or thirty-two ounces in a quart. In measuring volumes, he has the choice of using gallons, bushels, pecks, cords, or barrels, as well as the somewhat more reasonable cubic foot which contains 1728 cubic inches. These English units make an American child work like a Roman trying to figure out why XVI times LIII equals DCCCXLVIII.

Some of our most impractical measurements hide the simple, natural connection between length, area, and volume. They erect an artificial barrier that often diverts, blunts, and frustrates a youngster's interest in science.

Eventual simplification of our language to a phonetic system may be impossible. But eventual simplification of our methods of measurement to the metric system definitely is possible, and this simplification would help to eliminate one of the walls now standing between a child and science.

The United States should adopt the metric system. We have come closer to this goal in recent years than most Americans realize. Lewis Strauss, as President Eisenhower's Secretary of

Commerce, planned to ask the Bureau of Standards to investigate the best way to achieve a gradual but speedy transition of the nation's methods of measuring to the metric system. Introduction of the metric system would have many advantages outside the field of education. Most of the world now uses metric measurement. The competition for world trade is becoming keen. The nation that can deliver machinery and products measured in terms that most of the world's people can understand easily, eliminating arithmetic barriers to reorders and replacements, will be in a more favorable commercial position. But Strauss' appointment as Secretary of Commerce was not confirmed by Congress, and early adoption of the metric system in our country suffered another setback.

The United States, of course, could not adopt the metric system overnight. But we could start teaching our elementary school children the metric units of measurement right now. Children could be told about inches and feet and pounds, but these clumsy measurements should be presented as if they were about to be abandoned.

A good second step might be to erect new road signs and print new maps, giving geographic distances in kilometers rather than miles.

A third step might be to set a target date after which metric units would be used in all legal and governmental documents, providing an accumulating pressure for general adoption of the metric system. At the end of perhaps five years, all government orders for materials and supplies might use the metric system in the specifications, literally forcing companies dealing with the government to adopt metric measurement.

Our nation's complete change-over to the metric system probably would take a long time, perhaps a full generation of thirty-three years. Precisely because full adoption would require many years, we should initiate an exhaustive study of the possibilities and consequences of adoption now.

Our knowledge of the world, the universe, and of ourselves is being multiplied decade by decade. But most adult Americans hardly pretend to keep abreast of this amazing intellectual progress. Many find it easier to stop their education with graduation from high school or college, to accept scientific and technological advances without understanding them.

We should recognize that in this scientific age, no one can be called an educated person if he is not reasonably familiar with the laws of nature. And, more important, as long as most American adults remain uninformed strangers in their technological world, we cannot hope to recruit the young talent needed to regain our scientific leadership of the world. A large part of the responsibility for America's future lies with parents in the homes of our nation.

Parents may recognize that science is important to our future, and they may tell their children: "Study mathematics. Study physics. These are your best fields for the years ahead." And the children will judge this parental advice by parental action. If the parents know nothing about mathematics, care little about physics, have no understanding of the operation of such marvels as electronic computers, never talk about science in the home, the child will ask himself with some justification: "Why should I be different?"

In this way our scientific ignorance perpetuates itself. And, year by year, this ignorance adds to our weakness and to our confusion. Our democratic society has one sovereign: The people. If most of our countrymen lack a scientific education, then scientific questions vital to progress and survival will be judged without proper intelligence.

Our unscientific people today are represented and governed by unscientific politicians. These politicians hope to do their jobs properly by asking the scientists for advice. They ask the scientists: "What is your conclusion?" And scientists, like any other individual members of a group, differ in their conclusions. Then the politicians complain: "What shall we do? The scientists disagree!" If the question had been: "What are the facts? What are your arguments?" then the answers would have been more consistent. To evaluate scientific facts and scientific arguments, our politicians should know more about science. If our leaders and our people had a general understanding and appreciation of science, if decisions were reached by responsible policy makers who had developed an "ear" for science and could tell consistency and reason from emotion and prejudice, then our democracy could survive in a scientific age.

For all these reasons, effective scientific education must go hand in hand with adult education. We must bridge the disastrous gulf that has separated the scientist and the common man. A bridge must be built from both sides. The highbrow must learn to talk clearly and simply, and the general public should listen and discover that science is not only important but also more surprising and enjoyable than any contrived game or fiction.

The problem is difficult and pressing. Several approaches may be tried. One vehicle for adult education might be the commercial time of television stations. Most commercials are singularly uninteresting, and few are thought-provoking. Yet all people—children or adult, intellectual or uneducated—enjoy hearing about a surprising fact. We gladly concentrate, for at least a few minutes, on a new idea. And it takes only a few minutes to plant the germ of a thought. This would be a kind of subliminal education; people would not know that they were learning. For this very reason, perhaps, it would be effective both as education and as an advertisement. Instead of offering a meaningless cartoon or an offensive message about personal hygiene, a large company could present a brief talk by one of its practicing scientists on an intriguing project of the corporation's research department. An oil company's scientist, for example, might discuss methods of drilling holes in the ground and the means of deciding where to drill. He might describe the marvelous structures that act as molecular filters, allowing passage only to molecules of a certain size. Viewers would learn something—and at the same time they would get the idea that people in this company know what they are doing. The company might gain both recruits and customers while performing a public service vital to our nation. But, unfortunately, most television commercials today shout or titillate and attack all our senses except our curiosities.

Other ways could be suggested to spark and sustain interest in science and technology. The simplest and most obvious approach would be publication of large and inexpensive editions of books on popular science and on advanced science. We have begun to make real progress in this area. But Russian books on serious technical and scientific subjects still are one tenth as expensive as ours, and the Soviet editions are ten times larger. This has been going on for decades. Some of the hard work in Communist countries is worthy of imitation.

Adult education and advanced instruction are important. But our main task remains the education of our young children. For this, we need good teachers.

It frequently is said that a good teacher is a person who knows how to teach. The education of our teachers, in fact, is based upon this obvious doctrine. I think this doctrine does not accomplish much more than the elimination of the worst mistakes and malpractices from the schoolroom. Teaching is an art and cannot be taught by standard procedures.

Another common definition holds that a good teacher is a person who knows his subject. Knowledge of his subject certainly is an advantage to a teacher, but I think it is not terribly important. If a teacher makes a mistake during instruction in science, that only adds to the fun—as long as he does not insist that he is correct in his mistake. A good science teacher can use his factual errors as demonstrations that a scientist's most common experience is to make mistakes, recognize them, and correct them. Our teachers today, I believe, place too much emphasis on the techniques of education and on the infallibility of their knowledge of a subject.

A good teacher, to my mind, is a person who loves his subject and whose love for the subject is plainly visible to his students. If children see that the teacher has fun, they want to have fun, too. If their instructor thoroughly enjoys what he is talking about, the children will want to join in the game. Interest is the beginning and the most important step in the education of a scientist, professional or amateur.

Definitions of a good teacher may be debatable. But most people recognize a good teacher if they see one. And our lack of good teachers is painfully clear.

To find more good teachers in the immediate future we should, as a first step, recognize that in scientific education we have reached a state of emergency. To meet this emergency, we should adopt emergency measures. In most states, one is not allowed to teach in public schools today unless he has earned an official stamp of approval by having learned how to teach. As an emergency measure, we should abandon our insistence that teachers have certificates to teach. Anyone who holds an advanced degree in science should be allowed to teach in our public schools. I believe that many university professors of mathematics, science, physics, chemistry, and engineering would be willing and eager to sacrifice some of their time to deliver lectures or even to conduct regular courses in our elementary schools and high schools. Many of these eminently capable teachers now are barred from working in public schools because they have not taken courses in education and so do not hold the proper certificates.

Many industries, I know, would allow some of their scientists to take time from their regular duties without loss of pay to tell school children about the exciting and excellent research being done in industrial laboratories. Appearance of these industrial scientists in classrooms also might make education seem more practical. Children would realize that diligent study could lead to high-paying, exciting, and important jobs in industry.

Careers in teaching should be made financially irresistible to good teachers. Honor societies, for example, might be established for elementary and high school teachers. Society members would have no additional duties, but they might be paid double their regular salaries as long as they continued teaching. Society members should not be selected by academic examination. Rather, they should be selected after a study of the results of their teaching. Teachers are good teachers if their students are successful in colleges and universities, if their students gain honors in science fairs, if they do well in scholarship examinations. The quality of teaching is best measured by its success, and teachers of high quality should be given high rewards.

The thrill and excitement of intellectual achievement is not, and perhaps never can be, for everyone. All of our children, however, should be given a basic understanding of science and technology and an appreciation for intellectual achievement. More and more of the major decisions to be made by the citizens of our nation will be scientific. If these future problems are to be resolved wisely, people must know enough about science to be selective, to pick the right proposal from the wrong. The general public will have to be scientifically informed and capable of comprehension if they are to exercise their collective judgment as citizens of a democracy.

We might promote this kind of general appreciation for science in much the same way that we teach children to appreciate music. The enjoyment of music is an intellectual achievement and, as with all intellectual achievements, the taste for it is acquired. A person has to learn to like classical music, just as a person has to acquire a taste for abstract art or good architecture or for a theatrical performance that consists of more than showmanship.

How do we help our children acquire a taste for music? Do we tell them that to be good at music they must be able to play scales, and then seat them before a piano keyboard and make them practice the scale in C major for a few years so so they can play with speed and precision? If we did that, they never would listen to music again.

We give our children a taste for music by having them sing and listen and play—and if they make a few mistakes or do not fully understand a symphony, we do not worry. After they learn to appreciate music, some children develop an inner necessity to make music. This is their goal, and they willingly devote long hours practicing on a musical instrument. For them, the years of practice are neither dull nor unrewarding; they are the necessary means to a desirable end. Even while they practice, they hear and enjoy the more perfect music that their fingers cannot yet produce.

In the education of a scientist, we provide no such end-goal. We begin a youngster's scientific education with bits and pieces of knowledge, expecting him to memorize them separately, but we never fit the fragments into a picture of the orderly whole of science. We teach our children the multiplication table, in which they must never err. We tell them that force is mass times acceleration and that water is H_2O. But we have no course in mathematics appreciation and offer no glimpse of the adventurous spirit of science.

A phrase taught today's child early in his education, "exact science," convinces him that science and beauty are poles apart and that physics is in no way related to fun. Actually, the adjective "exact" more closely describes the work of a book-keeper, not the work of a scientist. To describe science, I should use the word "incredible." The scientist must be exact; otherwise, no one would believe him. His findings are so incredible that he hardly can believe himself. But of this, our children know nothing.

Almost none of our high school students are exposed to some

of the most exciting facets of modern knowledge. How many of our children have heard that mathematicians know of many sharply different infinities? And how does one infinity differ from another? How many high school courses in chemistry give an explanation of the different properties of a rubber band, a fiber, and a crystal—or between a metal and a semiconductor in a transistor radio? Do our children know what is inside the stars and what happens when a supernova explodes and shines with the brilliance of an entire galaxy? Hardly any child has heard in high school of the significant fact that atoms are as capricious as you or I, and that our knowledge of matter does not contradict our inner conviction that we possess a free will.

If high school science is barren, in our elementary schools we find a hopeless desert. Young children are puzzle addicts. Yet they never learn that puzzles and science are closely related, that science is nothing more than a pyramid of puzzles standing tier upon tier and reaching into the sky where paradox, knowledge, and understanding meet. Appreciation of science should be everyone's business.

We certainly should not make scientists of all our children. A small minority will suffice. But this small minority must be selected in the elementary schools. Some abilities appear early in life, and at an early age they start to decline. A language is most easily learned by the young, and the same holds for mathematics and other theoretical subjects. Pioneers in physics like Newton, Einstein, and Bohr made their greatest discoveries at an early age. The greatest mathematician, Gauss, planned most of his life's work in a notebook at the age of eighteen. And the French mathematician Galois died when he was twenty-one, having created some of the most fruitful ideas in modern mathematics.

Because scientific gifts bloom early, we must know how to

recognize this flower and how to help it grow. It can be recognized. Talent for science or mathematics consists of an interest, an addiction. A gifted person is one who has fallen in love with a subject. But though I think I can describe talent, I cannot explain it. I cannot say why the gifted one has fallen in love; I cannot guess what might have generated his interest. I can explain such important things only with memories of my own attraction to mathematics and science.

Like other children, I frequently was put to bed before I could fall asleep. The light was turned off, and there was nothing to do. I got into the habit of amusing myself in a strange way. I had heard that there were sixty seconds in a minute, sixty minutes in an hour, twenty-four hours in a day. I was perhaps four years old. I do not know why I should have known about those numbers or why I should have been interested in them. But I started putting them together. In the dark at night, I tried to figure out how many seconds there were in an hour, how many in a day. My answers were wrong, but I enjoyed the game. And I acquired the habit of mental arithmetic.

I talked to no one about my game. I played it alone. But my interest in numbers is one of my earliest memories.

When I was ten years old, my father discovered this strange proclivity. He was a lawyer and could not share my interest in numbers. But he had an old friend, Professor Klug, who taught geometry. My father arranged a meeting. Klug talked with me perhaps half-a-dozen times. He gave me my first book on algebra. I never shall forget him.

He was funny, and he was quite different from other grownup persons. Before I met him, I thought that only children could really enjoy themselves. But Professor Klug had as much fun as any child because he enjoyed playing with his formulas and proofs.

I knew, after meeting Professor Klug, what I wanted to do when I grew up.

In one important respect, most of our schools are doing a wonderful job. The companionship of children from widely varying economic, social, and racial backgrounds is an integral part of the education of our children. It is vital that our citizens of the future learn the lessons of companionship. Of all human abilities, the most important in the coming decades may well be the ability to get along with each other.

At the same time, we have misapplied the principles of democracy. It sometimes seems that in our schools we have distorted the ideal of equality into a veneration of mediocrity. Our children learn that it is wrong to be different. The one activity in which a child dares to be better than his friends is in athletics. If he excels in his studies, he is a "square"—and he may find himself excluded from the society of his classmates.

Many believe our children need more discipline. They may be right. There certainly is more discipline in Communist schools than in ours. But in this respect, I would hesitate to compete with the Russians. In the use of the whip, we cannot and we should not win.

Many others believe that schools should separate children according to their ability. The demand that special attention be given the gifted child is increasing. It seems to me that this would destroy much that is really good in our educational system. Such a procedure could introduce a new form of segregation. And besides, it is not so easy to tell a gifted child from one less gifted.

I do believe, however, that our schools should replace the emphasis on standard and uniform performance with a challenge to become excellent.

I like to believe that there is no such thing as an average child or an average individual. In his own way and in some endeavor, every one of us can and should be excellent. Excellence is a great and deep need of every human soul. The most important function of a good teacher should be to find out in which way each individual child wants to become and can become excellent. The teacher then should encourage each child to become outstanding in his own way. That we admire excellence in sports is right. That we do not admire excellence in learning is wrong. I do not object to the football hero, but the same admiration is due the precocious student.

It might be a good idea to require rather little of our children at school. Everyone must know how to read, write, do simple arithmetic, and get along with others. But beyond the bare necessities of education, we should not judge our children by their mistakes and by what they do not know. Learning is infinite, and there are gaps in the knowledge of the wisest and most erudite of us. We should judge our children by what they know best or whatever they can do best.

Outside the modest standard requirements of education, we should make every child feel that he must excel in something. That something may be swimming or science, history or painting, cooking or mechanical training, languages or mathematics, football or speech. Excellence could be acquired in a physics club or on the baseball field, in a drama circle or during music lessons. These student activities can be organized within the school system or independently of it. The discussion circles or science seminars should include youngsters of different ages. They may learn more from each other than from their teachers. Students should be allowed to change their chosen fields of interest, because it is natural that the interests of children should change from period to period, perhaps from year to year.

The important thing is that the child should be exposed at an early age to the company and example of those whom he can admire and imitate and whom—in time—he may surpass.

The method of education that I am proposing here may be short on method, but it may yield good results in education. By utilizing the enthusiasms of the youngsters, we can exploit most effectively the limited number of good teachers, counselors, and lecturers whom we can find.

To my mind, one point seems most important: We can surpass the Communists if we make the most of the inherent advantages of the democratic way of life. We believe in the individual. This belief can be justified only if we bring out the best in each individual. And what is best should be found and developed at an early age. This is how we should sow the seeds for tomorrow. The greatest accomplishments will be brought about not by conditioning, not by the whip, not by a search for a mysterious ingredient called genius, but by finding and nurturing the seeds of excellence in our children. When they grow up, they then will be driven by the greatest power on the earth: The force of inner necessity.

PART THREE:

The Counsel of Fear

CHAPTER NINE

The Fallout Scare

IN THE YEARS SINCE HIROSHIMA, a new factor has become prominent in American national policy. This new factor is fear. The counsel of fear has resulted in actions, plans, and institutions that are irrelevant, irrational, and even opposed to our national interest. Three examples are the fallout scare, the nuclear test moratorium, and secrecy.

Of these, the fallout scare is the least important. Release of radioactivity into the atmosphere was halted for three years with the test moratorium effective in October 1958. Safe methods of testing were developed. Most future weapons tests can be conducted underground or in remote space. No trace of radioactivity from such tests would reach the biosphere, the region of living beings. Simple measures of caution will eliminate all fallout from these tests. Radioactivity from nuclear explosions used for the needs of defense and for peaceful purposes can be held to an exceedingly low level. We have every reason to believe, furthermore, that safe underground experiments will result in the development of "clean" explosives. Once these are available, military experiments and the works of peace can be accomplished in a manner in which our safety from radiation damage will be complete.

There is no connection between world-wide fallout hazard and a rational program of future nuclear tests. We should not be intimidated by huge Russian explosions, but should consider fallout objectively, free from emotion, propaganda, and alarm.

Man, throughout history, has feared the mysterious and the unknown. Many natural occurrences—lunar and solar eclipses, thunder and lightning, birth and death—have caused terror. Scientific explanations have diminished many of these fears, but science cannot eliminate fear itself. In a rapidly changing world, old fear fixations are replaced by the new.

Radiation, as natural as an eclipse, has given rise to considerable fear in modern times. We have heard much about it in connection with atomic explosions. Scientists have discussed it in terms that gave rise to alarm. Radiation cannot be detected by man's senses. We cannot see it, feel it, hear it, taste it, or smell it. Yet we know it is there, and we know that an overdose can be dangerous or deadly.

Actually, there is no reason why a scientist or an informed layman should consider radiation a mystery. Our scientific knowledge about radiation is firm and detailed in many ways. We know, for example, that all types of radiation produce reactions in the human body that are almost alike. We know the levels at which radiation becomes a danger to humans, and we can predict the effects of certain kinds of radiation at certain levels with considerable precision. We have clear evidence that present levels of radiation in our atmosphere from both natural sources and from the radioactive fallout of nuclear tests are, at best, completely safe for humans or, at worst, are causing exceedingly little damage. We certainly know a great deal more about the effects and dangers of radiation than we know about any of the chemical or biological dangers of our environment.

Our bodies function and live because of an enormously complicated interaction of myriads of finely balanced chemical combinations and processes. Each of our functions—growth, breathing, motion, excitement—is connected with chemistry in which molecules enter the body's fine balance as a key enters a lock. The added chemical combinations may act as food that nourishes the body, as poison that kills cells, or as beneficial medicine; the final reaction often depends on the slightest change in chemical construction—like a small notch on a key. At a time when chemical additives and chemical sprayings of our agricultural products are in extensive use, the question of unknown biochemical effects is a thoroughly practical problem.

The body's chemical reaction to a foreign biological system like a germ or a microbe is even more complex. In the living microscopic world as well as in the countless inanimate molecules admitted to our bodies daily, we have friends and deadly enemies. An understanding of these chemical reactions and an orientation between them is the subject of several great—and incomplete—sciences.

The science of radiation biology is simpler. There are various kinds of radiations emitted by atomic nuclei and by the various processes in which atomic nuclei participate. Among the most important are alpha rays, beta rays, gamma rays, bombardment by neutrons, protons, fission products, and mesons. All of these have an important property in common: They are unspecific in their action.

We know a great deal more about the effects of these radiations on the body than we know about the effects of chemical compounds taken into the body. There are good reasons for this better understanding of radiation. It can easily be traced and measured in the body. And, in contrast with chemical reactions, the basic action of radiation is simple. A certain amount of radiation delivered to living tissue tears apart a proportionate number of molecules. Even the few exceptions to this general rule are predictable. We can anticipate the effects of radiation in stated dosages, because the effects at certain levels—with insignificant exceptions that are known and taken into consideration—are always the same. Radiation does not permit the kind of surprise so familiar in biochemistry, where a small change might convert nourishing foods and beneficial medicines into poisons.

Too much radiation certainly is dangerous. Excessive amounts of radiation can cause painful burns and lesions on the skin, leave the body susceptible to cancer or leukemia, cause the mutation of unborn children, or result in death.

In the event of an all-out nuclear war, we probably would be exposed to heavy and dangerous radioactive fallout. We can defend ourselves against this and at the same time decrease the probability of an all-out nuclear war. The necessary protective measures will be discussed subsequently. Here we are concerned with the world-wide fallout produced by nuclear tests, which gives rise to exceedingly small radiation effects.

From the very beginning of the atomic program in this country, we have been aware of the dangers of radiation, and we have been extremely cautious in the face of those dangers. Radiation, since it is invisible and insidious, demands respect. Its hazards, unfortunately, were neither understood nor respected by the medical pioneers of half a century ago who used radiation in the treatment of diseases. Many of the men responsible for early work in X-ray treatments were seriously overexposed to radiation, and the tragic results included lesions, cancers, and even some deaths. By the time we began our atomic program, the hazards of radiation were better understood and standards of safety based on the experiences of medical men had been established. We knew we had to be very careful, and we were. I doubt that men ever have undertaken as great a development with as few accidents. But, despite the precautions taken in our atomic work, there were mistakes and there were victims.

Our first great atomic accomplishment, the successful test at

Alamogordo, gave us reason for grave concern about radioactive fallout in the vicinity of explosions.

After the Alamogordo experiment, a cloud of radioactive contamination spread from the test site and fell back to the earth. The only sufferers, fortunately, were a few cows. After the radioactive dust settled down upon them, patches of fur fell out of their hides. The government purchased the cows, maintained them, and subjected them to close study. Their fur grew back, and the animals thrived. Except for the initial loss of fur, the radioactive fallout produced no other noticeable effects.

When the first big-scale tests of the hydrogen bomb were being planned, I proposed that they be conducted in Antarctica —as far as possible from any human settlement. But, for the sake of expediency, it was decided that the thermonuclear bomb should be tested in our established test area, the Marshall Islands. The tests were preceded by exhaustive studies of wind currents and other weather phenomena so that we could conduct the tests at a time when no inhabited locations would be endangered. These meteorological safeguards worked well in our first thermonuclear experiment on November 1, 1952. The overwhelming bulk of radioactivity produced in that experiment fell harmlessly into the sea.

Our next test of the hydrogen bomb, on March 1, 1954, was marred by a tragic error. That experiment was conducted on Bikini Atoll, an oval-shaped coral reef in the Marshall Islands. Large amounts of radioactivity were expected from the explosion, so the test was to be made only if islands and atolls in the downwind direction were uninhabited. A wind to the west might have endangered Eniwetok, about 200 miles from Bikini, where Americans were preparing for further tests. A wind to the east might have hurt people on the atolls of Rongelap and Rongerik, a hundred miles or so from Bikini; Rongelap, at the time, was inhabited by eighty-two people who lived in primitive palm houses, and twenty-eight American servicemen were stationed on Rongerik. A wind to the south could have affected Kwajalein, location of a busy base southeast of Bikini. The ideal wind direction would have been due north. On the morning of the scheduled test, the wind was blowing northeast. Meteorologists, knowing that a wind due north could not be expected for months, gave their OK to the test.

But almost immediately after the explosion, the wind veered. About six hours after the shot, the American servicemen on Rongerik noticed a misty fallout of radioactive dust. Aware of radioactive dangers, they washed themselves, put on extra clothes, and stayed indoors as much as they could. These precautions helped protect them against skin burns. Subsequent measurements showed that the Americans had been exposed to about 80 units of radiation. Such radiation units are known as "roentgens," a name introduced into medical science decades ago. This exposure was not too serious: A dose of fifty to 100 roentgens never is fatal and only rarely leads to any illness at all.

The fallout on Rongelap was much heavier, and the island natives did not know the elementary precautions against radioactive contamination. Fallout on the Rongelap people later was measured at 175 roentgens—not enough to cause death, but enough to cause sickness among some of the people. The situation was serious, and we narrowly escaped some dreadful consequences.

All of the Rongelap natives lived at the southern tip of the atoll. In the middle of the atoll, only about fifteen miles from the native villages, our measuring crews found that a person would have received 400 roentgens of radiation—a heavy dose that would have left its victim with a fifty-fifty chance of living. On the atoll's northern tip, only thirty miles from the native villages, crews measured the radioactive fallout at 1000 roentgens. Such a massive dose would have meant certain death in less than one month.

The Rongelap natives were removed to Kwajalein, and their medical history has been followed carefully. During the first twenty-four hours after their exposure, some of the victims complained of nausea and fever; these difficulties disappeared without treatment. Some natives also complained of itching and burning sensations on their skin, but these symptoms lasted only a couple of days. After a week or so, skin lesions and loss of hair began to occur. At the end of six months, the lost hair had grown out again in its previous texture and color, and the skin lesions had healed. Four Rongelap women were pregnant at the time of their exposure. Three of the subsequent births were normal babies; one was born dead. There was no evidence that the stillbirth was caused by radioactive fallout. The stillbirth rate among the Rongelap people is high, and one in four was not an unusual ratio. All the Rongelap and American victims of fallout from the Bikini test today seem to have recovered fully. No malignancies or leukemias have appeared, but an AEC medical team still is watching the victims for possible long-term effects.

No one suspected, before the Bikini test, that a Japanese fishing boat was in the area. Early on the morning of March 1, the boat was somewhere north of Rongelap. There were twenty-three men aboard the *Fukuryu Maru*, which in translation means the *Fortunate Dragon*. The boat was in a patrolled zone, but had not been sighted by our airplanes. The *Fortunate Dragon's* presence in the danger zone was discovered two weeks after the explosion, when the little boat returned to Yaizu Harbor. No one could tell then precisely how much radiation the fishermen had received, but the dosage probably was about 200 roentgens. By the time the *Fortunate Dragon* returned to harbor, the twenty-three fishermen were sick. One died. The other twenty-two, however, recovered their good health and went back to work. There is a possibility that the single death resulted from hepatitis, which may have been unrelated to the radiation exposure. But the world assumed that he died of fallout.

Every human life is priceless. But when a patrol plane's oversight and a shifting wind at Bikini appeared to have claimed the life of a single fisherman, the cries of protest were so great that this one death had a considerable influence on the policies of nations and on the fate of the world itself. The tragedy of this single death was compounded by national feelings of guilt and resentment. The thousands of wartime victims at Hiroshima and Nagasaki seemed to have died again in that single peacetime death in an isolated area of the South Pacific. The enormous emotional storm blown up over the fisherman's death was a psychological release of Hiroshima-born feelings of resentment on the part of the Japanese and of guilt on the part of Americans. The ghost of Hiroshima raised the fallout scare.

Tragic as it was, the effect of radioactive fallout after the Bikini test could have been worse. If the wind had veered a little more to the south, all of the people on Rongelap and Rongerik probably would have been killed. There was an obvious and urgent necessity, after the test, to avoid such close calls in the future.

Heavy radioactive contamination can be expected only close to the site of an explosion. Since our experience with shifting winds during the Bikini test of 1954, meteorological requirements for tests have become far more stringent. Under refined safety rules, many large-yield weapons have been tested since March 1, 1954, and we have experienced no further radiation accidents. According to present ideas and techniques, future explosions need not release substantial amounts of radioactivity into the atmosphere. We can be confident that dangerous contamination from fallout near test sites will not occur again.

The kind of radioactive fallout that has created the most alarm and the most controversy is world-wide fallout. Some radioactive particles from a nuclear explosion rise high into the atmosphere and are blown thousands of miles from the test site. Rain, fog, or mist can capture these particles and return them to the ground. It usually takes several weeks for this kind of fallout to occur. During this time, the radioactive particles may have encircled the earth near the latitude of the explosion.

Radioactive particles from the explosion of a hydrogen bomb rise even higher into the stratosphere. They may stay there for years, and the radioactivity is distributed like a blanket on top of the earth's entire atmosphere. It takes from one to ten years for the particles deposited in the stratosphere by the explosion of a hydrogen bomb to be returned to the earth as world-wide fallout.

The consequences of this fallout had to be investigated. The study was undertaken by Willard Libby, Hans Bethe, and others, and I participated in it in 1954. The results of the investigation were reassuring. Thousands of our biggest bombs could discharge their radioactivity into the atmosphere before biological effects on a world-wide scale could be proved.

The danger of fallout to the human body depends upon the rate of radioactive decay. A radioactive particle in the body is not harmful unless it disintegrates and releases its energy while the person is still alive. Most radioactive particles decay while they are still in the atmosphere—too soon to affect man. Other particles have an extremely long life—too long to affect man. Large quantities of Uranium 235, for example, are left in the atmosphere after a nuclear explosion. But 710 million years would be required for half of these radioactive U-235 nuclei to disintegrate, far too long a time to present any danger whatsoever during man's short life span.

Two products of nuclear explosions present unique threats to human beings. Strontium 90 and Cesium 137 have very dangerous half lives of about thirty years; that is, about thirty years are required for half the radioactive nuclei of these two elements to disintegrate and release their energy. These half lives are long enough so that radioactive decay is negligible between the time of the explosion and the fallout to earth, but short enough so that decay is probable between the time the particles contact humans and the time of the human's natural death.

After entering the human body, Strontium 90 gathers in the bones. Bones are sensitive to radiation, and an overdose can cause bone cancer or interfere with the production of blood cells in the bone marrow, causing leukemia. Strontium 90 is retained in the body for many years. It constitutes the immediate danger of fallout. Cesium 137, on the other hand, is deposited more or less uniformly throughout the human body, and is retained by the body less than six months before it is excreted. Although Cesium 137 presents a lesser immediate danger to the body, it can damage the human reproductive cells.

Our investigation of the actual dangers of world-wide fallout were aided by the case histories of men who had used radiation in medicine, by numerous animal experiments, and by our studies connected with safeguards for nuclear reactors. We had extensive experience with the effects of radiation upon the human body. And because various types of radiation have similar effects upon the body, we could establish simple standards of safe dosages by comparing the radiation from man-made fallout to the amounts of natural radiation that humans always have absorbed from minerals in the earth, from cosmic radiation that rains down on us from space, and from potassium occurring naturally in our bodies.

The dangers of big doses of radiation were and are well known. Exposure to 1000 roentgens over the entire body would cause almost certain death in less than thirty days. And exposure to 400 or 500 roentgens would leave a man with only a fifty-fifty chance of survival. A dose of 100 roentgens would not cause immediate death, but after years in a few cases could cause cancer. Although a person surely would die if his entire body were exposed to 1000 roentgens of radiation at once, there would be a much less than even chance that he would suffer at all if exposed to the same amount of radiation over a number of years.

Compared to the massive doses of radiation that can cause illness or even death, radiation from world-wide test fallout is exceedingly small. The bones of humans throughout the world today are getting an average of about 0.002 roentgens a year from Strontium 90 in the fallout. The rest of the body is being exposed to about the same amount of radioactivity, mostly from the fallout's Cesium 137. In certain areas there is a greater accumulation of fallout, but it would be difficult to imagine that anyone in the world could receive a lifetime dose of more than four or five roentgens of radiation from fallout. This still is less than radiation received from cosmic rays alone.

We found it enlightening to compare the human exposure to radioactive fallout with the human exposure to natural background radiation. The same doses of radiation from fallout's Strontium 90 and from cosmic rays will produce similar effects in human bones. People living at sea level in the United States are exposed to 0.034 roentgens of radiation from cosmic rays each year. This is seventeen times the amount obtained from the Strontium 90 in the world-wide fallout. Exposure to cosmic rays in Denver, about 5000 feet above sea level, is 0.05 roentgens a year. If such small doses of radiation really were dangerous, we had better evacuate Denver.

Radiation from radium is somewhat more dangerous to the human body than radiation from Strontium 90. But while world-wide fallout radiation to the bones from Strontium 90 continues at a dose of about 0.002 roentgens a year, radiation from radium in the drinking water in some parts of the United States has been observed as high as 0.005 roentgens a year. If such small amounts of fallout radiation really are dangerous, people in some United States communities should stop drinking their local water.

Brick contains more natural radioactivity than wood. A person living in a brick house rather than a wooden house is exposing himself to a considerably greater amount of radiation—perhaps as much as ten times the amount of the current dose from radioactive fallout. If fallout really is dangerous, we should tear down all of our brick houses. I would hate to do this, because I live in a brick house myself.

The comparisons are almost endless. A person wearing a wrist watch with a luminous dial is exposing himself to much more radiation than he is getting from the present level of radioactive fallout. If we really fear fallout, we should throw away bedside alarm clocks with dials that can be seen in the night because they are spraying the occupants of the bed with radiation.

If we had used natural background radiation as the standard in judging the danger of exposure to artificial radioactivity, the fallout scare might never have developed. Unfortunately, this was not done. Instead, arbitrary standards were decreed, and to make them safe they were set at a rather low level.

Radiologists in the early 1940s, taking their cue from the hard experiences of medical pioneers, considered one tenth of a roentgen-unit a day as the dose which for safety's sake should not be exceeded in steady practice. This was based upon observation. No statistical evidence could be found that a steady exposure to one tenth of a roentgen a day produced any harmful effects. This old standard of safety permits exposure to 10,000 times as much radiation as the average person now receives from world-wide fallout.

This medical standard at first was adopted in our work on atomic energy. I remember the first information I was given when I joined the atomic energy project in Chicago in 1942: "You must never exceed an exposure of one-tenth of a roentgen-unit a day. As long as you observe this rule, you are safe." As a theorist, I had little occasion to be exposed to radiation. But the general enforcement of radiation standards paid off in our atomic energy projects. We had no sad experiences comparable to those of the early medical pioneers.

Serious arguments later arose about possible long-range dangers of radiation exposure. The dosage accepted as safe, accordingly, was decreased to three tenths of a roentgen-unit per week. This standard still is several thousand times higher than the exposure to world-wide fallout. No harmful effects were observed, and this standard generally continues to be enforced in our laboratories.

But a question was raised: "When we consider whole populations rather than small numbers of professionals, should we not apply more cautious standards?"

The question appeared reasonable enough. It was decided that for whole populations only one tenth as much radiation should be tolerated as for small professional groups. This decision was completely arbitrary. It was based on no observed fact or general argument. It was guided by a desire to be absolutely safe even though we were virtually certain that these faint radiations were not dangerous. The authorities in subsequent years, trying to make safety multiply safety, further decreased this so-called "maximum permissible dose."

This designation, "maximum permissible dose," was most unfortunate. It suggested that anyone receiving more than this dose was in trouble. When, due to a local fluctuation, a small group of people received a sizable percentage of this "maximum" dose, there were feelings of alarm. When the "maximum" standard was lowered, there were feelings of uncertainty and distrust. Thus public confidence was lost, and exposure to small doses of radiation was firmly established as dangerous in the popular opinion.

The fact is that the "maximum permissible dose" is approximately four times the background radiation to which all living things have been exposed for all time. An exposure to ten times the "maximum permissible dose" certainly can be tolerated.

I do not propose that we relax our vigilance in guarding against possible dangers of radiation. But I do propose that the man-made and arbitrary "maximum permissible dose" should not be used as a measure or standard of danger. We should, instead, compare all exposures to the average background radiation. This radiation is a fact of nature. There can be little disagreement about its magnitude or its significance.

Our 1954 investigations of fallout effects was undertaken with a tremendous handicap: Secrecy. Willard Libby and others connected with our committee's work suggested to the Atomic Energy Commission that world-wide fallout was of world-wide interest, and that our facts should be made known so that fallout would not be feared.

Our arguments for openness finally prevailed. All the information we had gathered and all our calculations based on that information eventually were released and published. But declassification of secret material is a slow, bureaucratic process; and the spread of factual knowledge involving an understanding of mathematical equations is painfully slow. Bad news and scare stories travel much faster.

Democratic candidates in the presidential election of 1956 convinced themselves that radioactive fallout was a real cause for worry as well as a potent political issue. Although the facts on fallout by then were available, they either were ignored or suspected of being incomplete. Whatever the cause, an objective understanding of radioactive fallout suffered in the emotion of political debate.

Through the smog of debates since 1956, these facts remain visible:

Radiation from test fallout is very small. Its effect on human beings is so little that if it exists at all, it cannot be measured. Radiation from test fallout might be slightly harmful to humans. It might be slightly beneficial. It might have no effect at all. The smallest doses producing noticeable effects in animal experiments, approximately one tenth of one roentgen-unit per week, are more than a thousand times as great as world-wide fallout. These experiments produced a slight increase in the incidence of animal tumors—and a lengthening of the animals' average life. The living organism is so complicated and the intertwining of cause and effect is so intricate that we may never know the biological effect of so small a cause as world-wide fallout.

World-wide radioactive fallout can be expected to influence

heredity. Cesium 137 in the fallout, by affecting reproductive cells, will produce some mutations and abnormalities in future generations. This raises a question: Are abnormalities harmful? Because abnormalities deviate from the norm, they may be offensive at first sight. But without such abnormal births and such mutations, the human race would not have evolved and we would not be here. Deploring the mutations that may be caused by fallout is somewhat like adopting the policies of the Daughters of the American Revolution, who approve of a past revolution but condemn future reforms.

A really noticeable increase of mutations could give rise to understandable worry. But the effect of fallout on the mutation rate has not been observed. Only one tenth of a roentgen goes to reproductive cells from fallout during the lifetime of an individual. A dose fifty times greater is received during a lifetime from natural background radiation. Even higher doses would be required to increase noticeably the number of mutations.

Causes much less involved than radiation have the, effect of increasing the number of mutations. One such simple cause is an increase of the temperature of the reproductive organs. Our custom of dressing men in trousers causes at least a hundred times as many mutations as present fallout levels, but alarmists who say that continued nuclear testing will affect unborn generations have not allowed their concern to urge men into kilts.

There is serious reason to be concerned about people who are unnecessarily worried about fallout. Their needless worry has had tragic medical consequences.

It is reasonable to avoid unnecessary exposure to radiation. It is reasonable to obtain medical X-ray pictures with a minimum of exposure. But it is unreasonable and dangerous to shun medical X rays which give timely warnings of disease, and it is dreadful to allow fear to prevent the healing applications of radiation.

Convinced by the fallout fear-mongers that all radiation is dan-

gerous, too many Americans have shunned medical X-ray diag-
noses and treatments that could have helped prevent disease and
save lives. By far the greatest number of fallout casualties can
be counted among the thousands of people who have been
frightened away from their doctors' X-ray machines by the fallout scare. Those who pretend that they can trace the distant
consequences of nuclear tests in the uncertain effects on the incidence of cancer and the unknown fate of future generations
should consider the ultimate effects of their own actions. Their
ghost stories have frightened more people away from the saving
arts of medicine than ever could be harmed by radiation from
world-wide test fallout.

Considering the insignificance of the fallout threat and the
great proportions of the fallout scare, I believe that the general
concern about radioactive fallout is not objectively motivated,
but is rooted in the worries and tensions connected with our
first use of the atomic bomb. Hiroshima has become synonymous
with horror, and the story of Hiroshima has been told so often
that our responsibility for Hiroshima has tainted our judgment
of anything associated with nuclear development.

Many people are influenced by an unreasoning feeling that if
we can only purge ourselves and cleanse ourselves of radioactive
fallout, we will have made a great step toward a peaceful and
safe world. They behave like the neurotic who tries to cleanse
himself of guilt feelings by frequently washing his hands.

Such symbolic actions are of no help. Soap and water do not
wash away sin. Nuclear test bans cannot erase the memory of
Hiroshima.

If we consider radioactive fallout objectively rather than emo-
tionally, we know that it is not as dangerous as living in Denver
rather than San Francisco, that it is not as likely to induce cancer
as smoking a pack of cigarettes a day, that it is not as likely to

give rise to some harmful effects as are many unsuspected chemicals in the food we eat or in the air we breathe, that it is not as apt to produce mutations as wearing trousers. It is, in other words, not worth worrying about.

The fallout scare had one important practical consequence. It prepared the ground for the nuclear test moratorium. The logical connection is tenuous; we could conduct tests underground or in space with no additional radioactivity reaching any living being. But instead of adopting these unnecessary but still rational restrictions, the American people were carried toward the more radical alternative, suspension of nuclear tests. Thus from insignificant and doubtful medical considerations, there seemed to follow a political and military measure of the greatest importance, which has contributed decisively to our weakness and our danger.

CHAPTER TEN:

Mirage of Peace

BETTER PSYCHOLOGICAL propaganda for the cessation of nuclear testing than the fallout scare would be difficult to imagine. Still, during the years between Hiroshima and 1958, nuclear disarmament was supported by other plausible and popular arguments, and the American people were persuaded that the peace of the world depended not on preparedness but on unpreparedness.

Our people were convinced that the development of weapons was prelude and preparation for war. Most Americans subscribed to the idea that as long as opposing nations possessed and perfected nuclear arms, an all-out nuclear war was not only a possibility but a horrible certainty. There seemed to be a simple and radical solution for the complex problem that faced the world: Disarmament.

What could have been more logical? War's destruction is caused by weapons. We can abolish war and the fear of war's destruction if we abolish weapons. Of all weapons, nuclear arms are the most dangerous. They should be abolished first. It is true that nuclear weapons are relatively small and easily hidden, so there may be no practical way to destroy existing stockpiles. But a beginning can be made—we thought, at least, that a beginning could be made—toward disarmament by stopping nuclear testing and calling a halt to the insane competition in the manufacture and development of instruments for world-wide destruction.

Disarmament was and is a noble goal. It satisfies the strong desires we all feel for a peaceful world, and it appeals to our elementary human decency. The arms race has diverted us from the most essential task, the improvement of the lot of mankind. The comparative economics of the arms race recently was underscored by the Associated Press in a report that the world is spending fourteen million dollars an hour on arms and armies. The United States and the Soviet Union, according to this report, are pouring a total of about eighty-eight billion dollars a year into the arms race. The Associated Press concluded:

"If the world were to pool this money for peaceful purposes, the average annual cash income of 1,200,000,000 people who make less than $100 a year could be more than doubled. Adequate housing could be provided for 240 million families in under-developed nations. The hungry among the world's three billion people could be fed, the sick provided with medical care. An absolute end to the arms race would release the constructive energies of at least fifteen million men now in training to kill each other."

Every civilized man must desire effective disarmament that would eliminate the expensive and inhumane balance of terror existing in the world. But every rational man must admit that the terror would be greater if there were no balance, that the threats to peace would be multiplied if the instruments of terror were at the exclusive command of our enemies. One-sided disarmament is worse than no disarmament.

We thought, in 1958, that an effective world-wide disarmament was possible. At the very least, we thought that the further development of the most effective weapons could be halted with a suspension of nuclear tests. Many Americans argued that a test ban would prevent the further spread of nuclear knowledge, limiting the number of fingers resting nervously on nuclear triggers. Negotiation of a test ban was seen as a way to relax international tensions, as an opening to mutual understanding, as a possible conclusion of the cold war. The Russians said they would stop testing and meet us at the negotiating table. Some of our scientists insisted that a world-wide test ban could be supervised.

Unconscious and conscious forces, apprehension and logic, drove us toward the goal of disarmament, toward some accommodation with the Soviet Union, toward arms control or limitation if not total disarmament, toward a restriction if not an abolition of the instruments of war.

Disarmament is desirable if it promotes peace. But it is desirable only if it promotes peace. Historically there is no clear evidence that disarmament will ensure peace.

Most people believe that World War I was caused by an arms race, and there is good evidence to support this view. But World War II was caused by a race in disarmament. And with Communist Russia bent upon world domination, the tensions of the world today are similar to those created by the aspirations of totalitarian governments just before World War II. The situation before World War I was quite different.

Serious attempts at disarmament were made between the two world wars. Peace-loving nations disarmed after World War I, and they were too slow to recognize and react to the fact that Nazi Germany dropped out of the disarmament race. Germany, terrifyingly armed, was marching toward world domination before the peaceful nations began to realize the error of their own disarmament. During the same period, an agreed limitation of naval arms between Japan, England, and the United States was violated by Japan. Battleships are big, and the fact of their construction by Japan in violation of the naval agreement could not be kept secret. Still, we were unwilling to recognize the fact of violation. A violation recognized must be punished, and we were afraid that punishment of Japan might plunge our nation into war. Once the agreement on arms limitation was made, the agreement itself erected a barrier to recognition that the agreement was being violated.

Some of our people insist that nuclear disarmament is desirable at any price, and they advocate a simple approach to the problem: Unilateral disarmament. The magnificent example of Gandhi and the high moral principles of many of our most thoughtful people have inspired the idea that the United States should abstain from development and possession of deadly nuclear weapons no matter what other nations may do.

As late as September 1961, after the Soviet Union had publicly announced its continuance of nuclear tests but before the United States resumed testing, many Americans still urged unilateral disarmament on the grounds that if our nation refused to break our unilateral test ban of three years' standing, we could face the world as a nation truly seeking peace. The courage of anyone who holds this view while realizing the possibility of frightening consequences deserves a great deal of respect.

But at least one point cannot be forgotten: The story of Gandhi has two sides. Only one is told in a recounting of the sufferings, determination, and eventual success of this great man. The other side, in its way, is as admirable. This is the story of the British willingness to limit their own power and to permit Gandhi's movement enough freedom so that his ideas of peaceful resistance could take hold and achieve ultimate success. We know of no Gandhi in any Communist country. Many decades might have to pass before the high-minded advocates of unilateral disarmament can hope to find in the Soviet Union the liberalism and generosity which is necessary if passive resistance is to become practical.

Unilateral disarmament on the part of the United States would, indeed, prevent future war. It might even save us from attack. Disarmed, we would be unprepared, and we would have to submit and surrender to a mere threat of attack. A surprising number of our people profess a preference for crawling to Moscow in surrender rather than risking the dangers of a nuclear war. It is, of course, of paramount importance to avoid the great suffering of a third world war. That terrible conflict as well as an all-out nuclear attack on our nation can be avoided, I am convinced, if we are prepared. But if we are not prepared, if we were to disarm unilaterally, our only remaining alternative would be surrender or defeat. Disarmament is justified only if it decreases the probability of war without creating a situation in which surrender or defeat would be inevitable.

Total nuclear disarmament would be a unilateral act. Nuclear weapons are small. They are easily hidden. They are produced in secret. We can have no certain knowledge of the size and variety of the nuclear stockpiles of Russia. In fact, no nation could know if another nation decided to hold out on an agreement to destroy nuclear stockpiles. The dangers of such a hold-out are so great and so obvious that the question of nuclear stockpile reduction has been bypassed. To do otherwise would be to attempt enforcement of the unenforceable, to repeat the mistakes of the 1930s, to believe only what we wanted to believe and to see only what we wanted to see.

In the United States during the years after Hiroshima, hopes for total nuclear disarmament were replaced by lesser hopes. The dream that all nations might destroy their stockpiles was reduced to a hope for the limitation of future development of nuclear weapons.

In the spring of 1958, the Russians announced they would stop nuclear testing if we would. President Eisenhower responded to the challenge by proposing a summer conference of scientists from the nuclear nations to discuss the technical possibilities of policing a cessation of nuclear tests. The Conference of Experts reported that a test ban agreement was feasible, that enforcement was possible, and that the proposal showed promise.

In August of 1958, President Eisenhower invited the Soviet Union and England to a conference at Geneva to begin on October 31. Both accepted. The purpose of the conference was to draft a treaty agreement to end nuclear tests.

As an indication of good faith, the United States unilaterally initiated a test ban effective the day before the conference, October 30, 1958. The Soviet Union continued testing for a few days. After that, no further Russian tests were announced or detected.

Our voluntary moratorium on nuclear tests was to have lasted only one year. Within that year we hoped to reach an enforceable agreement with the Soviet Union that would ban nuclear tests forever, prevent the development of new weapons, and lead to a controlled disarmament. But an agreement was not reached during that first year. The Eisenhower administration agreed to the request of the Soviets and dropped its insistence that test cessation must be followed by other forms of weapons limitations within certain periods of time. Russian negotiators fought a bitter battle against United States' demands that a permanent test ban must be policed with on-the-spot inspections of suspected violations. The one-year time limit set on the Geneva conference, along with the time of our voluntary test cessation and the period of Russia's uninspected and unpoliced moratorium, was extended again and again.

The test ban negotiations, although futile, did bring to light the technical difficulties of policing and enforcing any agreement to end nuclear experiments. These technical facts are most important. They form the basis of any future discussion of test cessation. In a more general way, they illustrate the difficulties of any plan of policed arms limitation.

Nuclear tests can be conducted in four general areas: Above land or sea in our atmosphere, below the surface of oceans, underground, or in space. Each of the four presents particular problems of detection, and some of them offer opportunities to cheat on a test ban agreement and avoid detection.

Our first atomic bomb and our first thermonuclear bomb were tested in the atmosphere. The large majority of nuclear tests have been conducted in the atmosphere. In this area detection techniques are most refined. Atmospheric tests release radioactivity into the air. These radioactive particles decay at known rates. They can be gathered and their substance analyzed. The results fix the date of a nuclear test rather accurately. By plotting the flow of winds carrying the radioactive particles to the point of pick-up, the test site itself can be located. Verification of an atmospheric test can be made by correlating the information obtained from radioactive particles with the readings on instruments measuring disturbances in the air and in the crust of the earth caused by the test explosion's shock wave. All this was known long before the Geneva conference began in 1958. Some of these techniques, in fact, had detected the Soviet Union's first atomic explosion in 1949. Big nuclear explosions can be heard around the world—if not by human ears, then by the electronic ears of appropriate apparatus. Difficulties might occur when we try to detect "clean" explosions. But even in these cases, signals emitted from an atmospheric explosion probably could be noticed.

The Conference of Experts during the summer of 1958 reported that detection of atmospheric tests would be relatively easy, and it was on the basis of this optimistic report that the United States voluntarily undertook a unilateral test moratorium and invited the Soviet Union to negotiate a test ban agreement. The experts proposed installation of a moderate number of inspection stations throughout the world. These, in addition to appropriate flights of airplanes equipped with filters to pick up radioactive particles, could detect nuclear tests above the strength of one kiloton, explosions above the equivalent of 1000 tons of TNT. Smaller explosions, important for the development of tactical nuclear weapons, might go undetected. But an unexpected shift of the wind could carry telltale radioactivity from small tests to inspection stations, so the violator of a test ban would have reason to fear that even a small explosion might be detected. For an effective test ban, detection of each and every violation would be unnecessary. Not a great deal is learned from a single nuclear test. But it would be necessary to detect systematic violations and to prevent long series of tests from which a great deal might be learned. The atmospheric control system proposed at Geneva probably would be good enough to do that.

Nuclear explosions beneath the surfaces of oceans, likewise, are easily detectable. Water transmits sound so easily that an underwater explosion's noise and shock wave can be picked up even more effectively than the same disturbances in an atmospheric test. Once the noise and shock of an underwater explosion are recorded at several places, the arrival time of the shock wave at the various stations can be used to locate the explosion's site. Freedom of the seas would permit a check for radioactive contamination of the water at the determined location. The fact of a test ban violation could be established beyond doubt, although the identity of the violator working on the open seas might remain uncertain.

But the situation with respect to underground testing is quite different. Identification of underground nuclear explosions, large or small, presents serious difficulties. Underground tests can be hidden so effectively that a long and systematic series of experiments could be carried out without any real chance that they might be detected by any technical observation. Such a secret series, undetected and unknown, could yield practically all the information needed for successful development of nuclear weapons.

Actual detection of certain underground nuclear explosions is not exceedingly difficult, but identification and verification are.

There are three chief obstacles to the policing of underground nuclear explosions: Noise in the earth's crust may mean a test or an earthquake; a radioactive deposit is not easily located underground; and subsurface tests can be muffled.

According to present knowledge, it is very hard to distinguish disturbances created in the earth's crust by underground nuclear explosions from those caused by natural and frequent earthquakes. Earth's crust is not as solid as many people imagine. Slippages and upheavals cause thousands of disturbances each year, and these create noise which is picked up and recorded by seismographs.

Earthquakes and other natural movements in the ground cause different kinds of readings on seismographs in different locations. A seismograph to the east of an earth slippage, for example, might record the first movement as a compression, while a seismograph located to the north of the same slippage would record an opposite initial effect. If a disturbance is caused by an underground nuclear explosion, the first signal received by seismographs in any direction from the disturbance is expected to be a compression, because explosions push outward in all directions. But this distinction between nuclear explosions and earthquakes is neither definitive nor reliable. Underground explosions can be distinguished from earthquakes with today's equipment only if the first tiny wiggle of the record of the disturbance on all seismograms behaves in the same manner, indicating a compression in all directions from a given location. The steady background noises created in the earth's crust by pounding ocean waves and other causes, however, frequently resemble the compression wiggle of an underground nuclear explosion on all seismographs even when a natural earthquake actually has occurred. Conversely, the distinctive first wiggle caused by a nuclear explosion might be lost in the earth's natural background noise at some seismic stations and so the explosion may look like an earthquake.

Any nation determined to cheat a test ban agreement, furthermore, could easily camouflage nuclear explosions to resemble natural earthquakes. Explosions can be simply and effectively hidden in either of two ways: Two or more underground explosions could be set off almost simultaneously to produce the slightly more involved seismograms caused by earthquakes; or nuclear devices could be planted underground in earthquake-prone areas in such a way as to be triggered by a natural slippage. In either case, seismographs could be completely fooled, and the underground test would go unsuspected.

The second obstacle to successful detection of clandestine underground tests also involves the inexact art of seismology. Since seismograms can be fooled, the only sure way to tell an earthquake from an underground explosion is to send teams of experts to inspect locations of suspicious earth disturbances recorded by seismographs. If they could find traces of radioactivity, they would know a nuclear test had been conducted. But location of radioactivity would be difficult if not impossible. Our most efficient seismographs can localize disturbances only imperfectly, to within an area of about 100 square miles. An underground test within that area, need leave no mark on the surface different from those marks that might be caused by earthquakes. A nuclear explosion could be verified only if the inspection team located radioactivity at some depth below earth's surface. A one-kiloton explosion, equivalent to 1000 tons of TNT, buried at a depth of only 500 feet would push no radioactivity to the ground's surface after explosion. A one-megaton explosion, equivalent to one million tons of TNT, could be set off at a depth of 5000 feet without leaving a trace of radioactivity on the surface. Seismographs could not tell inspection teams at what depth the suspicious disturbance had occurred. Seismographs could not locate the disturbance except within an area of 100 square miles. Since radiation spreads only a few hundred feet from an underground explosion, inspection teams would have to drill to various depths all over the 100-square-mile area to prospect for radioactive particles that would give proof of a nuclear explosion. Proof would require this kind of desperate wildcatting.

The third obstacle to successful detection of underground tests is the established fact that explosions can be muffled. If nuclear tests are conducted in big underground holes, the seismic signal produced by the explosion can be decreased up to three hundred times. If a twenty-kiloton bomb, with an explosive force equal to 20,000 tons of TNT, were set off in a hole nearly 500 feet in diameter located 3000 feet below ground, it would be muffled so as to resemble an explosion of only seventy tons of TNT. Experiments producing such weak seismic signals probably could not be detected. Even if detected, the signals would be lost among thousands of minor, natural earth movements. It would be impractical to inspect them. Muffling, or decoupling, of underground explosions would permit the violator of a test ban agreement to conduct systematic nuclear tests in complete secrecy.

It would not be difficult to make the required cavities. The cheapest and most practical method of producing underground cavities would be to wash out thick deposits of salt. Underground holes big enough to muffle a twenty-kiloton explosion could be washed out in two years at a cost of about ten million dollars. Neither this length of time nor this amount of money would be considered excessive by a nation bent upon cheating a nuclear test ban. There are, in Communist territories, underground salt deposits extensive enough to be washed out as decoupling chambers. More underground holes could be produced at a somewhat higher cost by making appropriate cavities in widespread limestone deposits. Big holes would not always be needed to effectively cheat a test ban agreement. Maximum decoupling to a factor of 300 would not always be necessary. Cavities of one tenth the volume required for maximum muffling would be large enough to reduce the seismic signal of an explosion twenty or thirty times, and for smaller tests such cavities could be excavated easily by completely conventional means.

Muffling probably can be made even more efficient. Substances which absorb the energy of a nuclear explosion without producing a corresponding pressure could be placed in the decoupling chamber. Since it is the pressure of an explosion that is transmitted as earth motion, a reduction of pressure would decrease the seismic signal. It is entirely possible that the muffling can be increased from its present factor of 300 to a factor of several thousand. This might be done without an increase in the size of the cavity. In fact, the energy-absorbing substances would make it possible to reduce the size of the cavity.

Each of these obstacles to effective detection of underground explosions produced a particular effect upon the Geneva negotiations, and each made the likelihood of a test ban agreement seem more hopeless.

At the Conference of Experts in Geneva during the summer of 1958, it was agreed that 180 detection stations around the world would give a ninety per cent probability that underground test explosions above five kilotons in power, the equivalent of 5000 tons of TNT, could be detected. At the same conference, the Russian experts reluctantly agreed "that all events which are recorded by the control stations and which could be suspected of being nuclear explosions will have to be inspected on the site."

Even before the Geneva test ban negotiations began, we realized that the inspection system to which we had agreed was inadequate and could not detect five kilotons with anything like a ninety per cent probability. Our underground tests during October 1958, just before the Geneva negotiations began, demonstrated the difficulty of distinguishing between explosions and earthquakes. It became evident that agreed inspection methods would direct attention only to underground shots of above twenty kilotons rather than explosions down to five kilotons.

Early in 1959, a few short months after the Geneva negotiations began, the big-hole theory of decoupling was developed. Albert Latter of the Rand Corporation in Santa Monica, who had collaborated with our laboratory in Livermore for many years, found that nuclear explosions could be hidden underground simply and effectively by placing the explosive in a hole of an appropriate size. In January of 1959, the President's Scientific Advisory Committee visited the Livermore Laboratory. The committee's foremost expert was Hans Bethe, who had contributed throughout the years to many weapons developments. He also was a leader among those arguing that a test cessation was feasible and desirable.

Bethe listened to Albert Latter's idea and proof of decoupling, and then declared conservatively: "I shall have to make a decision about this." He did, several weeks later, and he confirmed Latter's findings.

Even before the theory of decoupling was verified experimentally, with small shots of conventional high explosives in Louisiana early in 1960, the idea that a nuclear explosion could be muffled in an underground cavity was presented by Bethe and Latter to the Russians in Geneva. Bethe later recalled the presentation by writing in an *Atlantic Monthly* article:

"I had the doubtful honor of presenting the theory of the big hole to the Russians in Geneva in November, 1959. I felt deeply embarrassed in so doing, because it implied that we considered the Russians capable of cheating on a massive scale. I think that they would have been quite justified if they had considered this an insult and had walked out of the negotiations in disgust."

Actually, it was the job of our negotiators to find out whether cheating was possible. If the Russians wanted to cheat, it became evident that they could do so with complete safety.

In Russia each year there are about 5000 natural earth movements that would give the kind of seismic signals produced by a decoupled twenty-kiloton nuclear explosion. Because of the unsatisfactory seismic discrimination between natural earthquakes and nuclear explosions, almost all of these 5000 movements would be suspicious, and this would pose an enormous problem of inspection.

Because of the accumulating difficulties of detecting small nuclear underground tests or muffled explosions, the United States on February 11, 1960, proposed conclusion of a partial test ban treaty. We sought an agreement that would ban large nuclear explosions, and we proposed that the nuclear nations should undertake intensive research on the improvement of methods to detect and identify underground explosions so that a ban in time could be extended to include all underground tests. This proposal was accepted by the Soviet Union on March 19, with an important modification: Russia asked for a moratorium on smaller nuclear tests for a number of years. While only big nuclear explosions would be prohibited in the test ban agreement itself, the Soviet Union wanted the nuclear nations to declare in a separate document that all would refrain from testing nuclear devices under twenty kilotons. The Soviet Union proposed a small-test moratorium of four to five years. The West said such a gentlemen's agreement should not extend for more than two or three years. The United States proposed that its partial test ban should be policed with about twenty inspections a year in the Soviet Union. The Russians, in July of 1960, said that within Soviet borders the annual number of on-the-site nuclear inspections would have to be limited to three.

Almost a year later, Soviet negotiators insisted that any ban on nuclear tests should be policed by a three-headed international commission, a "troika," composed of a Russian, an American, and a "neutralist"—and any one of the three could veto any inspection. The United States could not consider such an arrangement. Had we accepted, the Russians might have permitted inspection of genuine earthquakes. But if, by remote accident, we might have happened to pick out of the many disturbances one that corresponded to an actual test, the Russians certainly would have vetoed an inspection.

The Russian demands were extravagant, and the Russians knew them to be extravagant. Soviet leaders must have recognized that the United States would not consider a test ban treaty that would give Russians a veto over inspections on Russian soil.

Yet the Soviet Union insisted on the "troika." The talks were deadlocked.

And Russia got what she wanted: No nuclear tests in the United States, and no inspections in Russia.

At Geneva and in the public press so much attention has been focused on the difficulties of detecting underground nuclear tests that many people believe this to be the only serious hurdle to a test ban. It is not. The possibilities of treaty violations with underground tests are great, but the possibilities of illegal and clandestine tests are even greater in the fourth general area available for testing: Interplanetary space.

It would be possible to launch a rocket carrying a nuclear explosive and a compartment of observation equipment. Far from the earth, the nuclear device and the observation instruments could be separated and allowed to drift apart. When they were perhaps ten miles from each other, the nuclear device could be exploded and the observing instruments would radio the test results back to the earth. These results, vital as they are, usually can be conveyed in a brief message. They could be transmitted over the vast distances of interplanetary space with little power. They would arrive in a carefully coded form that would be inconspicuous and would appear as a meaningless, random noise to anyone except those who sent up the space experiment and who were listening for the results. At present, tests of almost any size could be carried out secretly in interplanetary space.

The possibilities of space tests are not fantastic. They are feasible. They would be largely undetectable. And an experiment in space could be as significant for a nation's armed preparedness as a full-scale hydrogen bomb test in the Pacific or in Siberia.

The expense of space tests would not be excessive. A reasonable cost estimate would be twenty million dollars for each test. This is somewhat more than the cost of each big nuclear test of the past. Actually, the money would go for different things. Space tests would not require the elaborate meteorological control or the great number of participants employed for all of our Pacific experiments. The biggest single expense of space testing would be the cost of thrusting the rocket beyond the earth's gravitational field to a distance of perhaps 100 to 200 million miles. And rocket thrust is a field in which Russia excels.

Space testing would allow violation of a test ban treaty on a really massive scale. The violator, to avoid detection, would need only rocket thrust and scientific patience. After a rocket carrying a nuclear device and observation equipment had left the earth's gravitational field, scientists would have to wait a few months for the rocket to drift 100 million miles from the earth before they could safely separate the rocket's compartments and detonate the nuclear device.

Nuclear explosions in space would produce intense X rays and electromagnetic waves. These would be absorbed in our atmosphere and could not be detected on earth. Police satellites carrying detection equipment could be launched and kept in orbit, at great expense, but their effectiveness could be thwarted. The test ban violator could shield his nuclear explosion, containing the X-rays and electromagnetic waves. Shielding would add to a rocket's weight and thus increase launching costs. But to a violator of a test ban, shielding would have a great advantage: Shielded explosives could be tested in far space without fear of detection up to 500 kilotons, the equivalent of a half-million tons of TNT.

There is a method of controlling nuclear tests in space that would be easy, practical, cheap, and almost foolproof. The experiment might be noticed before it left the earth. A network of observation stations could be established that would sight the firing of any rocket from any point in the world. An agreement might be sought permitting the inspection of each rocket before firing. In this way we could make sure that no nuclear explosive was aboard. Uninspected firings would be in violation of the test ban agreement. There is only one thing wrong with this simple and effective proposal: The Russians—who balked at adequate inspection of suspected underground explosions and who resumed atmospheric explosions—do not like it and have said they never would agree to it.

At a time when nuclear disarmament was so strongly desired by so many, when there still seemed to be some hope that a test ban might be possible, when our moratorium still was in effect and the Russians were insisting that they had abstained from nuclear tests, I was criticized for worrying about undetectable violations of a test ban agreement before such a treaty was signed.

I believe such worries were necessary and must be a necessary part of any future consideration of a test ban treaty. If a moratorium is to be checked at all, it is essential that we think about how an agreement's provisions might be subverted. To act otherwise would be as logical as to try to learn how to play chess while operating under the assumption that only the white pieces could be moved.

Is an effective nuclear test ban possible?

In the atmosphere and beneath the surfaces of oceans, yes. In these areas—the biosphere, the sphere of living beings—violations of a test ban could be detected.

But an effective ban of nuclear tests underground or in space is not possible. In these areas a test ban now could be violated without detection. We certainly should strive to improve detection methods. We should step up our seismological research, looking toward the day when we might be able to detect and identify underground nuclear explosions. We should search for better ways of detecting nuclear explosions in space. But until much better methods of detection have been developed, any test ban agreement could be violated. And an agreement that can be subverted in secret cannot be enforced and cannot be effective.

Nuclear testing, as a phrase, is a misnomer. It implies that scientists know rather precisely how a particular device will function even before it is detonated, that a test merely corroborates laboratory findings. Many people think of nuclear tests in the same context as the mileage tests they give their automobiles: They know the car will run and they know how it will run, but they conduct a test to determine whether it will run twenty or twenty-two miles on a gallon of gas. The development of nuclear explosives does not depend upon this kind of test. Each nuclear explosion in our development program, in fact, is an experiment, and the outcome is very much in doubt. We do not know in advance of the most important experiments whether the nuclear device will work. The explosive sometimes performs better than expected. It sometimes works less effectively. It sometimes is a fizzle. And we have learned at least as much from the failures as from the successes.

The aim of nuclear experimentation is a continued and rapid advance. Before the United States voluntarily stopped nuclear testing in October 1958, this aim was being realized. Impressive progress was being achieved, not by sudden break-throughs or unexpected strides, but by a steady accumulation of knowledge based upon an ever increasing understanding of the nuclear problems.

During the thirteen years of experimentation between the time of Hiroshima and our voluntary cessation, United States scientists learned how to increase the explosive force of a nuclear device a thousandfold. Great progress was made in reducing the weight of a bomb of a given power. Cost of the biggest nuclear explosives was reduced to a point where expense no longer was an essential factor. Experimentation was so effective and its cumulative results so pronounced that the nuclear arsenal of the United States today contains weapons that make those of 1945 appear completely obsolete.

This situation has led many people to conclude that further nuclear development is not important. The general opinion is that we have reached a state of saturation, that we possess more than enough nuclear weapons and that we need no more. This is, in part, true. The United States does have enough nuclear weapons to devastate all the cities of the Soviet Union. But we do not want to use our weapons for aggressive destruction.

We do, however, want to survive an initial attack that might be directed toward the United States. We do want to be able to strike back against any attacker. We do want to be prepared to participate in limited nuclear warfare for the protection of the freedom of our allies. These goals are more difficult to attain, and for these we are not yet appropriately armed. All involve the development and refinement of lightweight nuclear weapons. These weapons, so urgently needed as guarantors of freedom in the United States and throughout the world, can be produced only by nuclear experimentation.

Further nuclear experiments are essential to our security in several specific ways. A most important consideration is that the weight of nuclear bombs be reduced.

We have begun to disperse our retaliatory forces so that no initial attack, however swift and ferocious, could destroy our ability to strike back. Our nuclear submarines, armed with Polaris missiles, roam the seas far from important military targets; they are prepared to return any nuclear blow against the continental United States. Planes of the Strategic Air Command, armed with nuclear devices, are in the air twenty-four hours a day, serving notice that any attack upon our nation will draw a counter-attack. Advanced plans have been made for the continual shunting of Minuteman rockets about our nation.

The existence of these means of retaliation is the reason why

Krushchev's threats to bomb the United States today are empty threats. But our present retaliatory force is a wasting asset, and the Russian leaders know this.

As long as our nuclear explosives are heavy, they require big and heavy rockets to carry them. These missiles are not easily protected against the blast of Russian rockets. They must be installed in permanent sites that surely are known to the Russians. They cannot be carried around the country in an inconspicuous way. They require big and expensive nuclear submarines to keep them at sea.

Year by year the Communists can perfect the accuracy of their rockets that are aimed at our missile sites. We cannot prevent Communist espionage from detecting and reporting the locations of our clumsy instruments of retaliation. As the Soviet Union builds more nuclear submarines, the limited number of our oversized submarines will provide us with less insurance. The Russians cannot hope to destroy all of our nuclear striking power in an initial attack, but they may destroy such a great fraction that the remainder could be shot down in the air before reaching Russia.

Further tests will decrease the weight of our retaliatory nuclear weapons. This will multiply the effectiveness and divide the cost of this force. Lightweight nuclear explosives will allow a corresponding reduction in the size, weight, and thrust of our ballistics missiles. These smaller weapons could be carried around the nation on trucks and railroad cars with greater ease and with less likelihood of detection. More of these smaller nuclear weapons could be installed in more "hard" stations, shelters scattered around our nation, impervious to an initial attack, from which second-strike missiles can be launched. Smaller weapons would enable the United States to launch more decoys along with second-strike rockets, increasing the chances of thwarting an enemy's anti-ICBM system. Smaller nuclear weapons could be carried by smaller, much less expensive airplanes and submarines. A decrease of the sheer weight of nuclear explosives without a loss of power, resulting in a reduction of the necessary size of missiles and missile-carrying vehicles, could cut the cost of the retaliatory force which our nation so desperately needs by billions of dollars.

But our safety and survival should not be reckoned in dollars. The main point we must consider is this: We cannot be sure in a rapidly changing world whether our military strength is sufficient. By continuing nuclear experiments, we are much more likely to remain prepared for all eventualities.

Both United States and Russian strategists have recognized the possibilities of something less than all-out nuclear conflicts. With the world in a situation in which neither of the two greatest nuclear powers dares attack its opponent directly, the possibilities of limited wars continue as a menace to peace. Successful engagement in such limited wars would depend on lightweight, transportable, "clean" tactical weapons.

We have been told again and again that the United States is ahead of the Soviet Union in the development of nuclear weapons. Specifically, we have been assured that we are ahead in the field of tactical nuclear weapons of the type necessary for the successful conduct of limited wars. When our government ordered a moratorium on United States nuclear experiments in 1958, we might have been ahead. When our moratorium ended three years later, our lead certainly had vanished. It is highly possible that Russia today has more advanced tactical weapons than the United States.

Tactical weapons experiments are difficult if not impossible to detect because these nuclear explosions produce very low yields. Some of the most interesting tactical explosives produce yields of less than 1000 tons. If the most simple methods of concealment were used, we could not have detected explosions producing yields of 1000 tons during the years of Russia's supposed test moratorium.

We have good reason to believe that between 1958 and 1961, when the Soviet Union began testing openly, that Russia set off no big explosions in the atmosphere. But of experiments conducted underground or in space, we know nothing. Many continue to believe that the Soviet Union, true to its word, abstained from all nuclear experiments during these three years. Technically, this belief is unsupported. We have no way of knowing that it is true. The probability that a nuclear gap exists right now, in addition to a missile gap, is frightening and real.

Although nuclear experiments have been resumed, the clamor for some kind of a treaty banning tests continues. But there will always be limits below which an underground explosion could not be detected. This fact makes it certain that any treaty to end nuclear experiments never could be more than a gentlemen's agreement. An inclusive treaty could be neither policed nor enforced. It would place the United States in the untenable position of basing our national security upon Russian truthfulness.

From the outset of the Geneva negotiations, the thought prevailed that even if an agreement could not be reached, the very fact that the talks were in progress would restrain other countries from developing nuclear weapons. And, it was argued, if a test ban treaty could be negotiated by the existing nuclear powers, these nations would be able to prevent the spread of atomic weapons know-how.

These ideas were based on desire rather than fact. Ambitious nations like China were not included in the negotiations and were not bound by any possible agreement of the delegates. Knowledge spreads, and every nation capable of producing fissionable material has enough knowledge to build atomic bombs. So far, indeed, every nation that has acquired sufficient fissionable material of the right kind has succeeded in setting off an atomic bomb in a very short time. And in a dictatorship, any required experiments might be carried out in secret. To assume that knowledge can be confined or that clandestine misbehavior will not occur is similar to assuming that the morality of teenagers can be safeguarded by not telling them the facts of life.

Negotiation of a nuclear test ban cannot be regarded as a good first step toward better international understanding. It would be a step in the opposite direction. It would undermine the confidence in international treaties while setting a dangerous precedent. It would bind the United States to an agreement not similarly binding on others. We would abide by the agreement. So would other democratic, law-abiding nations. Others might not. Our way of life and our public morality would exclude the idea of systematic cheating. The morality in a dictatorship might not be so inhibiting, and the temptation of violation might be overwhelming—especially since violation could not be detected but could lead to great military strength. The result would be a dangerous amount of power in the hands of dictators.

International law hardly exists today. It certainly is not respected. It should exist; this is one of our most vital needs. But laws that cannot be enforced certainly will not increase respect for law. Unenforceable laws favor the lawless. Prohibition gave us an example of this in the United States. Unenforceable disarmament agreements could prove the truth of this statement on a disastrous scale.

The problem of an uncontrolled spread of nuclear weapons among the nations of the world demands an effective answer. The approach we have pursued in the past has proved impractical. If we continue on this approach, we may neglect more hopeful possibilities. Recognizing the futility of unpoliced arms limitations, we now should be able to concentrate on more realistic prospects.

It is my firm belief that the best answer to the spread of nuclear arms is co-operation between like-minded nations. By sharing our weapons with our allies, we can make our alliances more firm. At the same time, the motive for independent weapons development will disappear in the advanced democracies. Even more important, such sharing would be a long step toward effective co-operation between nations.

This would not solve the problem of nuclear weapons on a world-wide scale. But the remainder of the nations not yet in the Russian orbit would take a longer time to develop nuclear explosives. Our experience of sharing our nuclear explosives with our close allies would make it easier to agree on full nuclear co-operation with other free nations at the appropriate time.

The question of nuclear explosives in the hands of China and other Communist nations is one that the Russians must tackle. They have, so far, prevented the spread of nuclear explosives from the Soviet Union to other countries of the Communist bloc. Still, China may develop a nuclear explosive in the near future. This will greatly enhance China's prestige and will increase her nuisance value. But it will do little else. To develop an explosive is relatively easy. To acquire an effective delivery system is much more difficult. Chinese military strength will depend on the Soviet Union for many years to come.

During the critical days just before Pearl Harbor in 1941, Japanese emissaries were in Washington, assuring the highest United States officials that they wanted peace. During the critical years between 1958 and 1961, Russian emissaries were in Geneva, assuring us that they wanted a test ban and disarmament.

In 1958–61, as in 1941, we believed what we wanted to believe. For true peace, we accepted a mirage of peace.

We now know that our self-imposed moratorium on nuclear experiments during the Geneva negotiations was idiotic and dangerous, that we allowed our hopes to arrest our weapons development at the 1958 level while Russian progress was accelerating, that the Soviet Union never did stop nuclear tests but was conducting experiments all along.

All this was clearly indicated by the events of early September 1961 when Khrushchev announced that the Soviet Union would test explosives with yields in the 100-megaton range and Russia undertook a systematic series of nuclear experiments in the atmosphere.

During the long years of the Geneva negotiations, we had no way to detect Russian tests of moderate size. But tests of several megatons or more would have been difficult and expensive for the Russians to hide. Announcing their intention to conduct experiments with yields of twenty to 100 megatons, the Russians made confident statements about the results of these future tests. They could anticipate these results on the basis of earlier, clandestine tests with smaller yields.

The military value of 100-megaton tests is not particularly great. It is likely that the recent numerous tests of the Russians have produced more important progress. The willingness of the Russians to conduct such experiments openly, in spite of world opinion, was a clear indication that they had tested the more important small weapons while they could do so in secret.

The Russians must have known that their announcement and test series would lead to American resumption of nuclear experiments. They would have risked that only if they knew they were far ahead. An earlier, secret test program certainly would have put them far ahead.

We must assume that the Soviet Union actually is ahead of us in the development of nuclear weapons.

At the moment, we must bend all efforts toward stopping the increasing tide of Communist power. Stable peace and disarmament require that we should have the strength which will lend our voice proper authority.

But our present difficulties should not prevent us from trying again. We have attacked the problem of disarmament in a wrong way. Our next attempt should be more effective. We have learned that this important goal cannot be approached by trusting to the seemingly easy functioning of automatic means of detection. If we want controlled disarmament or even controlled arms limitation, we need one thing: Openness.

We need an open exchange of ideas between all people. If anyone can go to any country and any place in the world, if anyone can ask any question, if any person can answer without fear of reprisal, if secrets disappear, then no test or warlike preparation can go undetected. Openness will be of increasing importance, in the years ahead, as more and more nations acquire the capability to build and deliver nuclear weapons. Openness initiated now would eliminate possible errors in determining the source of a nuclear attack in the future.

The best and the only possible method of international arms control is based on this simple expedient, openness. Such openness is inseparable from our ideas of freedom. We should realize that in the long run our safety depends on the same openness.

Our goal, in the final analysis, cannot be merely to do away with arms and armies. We must, instead, work for the elimination of irresponsible and illegal acts of independent nations. We must work for establishment of a world authority sustained by moral force and physical force—a world-wide government capable of enforcing world-wide law and world-wide disarmament.

CHAPTER ELEVEN

The Quiet Enemy

OUR NATION IS VERY DIFFERENT today because of decisions made by scientists in 1939. We are, to be sure, stronger; the insight of scientists in 1939 resulted in a system of nuclear weapons without which the United States today could not stand before the world as a great and influential nation. But, as a corollary of this strength, these same scientists helped create a serious weakness. The strength is external, a force with which we will defend ourselves against any other country in the world. The weakness is internal, an influence that today is slowing our scientific progress and eating away at some of the basic institutions of our democracy. The strength is the nuclear weapon. The weakness is secrecy.

The possibilities of developing an atomic weapon and the desirability of doing it secretly were discussed at a Princeton University conference in which I participated in March 1939. The conference was called by Leo Szilard, and the participants included Niels Bohr, Victor Weisskopf and John A. Wheeler.

Szilard and Bohr differed rather sharply on the two basic questions: Can an atomic bomb be built? Should it be built in secret?

Szilard, who had discovered the production of neutrons in the fission process, maintained that the population explosion of neutrons in a chain reaction could produce an explosion of tremen-

dous force. He was sure the atomic bomb could and should be
built.

Bohr and Wheeler believed, correctly, that only a particularly
rare variety of uranium could be used effectively in the creation
of an atomic explosion. Bohr said this rare variety could not be
separated from common uranium except by turning the country
into a gigantic factory. Bohr was worried that this could be done
and that an atomic bomb could be developed—but he hoped that
neither could be accomplished. Years later, when Bohr came to
Los Alamos, I was prepared to say, "You see . . ." But before I
could open my mouth, he said: "You see, I told you it couldn't
be done without turning the whole country into a factory. You
have done just that."

Bohr in 1939 had an additional reason for hoping that an
atomic bomb could not be constructed: He dreaded the necessity of scientific secrecy. He knew that secrecy would clash with
the spirit of the scientific method. Science thrives on stimulating
and helpful discussion; secrecy would prevent discussion. Science
develops with both co-operation and friendly competition; secrecy would hamper both. Nuclear secrecy, furthermore, would
be difficult to achieve. Joliot in France was working on nuclear
chain reactions, and so was Enrico Fermi at Columbia University; both would have to be persuaded to impose secrecy upon
themselves if secrecy was to work.

In 1939, there seemed to be excellent reasons for undertaking
the atomic bomb project in secret. We could envision the terrible
destructiveness of the atomic bomb. We could imagine that a
single nation in possession of an atomic bomb might dominate
the world. We were afraid that nation might be Nazi Germany.
This fear was justified. Germans discovered the principle of fission. Germans had taken steps to secure large amounts of fissionable material. Nazi leaders, bent upon world domination, had a
strong motive for pushing development of an atomic bomb. We
were desperately afraid that Nazi Germany would be the first
nation to develop an atomic bomb and would use the power of

the atom to subjugate the peoples of the world. This fear prompted some of us at the Princeton conference to urge that our atomic work should be cloaked with a voluntary secrecy. Our concern for freedom, ironically, forced us to recommend abandonment of the traditional freedom of scientific discussion.

These arguments of the younger scientists at the Princeton conference finally convinced Bohr, at least partially, that in this case scientific secrecy was necessary. It was agreed that Weisskopf should try to persuade Joliot and his French colleagues to adopt strict secrecy. I was to discuss the matter with Fermi.

I left the Princeton conference and drove promptly to New York. There I found Fermi to be as displeased as Bohr about the prospect of scientific secrecy. But Fermi also recognized the dangers of openness. He finally agreed that if all others in the field would adhere to a self-imposed secrecy, so would he.

Weisskopf contacted Joliot in Paris. But he was not successful in convincing the French that nuclear secrecy was essential. So our first attempts to introduce secrecy came to nothing. In a few weeks, however, an organized effort to assure atomic secrecy was begun among a greater number of American scientists.

Created by fear in 1939, nuclear secrecy since has become an entrenched institution that costs millions of dollars a year to maintain, slows our scientific development, stands as a barrier between our nation and our allies and between our own government and the people.

Some secrecy, even in a democracy, is valid and necessary. Government crop reports are tabulated in strict secrecy to prevent profiteering by speculators with advance knowledge. Movements of troops and ships, along with details of other military operations, have been and should be secret. Location of our strategic nuclear weapons must remain secret; as long as the Russians do not know where our missiles and hydrogen bombs are, they dare not attack us and cannot blackmail us effectively.

The courses of our nuclear submarines must remain secret; as long as the Russians do not know where our submarines are or where they are going, they cannot render them ineffective. Such operational secrecy is normal even in a democracy, and it must be maintained as long as tensions exist in the world.

But the time has come for the United States to take stock of nuclear secrecy, to begin a serious re-evaluation of the services of secrecy in science and technology—and its disservices.

Nuclear secrecy performed a very real and valuable service to the United States from 1939 until the end of World War II. Then, in a way, scientific secrecy was operational secrecy. We were developing and perfecting a new kind of weapon during those years. We could use the bomb to hasten the war's end. An enemy nation might use it to turn the tide.

For a few short years after the end of World War II, justification for our continued nuclear secrecy seemed substantial. We had an atomic monopoly, and in our arrogance we believed that the scientists of other nations would require decades to rediscover our atomic secrets. Knowing that of all the world's nations only the United States had the secret of the atomic bomb and believing American know-how to be so vastly superior, the American people passed a judgment that was neither characteristic of them nor in keeping with the nation's traditions. The people approved of continued nuclear secrecy. Secrecy, it was thought, could perform a high service: It could provide security.

The perilous illusion that secrecy was security should have vanished, a few short years after World War II, in Russia's first nuclear explosion. With the evidence of that explosion came proof that our nuclear secrets were not secrets. It became hard to pretend that this kind of security made us secure.

But nuclear secrecy in this country, nevertheless, was continued—to our disservice. We know that Russian scientists are fully capable of unraveling nature's secrets. They can put their knowledge to effective use. They probably are ahead of us in nuclear developments. They certainly are ahead of us in space.

Probably there is no major United States scientific advance of which the Russians are ignorant. Still, the United States persists in spending millions of dollars a year to maintain a rigid scientific-technological secrecy.

The cost of maintaining secrecy in this country is high because the amount of secrecy is large. I cannot say just how many secrets the United States is trying to keep. Even that is secret.

Our concern, however, is not the amount of secrecy or even the cost of secrecy, but the fact of secrecy and the effects of secrecy.

The effect of secrecy upon our scientific development is ironic. Because we try to keep a potential enemy from knowing what we know, we know less ourselves. In a free country like the United States, people do not like to work in secret. By its very nature, secrecy involves rules and regulations that impinge upon freedom. Scientists, like anyone else, dislike regulations and restrictions. So scientists prefer to work in areas free of secrecy, where the interchange of ideas is encouraged and where they can become known for their achievements. By repelling some of our best minds from work that is badly needed for our defense, secrecy has performed a disservice to our nation.

Russian secrecy does not have the same effect upon Russian scientists. Secrecy was firmly established under the czars as well as under the Communists in Russia. Scientists working outside nuclear projects are just as restricted and as regimented as those who are engaged in these high-priority efforts. So Russian scientists are not tempted to abandon military efforts for the sake of personal freedom, because personal freedom simply does not exist.

Since the United States no longer has a nuclear monopoly, our safety no longer lies in keeping all we know to ourselves. Rather, our safety depends upon the rapid conception and utilization of ideas. The United States and Russia today are competitors in several races: The race in atomic energy, the race for space, a race for men's minds, a race to influence uncommitted nations, a race for national defense and survival. These are races of ideas, contests of the mind, and the winner of each race will be the nation which is the fastest producer of the best ideas. Because free discussion encourages progress and usually improves ideas, I believe less secrecy would mean more speed in our race for new and useful ideas. And the United States needs more speed in the races which vitally concern our freedom and survival.

Exaggerated nuclear secrecy not only slows our scientific development, but it also stands as a barrier between ourselves and our allies. Secrecy has forced the United States to assume the ridiculous posture of denying to our friends facts that are known to our enemies.

The United States has taken several significant steps to reduce nuclear secrecy, especially between ourselves and our allies. We published the relevant principles of reactor construction in the Smyth Report as early as 1945, and we took the initiative in revealing essential methods of reactor technology at the 1955 Conference on the Peaceful Uses of Atomic Energy in Geneva. The Atomic Energy Act was liberalized in 1958 to allow even more discussion of nuclear secrets with our allies. All this has helped alleviate the problem of nuclear secrecy but has not eliminated it. The barrier of secrecy still stands between ourselves and our friends, resulting in a duplication of effort, a waste of time, and a waste of money.

Our policy of continued secrecy, for example, forced the French to make an independent effort to explode atomic bombs. Surely it would have been wiser for the United States to have shared nuclear secrets with the French and freed France's scientists from the time-consuming rediscovery of facts and methods already known to us. The cause of freedom would have been advanced if our nuclear secrets had been used to unite rather than divide, if the considerable talents of French scientists had been utilized in a common undertaking aimed at increasing Western security rather than devoted to the rediscovery of known facts.

The disservice performed by secrecy in erecting artificial barriers between friends cannot be overestimated. We live in a time that demands common action among the free nations in the building of a lawful world community. It is self-defeating to permit nuclear secrecy between friendly nations to hamper cooperation.

Aside from creating a moral disunity among free nations and suggesting that the United States really does not trust its allies, our continuing policies of nuclear secrecy seriously weaken the West's defense against World Communism. We have convinced ourselves that we should not discuss all of our nuclear weapons even with our allies. The United States has weapons in its arsenal and on its drawing boards that have never been disclosed to friendly nations bound to us by treaties of mutual defense. Since secrecy is contagious, it is not inconceivable that these same nations may have developed some weapons that have never been discussed with us. I think we cannot expect the North Atlantic Treaty Organization countries to develop the best plan of mutual defense when the instruments of defense are not fully known to all NATO countries.

It is not enough to give our NATO allies some of the nuclear weapons we have developed and constructed. We also should discuss with them our future plans. Adaptation of a military organization to advances in weaponry often requires more time than development of the weapons themselves. If NATO nations are kept ignorant of advances in nuclear weapons, if they cannot plan ahead, NATO's military organization cannot be expected to make effective use of new weapons when they are developed. Our NATO defense cannot realize its full potential as long as we keep our nuclear plans and nuclear secrets to ourselves.

Free and open discussion of our nuclear work would certainly strengthen both the military defense and the political unity of the free world. To the extent that our secrecy isolates free nations from one another and creates suspicions between allies, it certainly performs a disservice.

Secrecy's most insidious danger, however, is to our own form of democracy. A bulwark of our system of government is the people's right to know. Secrecy, in effect, denies that right.

We have instituted safeguards which, to some extent, will prevent the subversion of democracy by our policies of secrecy. We have made our nuclear effort the responsibility of a civilian rather than a military agency. And the Atomic Energy Act recognized the danger of entrusting our atomic program to any single agency, civilian or military, functioning in complete secrecy. To avoid the dangers of centralized, secret power, the Joint Congressional Committee for Atomic Energy was established. This committee balances the power of the Atomic Energy Commission by making critical reviews of all important decisions. The committee and its staff—none of them scientists—have done a remarkable job of understanding, appreciating, and criticizing the complex field of nuclear technology. The committee and the commission constitute a team that often has been harmonious and almost always has been effective. Members of the congressional committee are empowered to penetrate the aura of secrecy that surrounds all nuclear matters and judge nuclear decisions and progress as representatives of the people.

But public representation, in this case, is not the same as public participation. Neither is it as effective. No matter how well the public's elected representatives perform their duties as nuclear watchdogs, a better system of checks and balances would be provided by an informed public opinion. The government often cannot act effectively without public support. It frequently cannot act wisely unless the public is informed. It must act either arbitrarily or unwisely if the public is misinformed. And secrecy breeds misinformation.

Misinformation has indeed flourished and multiplied in the postwar years. Secrecy is not entirely to blame. The American public has assumed that questions of nuclear energy and nuclear explosives are beyond the understanding and judgment of the average individual. Most people believe that these difficult questions should be left to the expert.

Besides, these problems are not merely difficult. They also are disagreeable. They force one to think of war, of nuclear conflict, of Hiroshima, of things that would be more comfortably forgotten. Better leave all these questions to the expert.

I cannot escape the suspicion that this public attitude is somewhat analogous to the behavior of an individual who has a disturbing problem. It is not unusual for such people simply to ignore their problem; the disturbing fact is shoved aside, forgotten. Psychologists have an expression for this phenomenon: Repression. And repression is not a sign of mental health.

Analogies are incomplete and even dangerous. But it seems to me that secrecy has become a psychological defense mechanism for a considerable segment of the American people. Secrecy is the vehicle of repression. It helps to make it possible and even necessary to forget what most people prefer not to remember.

Thus a great burden of responsibility was offered to the expert scientists, to a group which happened to live outside the main stream of American life. The responsibility was greater than that carried by any other group of citizens—with the single exception of the elected representatives of the people. And what did the experts do with the considerable share of responsibility that was thrust upon them? They did what most people would have done in similar circumstances. Many of the experts gladly accepted these responsibilities. They felt that scientists, the most intelligent of all citizens, had been entrusted with their due, the responsibility for important decisions that they could handle more capably than anyone else.

These attitudes and consequences have created a situation in which the common people, the sovereigns of our democracy, have abdicated. The right to know is a basic institution of our democracy. More than that, it is an obligation of every citizen. As long as governmental secrecy denies that right, as long as secrecy spawns a public indifference to that right, as long as most of our citizens ignore the obligation to know and leave vital decisions to be made by an elite of "experts," our secrecy is a threat to our democracy.

In addition to the experts, another, incompletely informed group participates in the molding of American public opinion. This group includes newspaper and magazine editors, reporters, commentators, columnists, clergymen, teachers, authors, government officials—almost anyone who has an audience and who has something to say. These opinion makers have continued to shape the public mind despite our government's official policy of nuclear secrecy, despite their exclusion by secrecy from knowledge of vital decisions and developments, despite the obvious limitations imposed by secrecy upon intelligent discussion. The result has been a misinformed public opinion still exerting its traditional influence on the formation of important national policies. This has been dangerous and could be disastrous.

Several recent examples can be cited of public opinions that were uninformed or misinformed and so led to trouble. The AEC, in its constant review of secret material, had declassified all of the facts about radioactive fallout before Democratic candidates made this topic the issue in a public debate during the 1956 presidential campaign. But because the facts once had been secret, the suspicion persisted that perhaps the government had not told all that was known about fallout dangers. This suspicion paved the way for the excited and unsupported predictions of some scientists that fallout could kill thousands of the living and make future generations grotesque. The result was a national bath in the emotion of fear that became known as the fallout scare, and a misinformed public opinion demanded that we halt nuclear tests.

Another example arose during the Geneva negotiations on test cessation. In the early months of 1959, we proved that underground nuclear explosions could be muffled and hidden from detection. But this knowledge was withheld from the American people, and the public opinion was allowed to form that violations of a test ban treaty could be detected and identified anywhere in the world. The detection difficulties were revealed to the American people by our government only after they had been discussed with Russia. And, by then, it was almost impossible to focus public interest on the technical difficulties and change the established and prevailing public opinion that, in safety, we could agree to ban all nuclear explosions. Our people could not have been misled and the public opinion would not have been wrong if all the facts had been available to all the people all the time.

Even today, a sound and rational public opinion on the need for certain nuclear weapons is greatly impeded by secrecy. And because the public cannot be fully informed of the need, public opinion cannot be aroused to the point of demanding the weapons. There is an urgent need for better tactical nuclear weapons. These weapons, I believe, must be developed as the tools of limited nuclear warfare. Beyond this, I can say little. Because of secrecy, I cannot be explicit. I suspect that Russian leaders know more about our nuclear weapons plans than do the American people. Our own policy of secrecy allows only a superficial description of our weapons needs for the benefit of our own people. Secrecy makes it difficult to awaken Americans to the real dangers and real opportunities of our atomic age.

There are two popular and powerful arguments for continuing nuclear secrecy.

One argument is that if we did not keep our nuclear secrets, more and more nations would produce nuclear weapons. This argument once had merit; today it has little. We could find assurance in our nuclear secrets only as long as we had a nuclear monopoly. But that monopoly has been broken, and every nation with the materials necessary for a nuclear explosive has succeeded in making a bomb. Production of the explosive materials is somewhat difficult, but they can be produced in any nuclear reactor. Since the United States published reactor principles in 1945 and revealed essential portions of reactor technology in 1955, there is little reason to believe that even a small nation willing to spend the time and money would be unable to put together a nuclear bomb. The number of nations winning membership in the group known as the Nuclear Club certainly will increase. Despite our zealous secrecy, more and more countries will achieve a nuclear capability. This is inevitable. We should realize now that when this inevitable development occurs, when additional nations that are both friendly and unfriendly succeed in constructing nuclear weapons and the means for their delivery, our policy of secrecy then might perform its greatest disservice. If we persist in nuclear secrecy, the nuclear capabilities of additional countries will certainly be developed in secret. This could lead to a tragic and perhaps fatal misjudgment on the part of the United States. Suppose a small but ambitious nation developed just one atomic bomb in secret and fired it upon a target in the United States. We would retaliate, but most likely against an innocent party, and the misjudgment prompted by secrecy could plunge the known nuclear powers into an all-out war. World-wide openness would greatly decrease the possibility of such a tragic error.

The other argument for continuing secrecy is more valid: If we tell the world our nuclear secrets and the Russians keep theirs, it is obvious that Russia always will be ahead of us.

This is a serious argument. If we abandoned scientific secrecy completely and Russia did not, the Soviet Union surely would have some advantage. But the degree of that advantage is questionable. It certainly would be a short-term advantage. Nations at about the same stage of technical development usually discover the same technical facts at about the same time. General scientific principles can be kept secret for only a very short time, because secrecy of itself does not prevent the spread of ideas or their rediscovery by scientists of other nations. When two or more parties have reached about the same level of development, scientific secrets remain secrets for only a couple of years.

This, then, is our dilemma: If we should abandon nuclear secrecy, we would give the Communists some advantage. If we retain secrecy in its present form, we slow our nuclear progress, erect a barrier between ourselves and our allies, force a deplorable duplication of time and effort upon the building of a common Western defense, and impede the formation of a well-founded American public opinion. There is no question, in my mind, that secrecy's service in giving us some scientific advantage is transient and limited. Secrecy's disservices, on the other hand, seem to me to be cumulative and substantial.

Important steps have been taken toward elimination of secrecy. But more should be done. At the very least it is necessary to apply our rules of secrecy in a more liberal manner. A more radical and persuasive suggestion has been made by Niels Bohr, a man who has always opposed secrecy in scientific matters.

Shortly after the end of World War II, Bohr suggested that scientific openness would be to the advantage of the democratic countries. In the hands of a dictator, secrecy can be an effective weapon. In a democracy, the weapon will backfire. Our natural weapon is openness. It may not seem completely obvious that openness can be used to fight dictatorships. But openness will make it easier to unite the free world in the interests of safety and progress. And openness may, in the course of decades, penetrate the Iron Curtain and help us defeat the spirit of the police state.

Acceptance of Bohr's advice would reduce secrecy to its normal and historic level in a democracy. We should re-establish the situation that prevailed in this country before 1939. We should completely abandon secrecy in science, retaining secrecy only in certain operational matters. And we should maintain operational secrecy only as long as this is made necessary by world tensions.

Such a radical suggestion may not be practical at the present time. But in at least one area we can and should make rapid progress toward elimination of secrecy. The strict code of secrecy we voluntarily initiated in 1939 still prevails in the Atomic Energy Commission. Under this code, facts about nuclear explosives are born secret. All new results and discoveries are classified as secret or confidential until it is conclusively proved that there is no danger in their release. In other scientific and technical fields, the burden of proof is on the party arguing for secrecy. Non-nuclear discoveries are considered nonsecret unless it is proved that secrecy is essential. This procedure should also apply in the nuclear field. We should create and continue secret classifications only if they are absolutely necessary for our defense. Publication of scientific results should be encouraged, whenever possible, in the nuclear as well as the non-nuclear fields.

In one respect, secrecy can continue to be helpful. Although general principles can be kept secret for only a short time, technical and engineering details can be guarded with greater success. These details, in aggregate, are important and have given us reliable equipment. Rediscovery of general principles is easier than reconstruction of equipment and hardware that make general principles useful. Since the accumulation of technical and engineering details can be guarded and does result in an important advantage, we should be more careful about revealing these secrets.

In the long run, openness will serve us better than secrecy. But how far and how fast we can proceed toward openness should depend upon a detailed study. Such a study is overdue.

This study should consider the probable advantage which we hope to derive from continued secrecy in each scientific and technical area. Only if this advantage is both substantial and highly probable should secrecy continue to apply.

The proposed study would also have to try to assess the reaction of the Soviet Union to a United States policy of nuclear openness. To expect that our complete abandonment of secrecy necessarily would lead to complete Russian openness would be recklessly naïve. There is, however, historical evidence that release of our secrets might be followed by revelation of Russian secrets. When we threw open the vast field of nuclear reactors during the 1955 Conference on the Peaceful Uses of Atomic Energy, Russia responded by opening the Iron Curtain wide enough for us to assess Soviet advances in reactor research. When we declassified Project Sherwood and revealed our efforts to control thermonuclear reactions in 1958, Russia told the world of its progress in the same field. Russia will be faced with a difficult choice whenever the United States declassifies any area of nuclear secrecy. It would have the choice of remaining silent and appearing less advanced than we, or it could follow our lead and reveal new information.

Communist countries do and must continue to interact with the rest of the world, and since Russia is not completely indifferent to world opinion, openness on our side could be expected to produce a favorable—if limited—Soviet response. However limited initially, this response might mature into complete openness under the prodding of Russian scientists who desire a free exchange of information and whose influence upon Russia's political leaders might make itself felt over the years.

Our policies of the recent past have been based largely upon an argument that seemed obvious: To reveal a secret is an act beyond recall; we must, therefore, proceed with great caution.

This caution has led us into difficulties and has profited us little. Our policies of nuclear secrecy have not significantly retarded Russian advances, but they have slowed our own development and that of our allies.

A spirit of caution should also prevail during a new study of secrecy. But the caution must be applied more broadly. The danger of openness may seem great. The danger of secrecy actually may be greater.

The safety and prosperity of an interrelated world depend upon international co-operation. This co-operation must, in the end, embrace all nations. But it is urgent that full co-operation be established soon between the free and friendly countries. Secrecy stands in the way of such co-operation.

While the world is divided into opposing camps, limitations of arms are desirable. But such limitations can be enforced only in an open world. Secrecy interferes with this necessary enforcement.

We believe in the virtues of openness and freedom not only because they promote human happiness but also because they are conditions for human dignity, for effective progress, for international co-operation, and for peace with liberty. Openness would be a great source of strength in our battle for the minds and hearts of people on both sides of the Iron Curtain.

PART FOUR:

Bulwarks of Peace

CHAPTER TWELVE

The Not-So-Absolute Weapon

AT THE END OF WORLD WAR II, our armed power melted away. The traditional and deep-seated opposition of the American people to a big peacetime military establishment asserted itself. Even in Los Alamos I felt the powerful current of the popular feeling. My good friend, Enrico Fermi, advised me: "Come with us to Chicago; in peacetime, it will not be pleasant to stay here and work on weapons."

We all wanted peace. We believed in peace. And we were convinced that peace had come. There was a massive and irresistible demand: "Bring the boys home." There was a successful effort to cut our defense spending.

It seemed that we could demobilize and remain safe. Only the United States, after all, possessed the atomic bomb, the absolute weapon. Strategic bombing had contributed decisively to our World War II victory. The American people were conditioned to accept the doctrine of massive strategic bombing. Now we had a weapon that made strategic bombing easy and irresistible. This absolute weapon guaranteed the peace and our safety. Certainly no enemy could mobilize and supply great conventional armies while we possessed atomic bombs with which we could attack massed concentrations of troops, wipe out their arsenals, and destroy their lines of supply.

These arguments were accepted as self-evident. It was fortunate for the strength of the United States that General Curtis E. LeMay did something about the obvious and necessary task of creating a powerful nuclear air force. While most Americans relaxed in the knowledge of our nuclear monopoly, LeMay with single-minded determination built a superbly trained force that was maintained in constant readiness to strike anywhere in the world. This Strategic Air Command became the enforcing arm of the Truman Doctrine proclaiming our intention of containing Communism. A slogan later was coined by John Foster Dulles for SAC's responsibility: Massive Retaliation.

During the years immediately following Hiroshima, all this seemed to make sense. It was necessary that Communism be contained. Churchill claimed that only the atomic weapon could limit Communist expansion. We took the position that if the Soviet Union attacked any of our free-world allies, the Soviet Union would be destroyed.

This was a strong position for us to take. It was, in fact, too strong—and we backed away from it. Our atomic club was too big, and we were afraid to use it. Russia subjugated the countries of Eastern Europe and Communism triumphed in China, but there was no armed reprisal. Even during the Korean War, when we still possessed many more atomic weapons than Russia, we made it abundantly clear that we were afraid to swing our big stick.

Actually, the idea of massive retaliation is in conflict with principles that are deeply rooted in our traditions. We condemn aggression. But we also feel that we must not and cannot reply to limited aggression with unlimited destruction. It is my firm conviction that we should meet violence with appropriate resistance; but we are not justified in meeting evil with greater evil. Many say today that atomic weapons certainly are a greater evil. This I do not believe. Evil does not reside in an instrument, but rather in the manner in which the instrument is used.

But that the wholesale bombing of Russia is a greater evil than limited Soviet aggression can hardly be denied.

In a dangerous world we must be prepared for all eventualities. To build a nuclear strategic air force was a necessity. Not to develop a more moderate response to limited aggression was a mistake. To believe that atomic bombs are absolute weapons to be used only as instruments of wholesale slaughter is dangerous confusion. That this confusion should have been firmly established in so many minds was one of the consequences of Hiroshima.

The United States, confident that Russia could not produce an atomic bomb until around 1970, probably would have continued its headlong plunge toward unpreparedness had it not been for the foresight of Lewis Strauss. Months before the explosion of Russia's first atomic bomb in 1949, Strauss persuaded the government to establish regular flights of patrol planes equipped with special filters that would pick up radioactive particles from the atmosphere. Knowing the rate of radioactive decomposition of these particles, we could date their creation back to one of our atomic test explosions. In September 1949 particles were collected that could not be dated back to one of our explosions. We knew, then, that Russia had the bomb.

President Truman told the nation on September 23, 1949, about Russia's unexpected accomplishment. In the next morning's newspaper, I saw a headline: THE UNITED STATES WILL HOLD ITS ADVANTAGE. A single Russian bomb, of course, could not wipe out our advantage. But it had been predicted that Russia would not have the bomb for many years. We had been overconfident. I wondered whether, in the face of the Soviet success, we would continue in our overconfidence.

Worried and anxious, I telephoned Oppenheimer. I had been asked to give him a message during a trip to England from which I had just returned. But the real reason for my telephoning was to ask the question uppermost in my mind: "What do we do now?"

Oppenheimer's answer was short and simple, and it cut off all further discussion. He said: "Keep your shirt on."

This answer worried me even more than the Russian explosion.

The day on which we heard that Russia had exploded an atomic bomb was a day like any other. It was impossible to realize that the world, suddenly, had become dangerous. Yet what had been only a future possibility now loomed as a concrete threat. Russia had the bomb. What was to have taken twenty years actually had taken only four. Atomic bombs in our possession had seemed absolute weapons. Atomic weapons on both sides now seemed to herald absolute uncertainty. The Russian achievement posed an urgent question: What should we do about the rapidly growing Soviet power?

The American reaction to this question was remarkable. It also was natural. Oppenheimer had sensed the mood of our people correctly. There was a ripple of excitement, comment, and concern. This passed, and the placid life of the United States remained undisturbed. Our response was a refusal to respond, and this was significant in leading us from our strength of 1945 to our weakness of the 1960s.

But what should we have done? Should we have taken the radical and rash way out of the problem and attacked Russia before the Soviet had a chance to bomb us? This cruel solution, a preventive war, was rejected before it was seriously considered. And no matter what the eventual consequences may be, I am convinced that in this rejection we were right.

As long as only the United States had nuclear bombs, as long as a few of our planes could devastate an offending nation, reliance on our strategic atomic bombers—if we really were willing to use them—appeared logical. On September 23, 1949, the day we learned that Russia also had an atomic bomb, the concept of massive retaliation was on its way to becoming illogical nonsense. On that day we had to recognize that if we bombed Russia, we would be bombed ourselves.

As Russia advanced in the fields of nuclear weapons, airplanes, and rocketry, massive retaliation was checkmated. The United States obviously would never punish Russia for launching a small-scale invasion if our massive retaliation would provoke a nuclear attack upon us.

We were at a standoff. The diplomats called it "mutual deterrence."

In an important respect, mutual deterrence is as impractical as massive retaliation. Neither concept is workable because each pretends to draw lines where no lines can be drawn—between war and peace, between aggression and defense, between significant and insignificant acts. Each leaves us unprepared for the ambiguous acts of the Soviet government: Acts which lead to extension of Communist power, but which nevertheless are not clear-cut acts of aggression.

In the long run, mutual deterrence will fail because the policy does not consider the very different aims of the United States and the Soviet Union. Nor does it consider the methods traditionally employed by each country to achieve those aims.

The Communists have a clearly understood, openly announced, and firmly held revolutionary aim: World domination. They pursue this aim with deep conviction, with impressive zeal, with religious fervor. They have imposed great sacrifices upon the Russian people in the interest of their long-range plan to dominate the world. But that plan tells them not to take extreme chances. Russia does not enter situations which do not hold out a great probability for Russian victory. Communists move when the odds are with them. They have a word for taking unnecessary chances. It is called "adventurism," and this is one of the most serious errors a Communist can make. Soviet leaders, unwilling to take chances that could defeat their long-range plan, are by no means careless about risking an atomic attack—not because they are necessarily concerned about the loss of human life, but because their hopes for world domination lie in the industrial complex built within Russia's borders. To lose these factories and foundries to our bombs would postpone and endanger the Communist prospects for world domination. But because they know American purposes, American methods, and American philosophies, the Communists realize they can move far and wide without risking attack. Mutual deterrence gives them the odds they need.

Our national purpose is peace, coupled with freedom and a decent livelihood for peoples throughout the world. To preserve world peace, we have adopted a policy in which I believe strongly and which I share fully: We must never strike a first blow. We are firmly convinced that it would be morally indefensible to start an atomic war. We have held to this policy. Even when the United States had a monopoly of nuclear weapons, we did not seriously consider using them although Communism used the force of arms to suppress freedom in Eastern Europe and to conquer China.

The policies of both massive retaliation and mutual deterrence carry the threat that the United States will fight if our allies are attacked. This is basically inconsistent with convictions which are strongly held by many Americans. It also is exceedingly dangerous. This threat, carried out, would expand a localized conflict into a world-wide nuclear war. I do not believe that the United States should unleash an all-out atomic attack for any lesser reason than to return a full-scale attack made upon us.

The crises of threat and counterthreat involved in mutual deterrence strongly favor Russia. No matter how often the United States sends strongly worded diplomatic notes, Russia knows that we will not launch the first nuclear attack. This leaves the field of ambiguous aggression open to them. Russia can support Communist revolutionary movements in the Congo or Cuba secure in the knowledge that the United States will not retaliate with nuclear bombs dropped on Russia. Soviet leaders are just as secure when they taunt us, when they insult our President and our nation, when they subject us to nuclear blackmail by threatening to bomb our country. They know we will not attack first. Ambiguous aggression may not appear to conquer the world for Russia in a hurry; but step by step, nation by nation, convert by convert, it will conquer the world eventually. And this our policy of mutual deterrence does not deter.

If massive retaliation and mutual deterrence are unworkable, what can we do? Many people believe this complex question has an easy and wonderful answer: The main threat is posed by nuclear arms. Let the world disarm, and the threat will disappear. Gradually this notion has become gospel. But disarmament, so far, has served us no better than our reliance on nuclear arms. Hopes of disarmament have persuaded us to lower our guard while conceding to the Russians the opportunity to gain strength with secret preparations for conflict.

This much is evident: Appeasement on our side and confident expansion on the side of the Communists have been the dominant themes of the postwar years. This situation must be changed; it can be changed. We must adopt methods in which we can have confidence and with which we can accomplish our main purpose: Stable, peaceful co-operation between nations.

An all-out nuclear war with Russia can be avoided. But I do not believe that this can be achieved by the threat of massive retaliation or by mutual deterrence. I do not believe that we can find a simple solution for a critical, complex problem.

Absolute weapons do not exist. But nuclear weapons are by far the most powerful instruments at the present time. It would be foolhardy for the United States to conduct its military planning as if nuclear weapons did not exist.

These four points, to be discussed in following chapters, are necessary for a strong United States position in the nuclear age:

1. We must have an adequate passive defense. We must anticipate nuclear attack and be prepared to survive it. A nuclear attack on the United States would be horrible beyond imagination, but we must imagine it. We must, in fact, plan against it. An unprepared nation invites attack. We must, therefore, prepare for an attack. Properly prepared, we can survive a nuclear attack.

2. Having survived an attack launched against us, we must be able to strike the second blow. The United States has started to build up a second-strike force, a strong nuclear force capable of immediately returning any attack made upon our nation. This would not be massive retaliation, which calls upon the United States to return any attack made upon any ally. Our second-strike force would be mounted to return an all-out assault only if our own nation or territories that share our loyalties and institutions were attacked. In making certain that we could absorb and return an all-out nuclear attack, we would attain a major but limited objective: Our survival as an organized society with an organized industrial complex and an advancing civilization. If we were properly prepared, Russia, of course, would know that we could survive an attack made directly upon our nation and would know we were capable of counterattack. The Soviet Union, knowing these things, would never attack the United States directly.

3. We must prepare for limited warfare—limited in scope, limited in area, limited in objectives, but not limited in weapons. A localized, limited nuclear war will be the answer whenever the Russian method of ambiguous aggression degenerates to an outright attack against our allies. It will be the alternative to a disastrous, all-out, world-wide nuclear war. To prepare for a limited war, we must develop new kinds of international di-

plomacy, new theories of battle tactics, new varieties of nuclear weapons, new kinds of fighting men.

4. We must realize that passive and active preparedness will buy us nothing but time. We must use this time to establish a lawful and prosperous community of nations to ensure peace. Our ultimate goal can be nothing less than world government based upon the principles of freedom and democracy. Of our four points, this last is the most difficult.

I believe that each of these four points is indispensable to our survival. Because we refuse to think and plan, our preparedness now is so lax that we could not survive an atomic attack upon our own country. There would be little benefit in surviving if we were not prepared to fight back with a second-strike force. We cannot afford to let Communism engulf the rest of the world either by ambiguous aggression or by attack upon our allies, leaving the United States an island in an unfriendly Red sea; we must be prepared to fight limited nuclear wars. And, although the difficulties almost seem insurmountable, we must strive for the ultimate objective of world peace through establishment of a world authority that wields moral and physical force to safeguard peace with freedom.

When we are faced with a great and terrifying development, we are apt to imagine that none could be greater. We have heard much of the absolute threat of absolute destruction by an absolute weapon. The atomic bomb, with the destructive load of a thousand blockbusters, at first was the absolute weapon. Then the hydrogen bomb, carrying the power of a thousand atomic bombs, became the absolute weapon. Now we know about the intercontinental ballistics missile, which can deliver its load of hydrogen bombs anywhere on earth in 20 minutes, and this seems to be the absolute among absolutes.

Actually, an absolute weapon does not exist. We live in an Alice-in-Wonderland world. We must run fast just to stay in the same place. If we stop, we are falling behind. A method of destroying ICBMs and rockets, a discriminating tactical nuclear weapons system, an adequate network of bomb shelters could upset any calculation based on absolutes.

The only absolute likely to defeat us is fear, the persuasion that we cannot escape. But even fear can be defeated by rational, planned action.

CHAPTER THIRTEEN

Off the Beach

AN ENGLISH NOVELIST, several years ago, wrote a book that had a deep and frightening influence upon the minds of men. The author, Nevil Shute, had written many vivid stories about the problems of our age—an age that has more questions than answers. This particular novel was built around an old theme: The end of the world and the ways in which men would face universal annihilation.

Considered coldly and factually, Shute's story has no relation to any possible future event. The catastrophe described in the book was caused by a world-wide conflict fought with cobalt bombs. These bombs do not exist. They would have no military usefulness. They would do their greatest damage not on the spot of a target, but around the globe; not immediately, but after the passage of years. The damage described in Shute's book could not have been caused by the bombs exploded during the war which, according to the narrative, results in the end of man. The cobalt bomb is not the invention of an evil warmonger. It is the product of the imagination of high-minded people who want to use this specter to frighten us into the heaven of peace.

In many other ways, Shute disregarded the real facts of life. Radioactive contamination is treated as a contagion. An exposed person—who actually could be decontaminated—is left to perish

as though he had the plague and as though we still lived in the
Middle Ages. But whatever Shute's book lacks in realism is made
up amply by its powers of persuasion. This work of fiction has
convinced multitudes that in the atomic age defense is useless.

The book was read by thousands, and its motion-picture
adaptation was seen by millions. Most people felt that the story,
persuasively told in the book and effectively presented on the
screen, had a specific relationship to our times. This was remarkable and revealing: We are obsessed by the idea of an
impending day of doom.

Shute's wonderfully human characters live in southern Australia, the southernmost portion of the civilized world. They are
the last survivors of an all-out nuclear war. But, although they
have survived the war itself, they know that their days are
counted. The atmosphere of the northern latitudes has been poisoned by radioactivity from the war's cobalt-bomb explosions.
Slowly and irresistibly the radioactive poisons are creeping south-
ward, and the people "on the beach" know they have only a short
time to live. Yet while life lasts, they live on in the old manner.
There is dignity in the way they spend the dwindling weeks,
and so we cannot help loving and admiring the last representatives of our race.

On the Beach is filled with touches of psychological realism.
Shute knows that only the fate of single people can give us the
feeling of a great tragedy. So he does not present the end of
the world in tragic colors. He tells his tale in a low, muted key
through the commonplace actions of individuals; the reader or
viewer acquires the distinct feeling: This is happening to me.

The people in the book know that their lives are coming to an
end. They even know when they will die. Yet they plan for the
future, anticipate the future, and think of the future. They behave as if there would be no end. They cannot face the facts. The
facts are too horrible for the children of a secure age. They make
a final, successful effort to escape the truth. Although this seems

illogical, it is natural and it is real. And the descriptions of people who delude themselves and try to escape unpleasant realities in a game of mental leapfrog are all the more frightening because they are psychologically sound.

There are some realistic preparations for the inevitable end. This part of *On the Beach* is the most dreadful. The only measure taken against the arrival of the deadly radioactivity is the distribution of suicide pills. The only protection provided against one kind of death is the substitution of a cleaner, quicker kind of death. No one thinks of prolonging lives. No one fights the battle of survival. No one tries to find a way, however improbable, to prevent the ultimate disaster. Make-believe psychological escapes are offered in fulsome detail, but no one suggests a realistic escape from death. In this universal fatalism, Shute's book is most unrealistic. Man's will to survive is deep and strong. If there is an overwhelming danger and a realization of danger, there always are attempts to survive in spite of the danger. Man's attempts to save himself may be irrational, useless, foolish, or even hopeless—but in the face of danger, the attempt always is made. I cannot help asking, as Shute's reviewer in *Pravda* asked: What manner of men will accept the end without resistance?

Although unrealistic, Shute's elimination of any practical attempt to survive is frightening because it corresponds with the attitude of the overwhelming majority of our people. A short time ago, I discussed some commonplace subjects with a young friend. We talked about salaries and savings. He could see no point in putting money aside, and declared: "The world is coming to an end. There's no sense in planning for the future." Such pessimistic personal conclusions are not unusual. There seems to be a prevailing and growing attitude in our country: Live to the hilt today, for tomorrow we surely will die. Americans are convinced that if an all-out nuclear war should engulf the world, human life would end. Some believe that even if human life survived, it would not be worth living in a world stripped of comforts and made barren by a nuclear disaster. Nearly everyone agrees that any preparation for survival is useless.

Nevil Shute's book is a prophecy. Some prophecies are misleading. They may come true, but not in the way that is expected. *On the Beach* may be correct in prophesying an end, but it will not be the end of the human race. It may be the end of our Western civilization, of our society with its ideals of human dignity and freedom.

Humans are tough and ingenious. The race certainly will survive. Our age of science and of scientific miracles is not headed for extinction. In our world, which is such a strange combination of the real and the fantastic, this one fact should stand out clearly: Man is here to stay.

It is repulsive to make calculations about millions of human deaths, but to conjure up nightmares about a radioactive doomsday is certainly worse. These nightmares have little to do with reality. If some maniac wanted to put enough radioactivity into the atmosphere to endanger all human life, he would have to explode the equivalent of at least 1000 tons of our present bombs for each and every human being on the earth. He would have to explode a bomb of more than Hiroshima strength on each square mile of the globe. This would not be impossible, but it would be exceedingly difficult and it would serve no military purpose. The aim of even the most savage wars is not completely indiscriminate and total destruction. What man, what organization, what nation would carry out a gigantic plan which has for its aim not defense, not victory, not power, but universal suicide?

We can safely ignore the modern heralds of the Apocalypse. But we cannot disregard the possibilities of war. Even though we can forget about a Doomsday War, we cannot discount the possibility of a nuclear war. We should realize, however, that even if the attempt were made during such a war to kill all people, the human race would not be wiped out. Some would have a place to hide, because there is a defense against nuclear bombs: shelters. Civilian defense methods can help people survive nuclear wars of almost any scale. The biggest nuclear conflict would be a catastrophe beyond imagination. But it will not be the end.

The United States today is not properly defended. We literally invite attack because our potential enemies know that the United States today could not survive a big thermonuclear attack. We have not made a serious attempt to save ourselves. We have spent less than one tenth of one cent from each tax dollar for civilian defense. Our danger is real, but we refuse to do much about it. We adopt the same fatalistic outlook as the last survivors in Nevil Shute's book.

The irrational refusal of the majority of our people to plan and act for their own survival is due to their unwillingness to face the terrifying prospect of an all-out nuclear war. They would rather not think about it. They have, in fact, declared that such a holocaust is "unthinkable." Quite the opposite is true. If the United States remains undefended and incapable of surviving a sudden attack, the prospect of an all-out nuclear attack not only is thinkable, it is more than possible.

Two defeatist arguments have convinced the majority of Americans that civilian defense is futile. Even if some of our people managed to survive a sudden attack, according to one argument, the world after a nuclear war would not be fit for humans: The atmosphere would be poisoned for years; food could not be eaten safely; our factories would be destroyed; there would be no creature comforts; unlucky survivors of a nuclear attack would die of starvation, loneliness, or sorrow. Another argument, because of its simplicity and frequent and skillful repetition, has been accepted widely. This argument holds that survival simply is impossible, that rapid development of nuclear weapons will make today's civilian defense preparations inadequate for tomorrow, that our adversaries can and will devise bombs to destroy any civilian defense shelters we can build.

No prophecy about a future war can be completely reliable. But this much is certain: Properly defended, we can survive a nuclear attack; we can dig out of the ruins; we can recover from the catastrophe. The shelters we need for our defense, properly constructed, will not be made obsolete by the development of new weapons. The strength of nuclear weapons since Hiroshima has increased a thousandfold. The increase of shelter depth required to withstand a direct hit by these bigger weapons has been less than tenfold.

As a nation, we shall survive, and our democratic ideals and institutions will survive with us, if we make adequate preparations for survival now—and adequate preparations are within our reach and our capabilities.

Mere survival, however, is not the only compelling reason for civilian defense. There is another reason that is even more important: Peace. If we are adequately prepared, if we cannot be defeated even by the most sudden and savage attack, then the main motivation for a nuclear attack upon our nation will have vanished.

Our Communist enemies are determined and dangerous. But they are not irrational nor foolish nor inclined to adventure. They are dedicated to the single goal of world domination. They certainly would prefer to achieve this goal without the horrors of an all-out thermonuclear war. There are, I believe, only two circumstances at all likely to prompt the Communists to mount an all-out nuclear attack against the United States. They will do it in self-defense, and they might do it if they were firmly convinced that only with these terrible means could they achieve their end-goal of world domination.

The policy of the United States, established and frequently alluded to, is that we never will deliberately provoke a nuclear world war by striking the first blow. Because of this policy, the

Communists know they never will need to strike us in self-defense. But as long as the United States is unprepared to absorb and survive an all-out attack, the Communists have a temptation that might prove irresistible: A quick and easy nuclear victory over the nation most effectively thwarting their aspirations for world domination. If we are prepared for an all-out nuclear war, if we know we can survive the most vicious and widespread nuclear attack, if we guarantee our ability to rebuild our industrial complex after an attack, then the only valid reasons for a Communist attack upon our nation will have been removed. If we prepare, this disaster will never come.

A civilian defense system protecting people all across our nation obviously will be a tremendous undertaking, but it must be undertaken. The task looms larger because so little has been done. We literally must start from scratch, because this peaceful, nonaggressive guarantor of peace has been neglected for so long. The United States today has no comprehensive plan for civil defense, let alone adequate structures for civil defense. But at least the general outlines are clear, and we know that a plan can be written and a civilian defense complex can be built.

What must be done?

An adequate defense demands that we have early warning of attack, shelters, organization, clean-up equipment, and a plan for reconstruction.

Before we can begin to save ourselves from attack, we must know that an attack is coming. We must have as much warning as possible because our chances of survival would be measured in minutes. A rocket's travel time from a launching pad in Russia to a target in the United States would be only about twenty minutes. Fired from a Russian submarine, a rocket could strike a target in the United States in even less time. Without a fast and accurate warning system, an enemy rocket could obliterate a large American city and its unsuspecting residents even before we knew we were being attacked.

The United States, fortunately, has established a complex and effective warning system. We have developed and are refining ways of detecting launchings from any part of the world as soon as the rockets rise into the air. Even more warning of an attack would save millions of lives, and more warning might be possible. The urgent need for the earliest possible warning of attack is one reason why observations of the whole world and all of the earth's activities—an "Open Sky" inspection from airplanes or satellites —have become so vital to our security. We have not yet attained an "Open Sky" inspection, but we have achieved a warning system that will tell us we are being attacked the moment rockets start to fly. So we can depend upon at least a little warning, and the short time we might have to save ourselves probably will not be shortened appreciably in the future because it would be exceedingly expensive to make rockets fly faster.

One of the most essential steps we must take is the establishment of reliable communications that would survive any attack. These communications should be used to warn our people of impending danger and to direct our essential post-attack efforts to save human lives and to recover from the blow.

In a sudden nuclear attack upon our nation, there can be no doubt that millions of Americans would die. But even the brief warning we would have if such an attack came tomorrow would be enough to save perhaps ninety per cent of our people—if they knew what to do in case of attack and had the means to protect themselves. The present warning system would alert our military establishment, but it would not save the majority of our people because they are uninformed about civilian defense methods and unprepared for survival. If we continue to neglect civilian defense, a nuclear attack on the United States could kill well over 100 million people. And the fate of the survivors would be no better than that of those who had perished.

In order to ensure ourselves against the horrors of such an attack by being thoroughly prepared for it, our people must be sheltered, organized, and educated.

Our most urgent need is a nationwide system of public and private shelters. To protect people in all sections of our nation from the expected and probable, a national program of shelter construction should be given at least as high a priority as any other project in our over-all defense effort. Detailed studies and plans are necessary. People in various sections of our nation will require different degrees of shelter protection.

Perhaps two thirds of our people live in the uncongested areas of our nation. Far from prime targets, people in these areas can be protected more easily. They probably would not be subjected to the blast of a direct nuclear attack. They might, however, be endangered by radioactive fallout of a very great intensity; after an attack, clouds of radioactive poisons could be expected to sweep over large portions of our country. They might also be exposed to conflagrations due to high-altitude explosions of the biggest nuclear weapons or carried to their neighborhoods by the winds.

Survival of people outside our cities would be favored by some circumstances: Time would be required for fallout to float downwind from the actual point of attack. In addition to the initial twenty-minute warning of an impending attack, these people could count on another half-hour, one hour, or even more time after attack before they would be endangered by fallout. This would give most residents time to protect themselves.

Effects of fallout often can be decreased simply by going indoors or taking shelter in a conventional basement. Protection almost always is sufficient in a fallout shelter built with thick but not necessarily strong walls and equipped with a filtered air system or properly designed ventilation. A reasonable measure of protection, in some rural areas, can be offered by simple shelters for individual families. These might resemble the storm cellars already built as tornado protection by many families in our Central Plains states. Or rural families could build simple and adequate shelters by piling sandbags around the walls of a small building. The best protection, however, would be in community shelters. All the people in a small town probably would have time to reach a community shelter specifically designed to protect against fallout. Community shelters would offer greater protection at a lower total cost than a number of individual family shelters. And, because fallout might continue to be dangerous for some time, it would be best for entire communities to plan together.

Even though blast would not be a danger in these areas, fire damage is a real threat. This argues for construction of shelters that could survive a conflagration. It would be a further advantage if the shelters contained their own air supply. In many cases, it would be simpler to build the shelter in a location that would not easily be reached by fire.

In cities and prime target areas, the problem of providing adequate protection is much more difficult. People in our urban and suburban areas, like those in our rural sections, must be protected against fallout and radiation. But the people in and near our cities also require protection against nuclear blast and the even greater danger following the blast: Fire.

Civilian defense shelters in metropolitan areas and near important targets must be shock resistant. They should be surrounded with loose material that would dissipate the shock of a nuclear blast, and the shelters themselves should be rigid enough to withstand the shock penetrating the surrounding cushion. Dirt is an excellent shock cushion, and the most effective shelters will be built underground. These need not be deep. People in well-constructed shelters only ten to twenty feet below ground would have reasonable protection from a thermonuclear bomb exploding only one mile away. In shelters 100 to 200 feet below the ground's surface, there would be greater safety. In a thermonuclear attack we cannot ask for complete assurances. But we can and should save most people.

Effective protection against fallout, shock waves, and fire produced by a nuclear attack upon a metropolitan area also can be provided above ground. Our skyscrapers could be built around a windowless, rigid core of concrete made sturdy enough to withstand a blast's shock after it had been dissipated by the offices and corridors in the building's outer structure. These concrete cores would offer substantial protection. And they would be readily accessible to people in the most congested parts of our metropolitan areas.

People in cities will have only a brief warning of an impending attack. Therefore, every worker and every resident of every large city in our nation should be able to reach protection in a five-minute walk. Sturdy shelters should be built to accommodate everyone living or working within a quarter-mile radius of the shelter site.

It is important to realize that not all of the dangerous effects would be generated by each exploding nuclear bomb. Conflagrations over the widest areas could be kindled by very high altitude explosions which create no fallout hazard and which may not cause great shock damage. Air bursts of moderate height produce the widest damage through air shock, but would not damage well-constructed underground shelters and would not be likely to create concentrated fallout. The explosion producing really dangerous fallout would be a ground burst. This explosion also would cause ground shock and could damage underground shelters in the vicinity. But the air blast and the fires resulting from such explosions would cover smaller areas. In constructing shelters, it is important to assess which of these possibilities is the most likely.

Even in target areas, mass shelters can be built offering a real chance of survival for $200 a person. On a national scale, an adequate shelter construction program would cost about twenty billion dollars. This sounds prohibitive. It is not. It is about half of our annual defense budget, and as a necessary insurance against nuclear attack, the cost of adequate shelter protection is cheap.

The price of survival actually might be considerably less than twenty billion dollars because there is no reason for shelters to remain unused except in case of attack. Shelters can be built for more than one purpose. They can be designed and equipped to provide protection if protection is needed, but they also can have other functions.

It would be particularly important to build adequate shelters in our schools. It might even be advisable to contemplate building the schools themselves, with modern lighting and air conditioning, underground. On the surface above the underground school, children could have a really adequate outdoor playground. The underground school, of course, would be constructed and equipped as a mass shelter. There would be no problem of getting the children from classroom to shelter after an alert, and we would be reassured by the fact that our children were given the greatest safety. The cost of this shelter would be reduced by the amount of money that would have been spent on a conventional school.

Dozens of other kinds of buildings, similarly, could be constructed underground and serve dual purposes as housing for normal functions and as community shelters. We could make mass shelters of underground theaters and auditoriums, supermarkets, parking garages, warehouses, hospitals, or any other kind of structure that will accommodate many people. Concrete cores of office buildings, likewise, could be more than shelters. They could be garages, easing congestion in the hearts of our large cities. Garage cores have been built in office buildings in our country, and they have been found to be practical and convenient. Office tenants of the Redick Tower in Omaha, Nebraska, and the Cafritz Building in Washington, D.C., can drive into their buildings and park on the same floor occupied by their offices. These are examples of garage cores; to be shelter cores as well, they need only more sturdy construction. Our cities are the great

American repositories of culture. In our cities are the large museums, the most valuable collections of paintings and sculptures, the great libraries of books, the best examples of our cultural heritage. Many of these same cities would be targets for a nuclear attack, and such an attack probably would destroy these cultural achievements of man. I would propose that our museums and libraries be built underground and equipped as community shelters. In case of attack, such shelters would save many lives while preserving some of the chief reasons for living.

Multipurpose shelters may reduce the cost of this phase of civilian defense. But even at a reduced cost, the question must be asked: Who will pay for it?

I don't know the answer to this question. The main concern is that an answer be found soon. The full bill, certainly, would not come due in any one year. Three to four years probably would be required to build the kind of national shelter network we so urgently need. The costs might be paid by the federal, state, or local governments—or shared by all three. It surely would be improper for any new federal or local government buildings—post offices, schools, courthouses, office buildings—to be built without shelters. Much can be done to encourage private individuals and businesses to build shelters. The builders of new warehouses, bowling alleys, theaters, parking garages, or supermarkets might find it to their advantage to build underground if the government offered appropriate subsidies. Real-estate tax exemptions might prove strong incentives for shelter construction. Shelter needs differ from place to place; so while all shelters should be a part of a national plan, details could be settled advantageously on local levels—by states, counties, cities, private individuals, and companies.

If we are attacked, heavy radioactive contamination of the ground and atmosphere may force people to remain in their shelters for days and possibly for weeks. Each shelter should be stocked with enough food, water, and medical supplies to meet the needs of the shelter's occupants for two weeks. It would be a very great help to have a filter system to remove radioactivity from air brought in from the outside, to have enough oxygen to provide an independent air supply for several hours—long enough to last through the fire storm—and to have chemicals which absorb the carbon dioxide exhaled by the occupants. Each shelter should also be equipped with an independent source of power to operate the air filter and to maintain radio communications with other shelters and with civilian defense headquarters. And, finally, each shelter should have a store of water and chemicals for hygiene; urban shelters should be constructed with several exits and stocked with dig-out equipment so their occupants would not be trapped by an explosion's debris.

A few days after an attack, people as a rule will be able to emerge from their shelters for limited times in limited places. Or they may have to remain in their shelters as long as two weeks. Shelters may have to serve as living quarters for months after an attack. Most buildings would be destroyed by an attack, and in many regions of our nation some radiation would remain, and time spent in these areas would have to be limited.

Shelters and equipment will not be enough for survival. We must have organization. All of our people should participate in a civilian defense training program. This is of the greatest importance. Every citizen must understand and practice civilian defense.

Either a limited or an all-out nuclear war would require the services of only highly trained, professional soldiers. General mobilization of manpower would be ineffective, unnecessary, and impossible. Instead of being available for conscription into the Armed Forces, our people should be drafted into civilian defense organizations. All should be trained in civilian defense fundamentals: All must know how and where to seek shelter. Once inside a shelter, our people must know how to organize for the safety of the group. They must be trained to follow the directions of a shelter leader and a shelter doctor. They must be trained to operate communications and air-filtering equipment. Before they can hope to emerge safely from the shelter, they must know how to measure radioactive contamination, and they must know how to wash it away.

An all-out nuclear attack upon our country would be terrible indeed. I do not believe it will come. But if it should come—and if we are prepared to shelter ourselves from its effects, if we are equipped and organized for survival—even an all-out nuclear attack would be no worse than some of the terrible events of past wars.

Radioactive contamination does not stay in the air over the target of a nuclear attack. It is blown away by the wind. It will pass over a given place in half an hour. Within three days of a nuclear attack upon the United States, airborne radioactivity would be blown away from our entire nation. But this is of little comfort because radioactive poisons, in addition to being blown away, can settle onto the ground.

The amount of radioactivity on the ground after an attack would depend upon the altitude at which the bombs were exploded and upon other factors. The post-attack fire storm, by creating an ascending air mass of considerable velocity, might help to keep the ground surface of a target area relatively clean of radioactivity.

But in planning our defense, we must assume that a nuclear attack would leave a good deal of radioactivity on the ground. A thermonuclear explosion would leave a city in rubble, and all or much of that rubble might be radioactive.

In urban areas this radioactive rubble could pose an additional threat to the survival of people who had been sheltered against the initial blast and the terrifying fire storm. In two weeks the radioactivity would have decayed to a level low enough to allow people to come out of their shelters and, in appropriate locations, resume work above ground. In the exceptional cases of very high radioactivity, bulldozers could be brought in and used to clean up essential areas or escape routes by pushing debris and topsoil aside. Radiation, in any case, will decay a little faster than the inverse proportion to the time passed. After one day, only three per cent as much radiation will remain on the ground as was there an hour after the explosion. After a week, the amount of radiation on the ground will be ten times less. After two months, the activity will be ten times less again.

We can save most of our people, and the survivors soon could turn to the problems of the new days to come. They must know what to do and how to do it.

While the majority of our people can be saved from an all-out nuclear assault, we cannot hope to save most of our goods or the factories that manufacture our goods. In an all-out attack, our industrial complex probably would be effectively destroyed. It can be rebuilt if we provide for its reconstruction. But it cannot be rebuilt and survivors of a nuclear attack will be without support and may face starvation if they have to start the task of reconstruction from scratch with no better tools than their bare fingers.

Much of the strength of our industrial society, fortunately, is not in our industrial plant. Our factories are expendable. Our strength is in our know-how and in our organization. Our gross national product, the value of everything manufactured or mined or produced in the United States, now is more than 500 billion dollars a year. But the total value of everything that exists in the country—all the houses, clothes, food, factories, minerals, farms, services, cars, everything that can be bought or sold—is only about 1500 billion dollars. Everything we have, in other words, could be produced by our present industrial complex in only about three years. This means our present standard of living is extremely high and our rate of consumption is prodigious. This also means that survivors of an all-out nuclear attack, given food and a bare minimum of essential tools, could rebuild our industrial complex in a very short time. Even if our industrial plant were totally destroyed in an all-out attack, properly fed and equipped survivors living in austerity and working with complete dedication could rebuild our industrial plant to its pre-attack productive capacity within five years.

Just as we need to plan the construction of shelters to protect our people, we should begin a searching and exhaustive study of the things those people would need to survive after an attack and to rebuild our economy. We should plan and provide for our economic survival as well as for our personal survival. A thorough study must precede a complete plan for economic survival, but some potential needs already are obvious.

Survivors would need food. Shelters, hopefully, would be stocked with enough food to sustain people for two weeks after an all-out attack. This would feed them during their confinement in the shelters, but more food must be easily available after they emerge. Fortunately, we have a solution at hand. We have a national treasure that is considered an embarrassing political liability, but it could be converted into a great asset: Our agricultural surpluses.

The government today is storing enough surplus food to sustain the survivors of an all-out nuclear attack for perhaps two years. But it is not distributed so as to be available in all parts of the nation. It should be. Our surplus foods should be safely stored and located throughout the nation, making supplies of food available to all survivors. Wheat and other raw foodstuffs, furthermore, should be partially processed or stored with processing equipment so that survivors would not starve next to a filled granary.

Survivors would need tools and machines. These needs, likewise, can be met rather easily. Our government has moth-balled billions of dollars worth of equipment used during World War II and the Korean War, and we have stockpiled machine tools and strategic raw materials. Most of this storehouse of equipment, tools, and materials would be useless during a nuclear war, but it would be most useful for survival after a nuclear war. Our moth-balled fleets, our desert dumps of outdated aircraft, our entire inventory of military surpluses and stockpiles should be carefully studied. Tools and parts and machines and materials that might be put to work after a nuclear attack should be distributed over the nation for safe storage.

Private industries should be given tax write-offs as an incentive to save equipment from the junk heap today for survival tomor-row. American industries are making steady advances in engi-neering and technology. Machines are being discarded and replaced as manufacturing methods are modernized. These work-able machines should be stockpiled rather than junked.

We could store our old machines in simple, weatherproof, and widely dispersed structures. Fallout would not harm these ma-chines, nor would moderate blast pressures destroy them. When needed, they would be ready for use. Equipment considered ob-solete today would be invaluable to the survivors of a nuclear war.

Survivors would need transportation. Safely and speedily, they would have to be able to get to underground supply dumps of food, machines, and raw materials. Our systems of roads and na-tional highways probably would not be destroyed by an all-out attack. But key links in our highway system probably would be knocked out. Our economic reconstruction would be accelerated if destroyed links in the transportation system could be repaired speedily. Repair equipment and materials should be safely stored near anticipated trouble spots. Materials necessary for the build-ing of a simple pontoon bridge, for example, should be stored now near bridges likely to be destroyed in a nuclear attack. Our refineries and our stores of gasoline may be lost. But we could encourage each filling station outside our cities to store gasoline in a reasonably safe place now. If all these stations would carry ten times their present stocks of gasoline, a small but valuable contribution to our recovery would have been made.

Survivors would need energy. Reconstruction of a factory would be of little use if there were no power available for its operation. Revival of our industrial capacity would be agonizingly slow if our people had to depend upon water wheels and other primitive power sources. Our best guarantee of an efficient and effective postwar source of energy would be the construction, now, of underground nuclear reactors. Most nuclear reactors today are built above ground, and must be enclosed in a gastight sphere for absolute protection against an accident that would release radioactivity. This sphere is expensive. Construction of reactors underground, where no sphere would be needed, would be not much more expensive and might be even cheaper than aboveground construction.

Many individual parts of our recovery plan must be worked out and fitted together. There can be no doubt that industrial production will eventually recover after a nuclear attack. But if we prepare properly, the recovery could be fast.

Survivors, above all, would need organization. They would emerge from their shelters into a kind of world man has never known. Millions would be dead. The standard of living, highest in history only two weeks before, would be near zero. Things our people long have considered as necessities suddenly would have become the hoped-for luxuries of the future. Life would be bleak and cheerless, and life's prospect would be the necessity of rebuilding our productive capacity before stored supplies of food were dissipated.

In such a world, people would have to live and work according to a plan. Teamwork would be essential. The pressing goal and aim of our people would be group effort and survival.

If we wait until we are attacked to plan our postwar organization, there is a very real danger that we might lose our individual liberties and freedoms permanently. The postwar society will need rigid organization for its own survival, and rigid organization usually leads to tyranny.

If, on the other hand, we plan a postwar organization before we are attacked, our liberties can survive.

When young men and women join the Armed Forces today, they lose many of their rights as individuals. They must subject themselves to a rigid discipline. But they know that this discipline is only temporary. They know that when they leave the Armed Forces, their full rights will be restored.

It is this kind of postwar organization we must plan now. We must anticipate a strict state of emergency, but we must limit it to the time of the emergency. We must understand that during the critical five years after attack, when the needs of the group and of the nation are paramount, the individual will have to make great sacrifices. But we must guarantee that after the emergency has passed, after our economy has been rebuilt, our way of life, our right to the pursuit of happiness, will be restored.

We should define the necessary emergency measures while we can do so rationally and in freedom. In this way, we can be sure that the emergency measures will be properly limited.

Our almost total lack of civil defense is the weakest link in our national security, and so it is the greatest danger to peace. In an area where so much needs to be done and so much should be done, we have done practically nothing. Russia, on the other hand, has done much.

Our Office of Civil and Defense Mobilization says: "Official Soviet interest in new shelter construction has been apparent since about 1950. New building construction in some Soviet cities is known to include shelter as a matter of routine. . . . The impression is gathered that the inclusion of protective construction features in new buildings is a standard practice in many centers of population and industry, and that basement shelter of some kind already is available to an important segment of the population of urban areas of the USSR." The average adult Russian is given about sixty-four hours of civil defense training each year. The Soviet government has distributed plans for "hasty shelters" that can be erected to protect Russian families against fallout within twenty-four hours after warning of an attack. An estimated fifty million Russians participate in some phase of the Soviet Union's civil defense program; the United States has only 2000 professional civilian defense workers, and private citizens now are given almost no training.

Even though Russia is struggling to build her economy, even though it is more painful for the Soviet Union to spend money for civilian defense, Russia has spent much more than the United States on shelters and on an effective civilian defense organization. Unless we change, unless we spend vastly greater amounts, it is likely that Russia would survive an all-out nuclear war and we would not.

It is useful to compare the economies of Russia and the United States. We are fat and Russia is lean. In a conflict, to be lean is an advantage. But our wealth can enable us to put things aside for a dreadful rainy day, helping to ensure that we will never meet the lean ones in conflict. To stockpile food and machinery for survival is incomparably easier for us than it is for Russia. We have surpluses. Russia does not.

Judicious stockpiling in the United States during the next few years would make it completely clear to the Communist nations that we could recover faster and more effectively after an all-out nuclear war than could Russia.

I believe that the Soviet Union is not anxious to participate in an all-out nuclear war for an important economic reason. The Russian people have made tremendous sacrifices to build up the Soviet industrial plant. Russians are proud of their new factories and of their new products, and they do not want to lose them. Those factories and those products are important Russian assets in their fight for world domination. With adequate civil defense preparation and organization, we can assure ourselves and the world that after an all-out war the United States would be able to re-establish economic strength sooner than Russia—and so the United States would remain by far the strongest nation in the world. Thus every trace of motivation for Communist attack upon our nation would vanish.

Fortunately, our civilian defense effort is no longer completely paralyzed by fear and despair. On May 9, 1961, President Kennedy proposed to triple the budget. In New York State, after years of careful preparation, a vigorous program was undertaken by Governor Rockefeller. Throughout the nation, common sense and the will to survive have begun to reassert themselves. We are moving off the beach.

Even in case we are attacked, we can survive if we are determined and translate our determination into action. The first and basic objective of any defense is survival. If our individual and national survival is assured, we can proceed with confidence to build all the other bulwarks that are needed to maintain peace.

CHAPTER FOURTEEN

An Eye for an Eye

MOST OF MY KNOWLEDGE and most of my convictions have been acquired during an imperceptible process of growth. But in a few instances I have learned something at a clearly remembered time. One such instance was when I asked my grandfather a question about the Bible. I was fourteen years old. It was on a different continent, and it seems to have been in a different age. Yet what I believe today about nuclear war was determined for me at that time.

I was concerned about the well-known phrase in the Old Testament: ". . . eye for eye, tooth for tooth, hand for hand, foot for foot." I asked my grandfather what this meant. Should one put justice before mercy?

He replied: Mercy is more than justice. But the law, to be just and merciful, must be binding on every man; and the law can demand only what every man can obey. To act with mercy is best. But the Old Testament tells us that under no circumstances whatsoever should a man take *more* than an eye for an eye or a tooth for a tooth. That is the law.

This is the law that the doctrine of massive retaliation has disregarded. We never should have subscribed to this doctrine. We never should have declared that we would respond to limited

Soviet acts of aggression with a massive, all-out attack. Under no circumstances would we be justified in striking the first blow in an all-out war. If we had certain knowledge that the Russians would unleash the full fury of an atomic attack against us tomorrow, I still would say that in anticipation we should not strike the first blow today. My reason for saying this is not practical. I say it because I think this is right. But I believe that to abstain from striking the first blow also happens to be the only practical policy.

No prediction of the future can be absolutely certain. But if any one thing would make a bombardment of the United States unavoidable, it would be an attack launched by us against Russia. If, on the other hand, our civilian defense were adequate and if our retaliatory force were dispersed, mobile, and protected, then we would not need to strike first. We could absorb the attack against us, make as sure as possible that we knew where it came from, and then strike back.

Even after suffering the first blow, we would be able to strike back. If that first blow comes, we must strike back. And we must make sure that the Russians know that we are able and determined to strike back, so that they will have the strongest argument to leave us alone. If we were attacked, our second-strike actually must destroy the Soviet armed forces and industrial plant so that they would be unable to conquer the world. An all-out war would be dreadful for all participants. But there would be a winner, and there would be a loser.

If we had the most excellent evidence that a Communist attack against us was imminent, we should send our people into shelters, put our strategic force into readiness—and then wait. Our preparedness would give our enemies the most excellent reason not to attack. If they still did attack, our country could and would react with unity and determination; in the end, we could win the hard struggle for the future of freedom.

If we saw signals on our radar screens and received information from our satellites that could mean only that Russian rockets were on their way, we still should not attack Russia. The possibility of error might still exist, and we must do everything humanly possible to avoid all-out war by mistake. Once Russian rockets were flying, we could not save our cities and prime target areas with a counterattack.

By following this policy of never striking first under any circumstance, we would have strength in the knowledge that all-out war was not our doing. But to follow this policy, to act in this way, and to have confidence in the future, we must be strong.

Our strategic retaliatory force must be able to survive any attack. It must be a true second-strike force. We are negligent today in building and securing such a second-strike force.

During an unpoliced and unpoliceable moratorium on nuclear tests, we refrained from testing and therefore did not decrease the weight of our retaliatory bombs. We did not complete the development of "clean" explosives, although such explosives are practical and would assure us that a bomb launched against Russia would not deposit its radioactivity in a neighboring, friendly country.

The long moratorium on tests might have given us some propaganda advantage. If so, we have sacrificed strength and justice for propaganda. Our second-strike force has not had full and proper priority.

Even with full priority, it will not be easy to build a really reliable second-strike force. The best future plan will depend upon future technical developments. And no one can predict these developments. Some general observations, however, are possible.

Any defense can be outwitted. But a multiple defense is hardest to defeat. We should put our retaliatory force into airplanes, many of which should be in the air constantly; we should put bomb-carrying missiles into many small nuclear submarines, into many inconspicuous carriers such as trucks and railroad cars.

Development of lightweight, mobile retaliatory missiles would improve our chances of defense because such targets could be maintained as moving targets. Additional retaliatory bombs should be located in many solidly built and well-defended bases. It may be impossible to shoot down all approaching missiles. But if a missile has to make a precise hit on a missile base to be effective, there is a real chance for an anti-missile defense protecting a sharply defined point. Much thought and work will have to go into this second-strike force, but better nuclear explosives are the beginning and the end of every improvement. Smaller explosives will make our missiles more mobile and easier to defend. Better explosives will make the hard task of point-defense against missiles somewhat easier.

The plan to launch our counterattack only after we have been bombed decreases the chances of accidental war. But a second-strike force requires many retaliatory missiles which must be kept in constant readiness. This may seem to increase the chances of a tragic mistake. Actually, a great deal of thought has been given to devices which will eliminate the possibility that the human error or aberration of a single person in charge of a retaliatory missile could unleash a war. Using past accomplishments and future progress, we can make absolutely sure that our government has a restraining power and that as long as our government is functioning, only the most responsible persons to whom we have entrusted our fate can order a counterattack. Our strength would give these men the assurance that they never need act in haste.

On the other hand, we need not worry that the Communists can defeat us by knocking out our government and eliminating those empowered to order a counterattack. The safeguards against an unauthorized launching of our second-strike force can be so arranged that as soon as our government ceases to function, the safeguard also ceases to be in effect. With the country in flames, the dispersed units would be free to do their duty and strike back.

The problem of creating a second-strike force that can *never* strike first but that can *surely* strike in retaliation is not easily solved. But it can be solved.

There remains a question that is most disturbing: What should we do if one of our closest friends were subjected to an all-out bombardment? What should be our reaction if England or Canada were attacked?

One possible answer would be our declaration of a limited war. We must try to limit the territory and the aims of such a war, and we must do all we can to help our ally without allowing the conflict to become world-wide. How this might be done will be discussed in the next chapter.

This answer may be logical. But it will not satisfy everyone. It does not satisfy me. Unfortunately, I could accept only one alternative. And this alternative, while probably the right one, is most difficult.

If two countries are so closely tied together that nuclear bombardment of one necessarily will lead to nuclear bombardment of the other, then these two countries in reality are not two but one. In this case, the policies of the two countries must be shaped by common participation and consent. Instead of two separate loyalties, there should be a single loyalty. The governments of the two countries in many respects may continue to function separately. But in the most important areas, in the questions concerning survival, there can be but a single government for the two countries. In that case, effectively and morally, an attack on one would be considered and announced as an attack on both. A union would in fact be created, and the ambiguous situation of an attack on an ally would be replaced by the straightforward demands of self-defense.

The stability of the world, in the long run, demands a suprana-

tional authority. It can be argued—indeed, it has been argued—
that the time has come to establish a single government responsible for the survival of England and the United States right now.
It might be possible and necessary to establish an even more inclusive union at the present time. My own belief is that such a
step would be an early recognition of an inevitable development and would greatly increase the chances of continued peace.

The choices that are before us are not easy, and we cannot
make progress toward a stable world without sacrifices. But this
much is clear: Our position will be more firm, secure, and right
if we establish a strong second-strike force and if we develop
our ability to fight a limited war in order to defend our allies.

CHAPTER FIFTEEN:

Limited Warfare

THE KOREAN WAR TAUGHT the United States two great and valuable lessons. We would do well to remember them.

Conditioned by two global conflicts, the American people in 1950 had a big-war mentality. They could not conceive of a conflict limited both in political aims and in geographical area. The opinion prevailed that any kind of war almost automatically would become a world war. Korea, politely termed a "police action," was a practical and effective reminder that we could participate in a limited war without becoming embroiled in a world-wide catastrophe.

Korea taught the American people another and more bitter lesson, one that military leaders always had accepted as axiomatic: We should, if possible, avoid fighting on the enemy's terms. The enemy in Korea had tremendous advantages. He could select the place for war; he could set the time for attack; he could effectively dictate the scale and the method of war. Fighting an enemy with these considerable advantages, the American people learned that we cannot allow future enemies to dictate the terms of future wars. It was a difficult lesson to learn. It cost three years of hard fighting and 33,629 American lives. Still, it is not completely clear that we have learned this lesson.

The Korean War demonstrated these two important lessons, but it also implanted a grave misconception in the minds of most

Americans. At a time when we had a clear-cut atomic advantage over the enemy, President Truman stubbornly and steadfastly refused to authorize the use of nuclear weapons against Communist forces in Korea. Military men, anxious to use their most effective weapons to shorten the war, were unable to persuade the President who had taken full responsibility for the surprise nuclear devastation of Hiroshima and Nagasaki. He was adamant, and nuclear weapons were not used in Korea. Use of atomic weapons at that time, indeed, might have turned millions of Asians against us. But Truman's stand gave birth to an idea which has become generally accepted but which is, nevertheless, invalid: If neither side uses nuclear weapons, there is real hope of keeping the scope of a war limited; but the moment either side does employ nuclear weapons, nothing can prevent expansion of a limited war into an all-out nuclear catastrophe on a world-wide scale.

Korea established two precedents and proved two principles of limited warfare. We learned, in Korea, that wars can be limited in area: Rightly or wrongly, the area of fighting in Korea was limited to one side of the Yalu River. We learned that wars can be limited in their political aims: The fighting, clearly, was for Korea and nothing else. These precedents both are valid. But Korea also gave rise to the popular idea that a war can be limited only if it is non-nuclear.

This last idea is not only invalid but dangerous. The misconception that *any* use of nuclear weapons would expand a conflict and inexorably trigger an all-out global war has been accepted as an unquestioned fact by many of our highest government officials and has been a prime consideration in our international conduct and military planning. As a result, we have concentrated on preparations for a kind of war that I doubt will ever be fought again. We have continued to draft thousands of young men and have taught them to stand at attention and march eyes-right. We have continued to build and man aircraft carriers and other huge surface ships. We have spent billions of dollars on conventional arms for a conventional force, acting on the assumption that wars in the future will be fought like wars in the past. History differs, and tells us that the ways of fighting wars change. But this lesson of history has been largely ignored, and we have continued preparations for a non-nuclear conflict at the expense of the development of the kinds of effective nuclear weapons and other military methods that surely will be employed in future wars.

We must recognize that Russia inevitably would have three overwhelming advantages in a war fought by conventional, historical means. The massive, disciplined manpower of the Communist countries has given the Soviet Union far and away the most powerful peacetime army in the history of the world. Russia is in a central, strategic location—near the countries in which a limited, conventional war would most likely be fought. And, finally, Russia is not unwilling to take the initiative.

The United States is strictly circumscribed by traditional and historical principles. Our people have strong feelings against aggression. Russia is not so circumscribed nor so hampered. On the contrary, Russia is opportunistic and is capable of grasping the initiative whenever a nation's internal politics or external defenses seem to assure Russian success. Combined with the Soviet's strategic location, this willingness to take the initiative would give Russia a tremendous advantage in a conventional war limited in scope to one of the nations on the periphery of the Communist empire. Before we could get our conventional forces to the front in sufficient numbers to wage a non-nuclear war, the Communist armies would be firmly entrenched.

Two imaginary future wars might demonstrate our alternatives. The outcomes are quite different, but they are not difficult to imagine because one or the other is being written by our military planners today. One outcome would be a death-blow to American prestige, and would lead to the eventual extinction of our national government. The other outcome would enhance America's position of world leadership, guarantee our existence, and preserve our freedoms. We will consider the two distinct possibilities as histories:

A CONCISE HISTORY OF THE WAR OF BRAVADO

The country of Bravado was a small but strategically located nation adjoining Communist bloc countries near the Scrobean Sea. The democratic government of Bravado outlawed the Communist Party, but the Bravadonian Communists continued to function underground and attracted some support among student organizations.

On September 13, 1965, these Communists, in an internal uprising, usurped the established government and precipitated the War of Bravado, the shortest war in the world's history. The Communist uprising was well co-ordinated. Various Communist units, carrying small arms made in Russia, simultaneously took control of Government House in Scrobea, the nation's capital, and captured the city's two newspapers and three radio stations. Loyalist officials found just enough time, before fleeing Scrobea, to send an urgent message to Bravado's ambassador in Washington, X. G. Strunk.

Strunk won an immediate audience with the President of the United States. The mutual defense treaty between Bravado and the United States was invoked. The President, acting as Commander in Chief of the Armed Forces, ordered American troop transports and aircraft carriers to sea, then placed our Air Force bases overseas on an alert for a possible attack against the Bravadonian Communists. While our warships were steaming toward Bravado, the President called a special emergency session of Congress. He wanted the legislators to issue a Declaration of War before actual fighting began. As congressmen converged on the nation's capital for the historic session, Air Force reconnaissance planes roared from the runways of U.S. bases in England and flew toward Bravado with rather ambiguous instructions to "report" on the "strength" of "Communist forces."

Three hours after Ambassador Strunk had called on the President to ask for U.S. aid, Radio Scrobea said that a large force of Russian paratroopers had landed in the capital of Bravado after a short flight from Communist territory. Within minutes after this report was picked up by U.S. radio monitors on Long Island, the Kremlin announced through regular diplomatic channels that Bravado was a Russian protectorate. The Soviet government recognized the new government of Bravado and warned all nations that it would be defended against any aggression.

Five hours after the President had acted on Ambassador Strunk's request for aid, the Air Force reported to the Pentagon that communications with U.S. reconnaissance flights had failed. The new Bravado government subsequently revealed, over Radio Scrobea, that the United States reconnaissance planes had been shot down as aggressors and that five surviving American pilots had confessed that they had been ordered to fly over Bravado as spies.

Congress had not yet convened in Washington. On the heels of Radio Scrobea's spy charges, the Kremlin issued Russia's famous White Paper. The White Paper formally accused the President of the United States of "shameless aggression" in Bravado. As a peace-loving nation, the White Paper declared, Russia was determined to halt any aggression that might lead to World War III. Russia would torpedo and sink any warships or aircraft carriers approaching Bravado with aggressive intentions, and would "regretfully" undertake the nuclear punishment of any nation that threatened the peace of the world. The White Paper vowed that if American forces were not ordered to return to American shores at once, Washington would be subjected to massive attack by nuclear rockets. The Paper concluded with polite diplomatic language asking the President to reconsider his "rash actions threatening world peace."

The President, knowing that Washington could not be adequately defended against massive nuclear attack, complied with the demands of the White Paper. The War of Bravado was over. It had lasted less than one day.

Short as it was, the War of Bravado was the beginning of the end of world leadership for the United States. American prestige nose-dived throughout the world. In the months that followed, the United States Government passed legislation drafting men and women to bolster our cold-war effort, but the drastic attempts to build America's defenses against nuclear attack came too late. A little more than three months after the War of Bravado, on Christmas Day of 1965, Russian armed forces landed in Iran, Iraq, Kuwait, and Saudi Arabia. The governments of these countried appealed for American aid.

The President called Congress and the NATO high command into emergency sessions to choose between the alternatives: An abandonment of the Near East that would cut Europe off from its oil supply, or a declaration of war that would provoke an all-out attack on the United States and our allies—an attack which neither our nation nor the other members of NATO could survive.

The Near East was abandoned.

Three months later . . .

A CONCISE HISTORY OF THE CROSTIC UNION WAR

History's first limited nuclear war began on September 13, 1965, in the Crostic Union, a federation of strategically located provinces near the border of Russia. The Crostic Union War was launched when the outlawed Communist Party led a revolution against the established government of the Union. Within hours after the uprising began, the insurgents had captured the government buildings in the capital, Union City, as well as the capital's leading newspapers and radio stations. Leaders of the established Loyalist government, however, managed to escape to provincial cities.

Both sides called for outside aid. The Communist insurgents, entrenched in Union City, asked neighboring Russia to declare the Crostic Union a Soviet protectorate and to supply military support. Loyalist leaders in the provinces radioed their ambassador in Washington, Dr. Magharta, to secure immediate aid from the United States under terms of a mutual defense treaty between the two countries.

Both Russia and the United States acted swiftly. Three hours after Soviet aid was sought, Russian paratroopers floated down over Union City to give ground support to the rebel forces. The Soviet Air Force gave the paratrooper transports more than adequate protection with fast fighter jets. On the diplomatic level, Russia recognized the rebel government in Union City and declared all of the Crostic Union as a Russian protectorate. A Russian army of 100,000 men began marching toward Union City.

In the United States, the threat to world peace was met with equal effectiveness. Congress, years before, had given the President and a small permanent committee from the House and the Senate the power to declare war by Executive Order anywhere in the world—providing that the war was limited in area and in scope, neither of which could be enlarged without provocation from the enemy and without subsequent ratification by Congress. While the President received the ambassador from the Crostic Union, the situation in Union City and the facts of Russia's intervention were confirmed by our Central Intelligence Agency. The President, by Executive Order, immediately declared war. In the declaration, he limited the fighting area to the boundaries of the Crostic Union. He carefully limited the political scope of the war to re-establishment of the Loyalist government. He affirmed that the United States would use all the means at its disposal to achieve these objectives.

The President's declaration set the well-oiled machinery of the Pentagon into action. No warships or aircraft carriers were launched. Military planners, in fact, had decided years before that such cumbersome and slow-moving ships would be nothing but good targets in a nuclear war. But great numbers of transport planes took off from bases within the continental United States and flew toward the Crostic Union at speeds that would have been thought impossible four years before. These planes were armed with atomic air-to-air warheads. In fierce nuclear dog-fighting over the Crostic Union, both Russia and the United States suffered air casualties. But about a hundred United States transports got through Russia's air-to-air barrage and dropped 3000 American commandos over the Crostic Union. Strategic supplies, including lightweight nuclear weapons, were parachuted along with the commandos. The United States commandos spread over the country to perform the job for which they had been thoroughly trained: Organization and leadership of Loyalist guerrilla fighters.

The United States and the established government of the Crostic Union had worked diligently over the years to plan the military defense of the small nation. This careful planning paid off during the world's first limited nuclear war. The airborne commandos knew where to contact Loyalist leaders, and knew exactly where small arms had been cached for Loyalist guerrillas.

The Russian army of 100,000 marching double-time from the border to Union City, the only Communist stronghold in the nation, met only guerrilla resistance—with one devastating exception: United States commandos assembled one of the lightweight nuclear weapons which had been parachuted to them and destroyed a large supply depot upon which the advancing army depended.

Russia, through diplomatic channels, immediately objected to the use of nuclear weapons in the war. The United States replied by pointing to its declared intention of using all possible weapons against strictly military targets during the limited war. When the United States ambassador to Moscow delivered this reply to the Kremlin, the Soviet Premier was beside himself with rage. He pounded his desk with both fists and shouted that if one more nuclear weapon were used in the Crostic Union conflict, an all-out nuclear retaliation would be hurled against the United States.

The Russian ultimatum was received in Washington. Before replying to Russia's nuclear threat, the President ordered the United States on a nationwide atomic alert. The country was ready. Civilians quickly moved into bomb shelters that had been constructed near their homes and the places where they worked. Previous peacetime drills had taught them what to do in such an emergency.

The President also alerted our second-strike force—an arsenal of nuclear warheads aimed at Russia from nuclear submarines, airplanes, and mobile launching pads in the United States.

And then the President rejected the Russian ultimatum.

The United States preparedness took the teeth out of the Russian threat. The effective alert left the Russians no strategic reasons for bombing the United States, no hope of inflicting damage that could not be eventually repaired, no hope of crippling the nation. The poised second-strike force was recognized by the Kremlin as a counter-ultimatum. Russian leaders nobly announced that the peace-loving Soviet Union would not plunge the world into war by bombing the United States.

Russia turned her full attention to the war for the Crostic Union. The rebel Communist government controlled only the capital, Union City, but Loyalist guerrillas aided by American commandos controlled the rest of the nation. Neither the guerrillas nor the American commandos presented targets large enough for nuclear weapons. The Soviet Union found it impractical to use her most effective arms at any time during the war except in the air-to-air missile battle over Union City. This air battle was fought by the Russians to protect Soviet planes dropping food and supplies to rebel forces in Union City, which was besieged by Loyalist guerrillas and American commandos. Russia, equipped with better fighter planes and better air-to-air nuclear missiles, was winning the air battle over Union City; but American commandos using nuclear ground-to-air missiles downed many of the Soviet's flying boxcars. Russia determined to break the deadlock siege of Union City, and 400,000 Soviet troops poured over the border into the Crostic Union. Natives in villages along the border, who were in sympathy with the Loyalist cause, reported the Soviet troop movements to American commando teams in the area. United States forces used nuclear bombs to halt the massive Russian land attack. Those Soviet soldiers who survived the nuclear attack retreated beyond the Russian border.

Russia withdrew all land and air forces from the embattled country, and then went before the United Nations to brand the United States as an aggressor against the government of the Crostic Union and to protest America's use of nuclear weapons during the limited war. The United States proposed in the United Nations that the world organization should oversee free elections in the Crostic Union, elections in which all parties, including the Communist Party, could sponsor candidates. The free election was held on the day before Christmas 1965, and Loyalist officials who had been defended by the United States were returned to office by an overwhelming majority.

The conduct and consequences of these fictional conflicts are easy to imagine, because they accurately reflect the difficulties now faced by the United States. If a localized, brush-fire war should break out almost anywhere in the world, Communist forces would have the tremendous advantages of concentrated manpower, centralized location, and an initiative devoid of moral considerations. To overcome these dangers, the United States would have to use every means that technology can give us. Among modern weapons, nuclear arms stand out because of their light weight and unmatched power. They would give us the high degree of mobility we would need to stop Communist aggression anywhere.

Why, then, has the United States not planned and prepared to use nuclear weapons in limited warfare?

Four powerful objections have convinced most of our people that nuclear weapons should not be so used. They are the following:

Any use of nuclear weapons would provoke nuclear retribution. If nuclear arms were used in limited warfare, the localized conflict would grow into an all-out nuclear holocaust engulfing the world.

Nuclear explosions would leave the scene of a limited war in total ruin, and a people would not want to be defended if it meant their destruction.

The United States, in the final analysis, could not hope to win a limited nuclear war because the Communists also have nuclear weapons. With nuclear arms available to both sides, we could not hope to neutralize the Soviet advantages of manpower, location, and initiative.

The United States actually is not prepared to fight a limited nuclear war, so we cannot engage in this kind of warfare.

These four arguments are so popular and so persuasive that each deserves a detailed discussion.

First, make no mistake: We do not like or want limited wars. We do not want any kind of war. But the horrors of war can be limited, and if some conflict is inevitable, we should strive for limitation. We must do everything in our power to prevent local conflicts from becoming world-wide catastrophes.

Any limitation, to be effective, must be clear-cut and enforceable. Limitations on weapons are extremely difficult to enforce, but limitations of the territory and aims of wars have had frequent success.

Most people, when they think of nuclear weapons, think of mushroom clouds and massive destruction, of dramatic after-effects that would make it easy to determine whether a conflict's restriction to conventional weapons had been violated. So, in the popular mind, the use of nuclear weapons has become the line of demarcation, the detectable shutoff point of a war's enlargement. But the development of new tactical weapons and the possibility of using plentiful small nuclear explosives against relatively minor targets make this shutoff point less impressive, less detectable, and therefore less enforceable. Radioactive fallout might diminish or disappear with development of "clean" bombs. New scientific surprises might be used in battle, and the attacked might not know what hit him—a nuclear or a non-nuclear weapon.

Retaliatory nuclear attacks would be made on the basis of guess, suspicion, and rumor. And, once nations are at war, even the craziest rumors are accepted as facts. During the Korean War, for example, many of the world's peoples believed the outrageous accusation that the United States had resorted to bacteriological warfare. And during World War I, the American people got fighting mad over the fabricated report that Kaiser Wilhelm had ordered his troops to cut off the hands of Belgian children. It would be too easy for the commander of conventional forces in a war limited to conventional weapons to say that he had been driven to the edge of defeat by an enemy using illegal nuclear arms. At that point, nuclear weapons might be used without previous planning. An unplanned expansion of the war may indeed have tragic consequences, and the limits of these consequences would not be easy to foresee.

Although limitations on the weapons of war are very difficult to enforce or maintain, wars can be limited in geographical territory and political aims. The losing side in any war is strongly tempted to use the most effective weapons to turn defeat into victory, but the last to want either the area or purpose of the fighting enlarged. Weapons cannot be limited, because this kind of limitation assumes that the defeated will consent to defeat. But area and aims can be limited and have been limited.

The United States would want to maintain the limitations of a conflict whether we were winning or losing. The Communists would want to limit the territory and aims of a war if they were losing. Lenin recommended, many years ago, that Communists faced with heavy odds should take one step backward in order to take two future steps forward. This has been preached to Communists and practiced by Communists. It has become a Communist doctrine, and Communists would accept defeat in a limited nuclear war without attempting to enlarge the war's scope, hoping they could consolidate their forces for future advances. But the Soviet Union would be tempted to expand the scope of a limited war if they were on the victorious side, and this we might be unable to prevent. The defeated cannot prevent expansion of a limited war's scope. Precisely for this reason, our best insurance against expansion would be our preparation and willingness to fight a limited war with whatever weapons are most likely to win.

To be effective, limitation of a war's geographical and political areas must be announced. Whenever the United States is drawn into any conflict, we should recognize and proclaim that our wartime effort would be conducted in a specific territory for specific purposes, and we should make it clear that we would not take the initiative in expanding either. If Communist forces should again push over the 38th Parallel in Korea, for example, our clearly stated objective in fighting might be to liberate all Korea. If another Asian nation were attacked, our stated purpose in declaring war might be purely defensive. If we undertook the armed defense of West Berlin against Communist aggression, we probably could not fight for anything less than for all of Germany. In any case, the area of the limited war would be circumscribed by our objective in fighting.

Russia, before moving to expand Communism anywhere in the world, would have no knowledge of the United States countermove in each specific situation. The price for a move into West Berlin might be the potential loss of all Germany. But Russia would learn the price only after its move had been made and the President had declared a limited war, stating the United States' objectives and limiting the area of the fight to win those objectives. We would be bound by these limitations, however, only as long as they were respected by the Communists. They would realize that every Communist expansion of the conflict beyond our stated limitations would expose them to additional and unknown risks. This uncertainty would greatly reduce the likelihood of a limited nuclear war and of its expansion. In fact, the worst time for the Soviet Union to undertake a further expansion of Communism, the worst time for Russia to touch off a world-wide nuclear war or launch an all-out attack upon our nation, would be at a time when a limited nuclear war was in progress. At that time, we would be most alert and least likely to be caught off balance.

Our best insurance against a nuclear attack upon the United States, however, remains civilian defense and the establishment of a second-strike force. The very existence of this force of hidden, poised, invulnerable missiles would serve notice upon the Soviet Union that if we were attacked, Russia could not escape attack. A strong second-strike force would deter the Communist temptation to disregard the limitations of a localized war. Our ability to survive an initial attack and rebuild our economy would make a Russian assault upon our nation futile.

If we are prepared and can survive, I am convinced that we will not be attacked under any circumstances. And our strength and passive preparedness will give us a reasonable guarantee that a limited, localized nuclear war will not grow into a global conflict.

The second objection to limited nuclear warfare is that it would leave the territory of the fighting in ruins. A limited nuclear war conducted by the United States, according to this argument, would kill the people we were trying to save and destroy the country we were trying to defend. And what, after all, is liberty without life?

This argument disregards the nature of nuclear warfare and of nuclear weapons. It assumes that wars of the future will be fought like wars of the past.

Strategic bombing contributed to our victory in World War II. It interrupted the mass production that supplied massive armies, and broke transportation systems connecting factories with the front lines. Strategic bombing left the World War II armies of the enemy like the hands of a man with the blood vessels and the muscles of his arms severed.

Strategic bombing was effective in the last great war. But it does not follow that it would be effective in a limited nuclear war. Cities will not be arsenals for future wars, and fighting men no longer will depend upon lines of supply. There would be no military justification for the large-scale bombing of cities and transportation systems. Fighting forces in a limited nuclear war would be widely dispersed and highly self-reliant. They would not need materials being manufactured in cities' factories, so the cities themselves and the country's transportation network would not be important military targets.

Nuclear weapons used in limited warfare, as a matter of fact, would do no more damage to the face of a nation than conventional weapons. They might, indeed, do considerably less damage. The United States today has nuclear weapons in great numbers and in a great variety of sizes. We can adjust weapons to the specific purpose for which they are intended. For example, we can conceive of a nuclear explosive so small that it could be fired by one man from a weapon similar to a bazooka against a target no larger than a single tank. The amount of additional destruction, in the firing of either conventional or nuclear weapons, would depend upon marksmanship.

Our fighting forces in a limited nuclear war would not be measured in battalions and divisions. They would consist of commandos, and in each group there would be as many as fifty or as few as five men. They would be air-dropped, air-supplied, and if necessary, air-evacuated. American forces fighting a conventional kind of war for the liberation of an ally, on the other hand, would consist of many thousands of men in the front lines of battle, and they would depend upon long lines of supply furnishing them with hundreds of thousands of tons of the materials of war. These supply lines themselves would be military targets; their defense would depend upon additional multitudes of soldiers. A conventional war thus would be fought not only at the front, but also along the lines of supply. This kind of warfare converts an entire nation into a huge battlefield. This has happened again and again in our century. And this inevitably would do more damage to the face of a nation than would a nuclear war in which the battle for liberation would be fought at specific points on the ground and the battle of supply would be fought in the skies.

Although cities and transportation systems would not be military targets in a limited nuclear war, although the nuclear weapons used by the participants may do no damage beyond military needs, although small groups of fighting men would not be as destructive as massed armies, there remains another reason to fear that even a limited war might lay a nation to waste: Cities might be bombed to frighten citizens into submission.

The devastation of cities and the planned annihilation of civilian populations in a limited war cannot be justified. And it seems likely that psychological bombings might be ineffective; the survivors of such attacks might emerge more enraged than terrified, as they did from the London blitz. There is serious doubt about an indiscriminate nuclear attack's psychological effect, but no doubt about the effect it would have upon world opinion. Any nation considering a terror raid would have to weigh its value and consequences. The wise decision would be not to provoke the anger of the world but to preserve the face of the nation embroiled in the war.

According to the third argument, the United States could not hope to win a limited nuclear war because the Communist forces would also be equipped with nuclear weapons.

Actually, with both sides using nuclear arms, we cannot hope that nuclear weapons alone will win wars for us. But they will enable the United States to fight limited wars on our terms. They will give us a chance to win conflicts that otherwise would be lost.

Our nuclear power would force dispersion of any massive Communist armies. Our lightweight, easily transported nuclear weapons and our ability to rush small groups of fighting men equipped with those nuclear weapons to troubled areas would eliminate the Communist advantage of location. Our ability to move fast and to strike effectively would reduce the Communist advantage of initial action.

It is now generally accepted that in order to participate effectively in brush-fire wars, the United States must develop and train guerrilla forces. If we should try to use guerrillas without using nuclear weapons in the conduct of a conventional war, the small and dispersed groups of fighting men would be overwhelmed by the concentrated armies of the enemy. But nuclear power would change the war's character. It would make concentrations of enemy manpower completely impractical, and at the same time it would multiply the effectiveness of our dispersed guerrillas. Armed with nuclear weapons, very small groups of American fighting men could spread over the countryside and could destroy any military target—including a marching army of enemy soldiers.

Nuclear arms used by our hit-and-run guerrilla fighters would not win a war by themselves. Our ultimate success would depend on the people for whom we would be fighting. They would have to be with us. They would have to give us information on enemy tactics and troop movements, take up arms themselves, and defeat the enemy dispersed by our guerrilla forces.

The United States could not be confident of victory in a limited war fought within the borders of a nation whose people were not wholeheartedly on our side, where the majority actually was inclined toward Communism, or even where most people simply were apathetic about Communism and unwilling to fight for freedom. America's determination to contain Communism, to prevent the Soviet Union from using ambiguous aggression and outright attack to conquer the world, is predicated on the assumption that the peoples of the world would rather be free than enslaved. We must be sure that this assumption is correct before we allow ourselves to become involved in any limited nuclear war. Our success in any such war would depend upon the support and active participation of the people in the involved nation.

The powerful strength of a home guard of freedom fighters has been demonstrated again and again throughout history. In the beginning of our own national history, freedom-loving men used inferior arms and equipment, guerrilla tactics, and a great deal of ingenuity to defeat the superior forces of the British. In 1956, the dedicated zeal and largely unsupported efforts of patriotic Hungarians won a brief, bitter victory for freedom. At the beginning of the Hungarian revolt, when a single Russian tank no longer was safe in Budapest, Russian soldiers realized that the popular will was against them, and they no longer wanted to fight the people. These Russian soldiers were withdrawn and replaced with fresh forces that concentrated tanks south of Budapest for a single assault that crushed the Hungarian revolt. The success of freedom fighters against individual tanks and dispersed forces showed the effectiveness of a home guard. Their failure before a concentrated array of tanks demonstrated the limitations of even the most zealous unsupported force. If concentrations of enemy forces can be prevented, the will of a determined people is going to decide the outcome of any future limited conflict.

According to our ideals, we should support only nations controlled by true governments of the people. But we also have supported strong-man governments, dictatorships and monarchies, that could not claim wide popular support and were in no way governments of the people. Since success in any limited nuclear war would depend upon the people of a foreign country and not upon the titular head of that country's government, we should cement relationships and improve our position by increasing military and economic aid to governments fully supported by the popular wish. Conversely, we must never make the suicidal error of attempting to defend a government that is not supported by the people and whose leader is afraid to put weapons into the hands of his people.

We never must try to protect a people from Communism if the people want Communism. Our best international defense against war is an international desire for freedom. The ideological conflict that has engulfed the world can be bloodless. We can win the battle with Communism for the hearts and minds of men. If the people of the world really want freedom and are on our side, and if our nuclear forces can stop massed Communist manpower, I am convinced that our victory would be assured in any limited war. And with our victory assured, I believe that the Communists never would provoke such a war.

Three of the objections to limited nuclear warfare are invalid. A limited nuclear war, I am convinced, would not automatically trigger an all-out global conflict. The battleground of a limited nuclear war would not be left in utter ruin. We could win such a war if the people of the embattled nation were on our side. A last objection remains to our participation in limited nuclear wars: We are not prepared for it.

I must agree that this final objection is correct. At a time when limited nuclear warfare looms as a distinct possibility at any of a half-dozen of the world's troubled areas, the United States in truth is not prepared to participate, and the truth of this unpreparedness is frightening. The United States today would be totally incapable of declaring or fighting a limited nuclear war. We are unprepared politically, diplomatically, militarily, and psychologically.

We must prepare politically. If provocation for a war comes, the United States must be ready to move fast. We must prepare to do this by slashing through the red tape now required to place the United States in a state of war. The President should be empowered by Congress to declare war on his own initiative at any time and at any place in the world to achieve limited and predetermined purposes. Congress should retain the right to criticize and ratify the presidential decision, but should not be required to make the split-second determination to fight a limited nuclear war. The Departments of State and Defense, in consultation with other affected governmental agencies, should outline several limited objectives for each of the many possible provocations for war before hostilities actually begin. American forces waging wars under presidential declaration should not exceed these limited, predetermined objectives. Purposes and goals of our fighting would be different in each possible situation, and up to the time the President made a decision between alternative objectives and we entered the conflict, the enemy would be ignorant of our demands as victors. Investment of new powers in the presidency is a legislative matter. Assessment of the extent of American interests in each of the danger spots of the world is a matter of administrative consideration and mature judgment. Both are necessary ingredients of political preparedness.

We must prepare diplomatically. The necessity for home-guard support for our commando forces in a limited nuclear war will inevitably dictate a change in America's international diplomatic posture. Since victory would depend so largely upon other people, we must make diplomatic preparation for war by improving understanding and co-operation. Our allies must realize that their freedom depends on their own people. They also must be firmly convinced that we can help to defend them from a concentrated onslaught of their enemies.

We must prepare militarily. This preparation will be difficult and will have many aspects.

The United States today does not have the best possible arms and does not have the military organization that would be needed for the successful waging of a limited nuclear war. The prevailing American philosophy of mutual deterrence has prevented proper preparation for limited wars. We have concentrated on big weapons for big nuclear conflicts. Some good work has been done on small, lightweight nuclear weapons of the type that would be used in limited warfare, but in this field the future possibilities greatly exceed the present accomplishments.

The little work done in the field of advanced weapons has been secret, but one phase has been discussed publicly: Development of a "clean" nuclear explosive producing little or no radioactive contamination. Suppose the Soviet Union were the first to develop the kind of "clean," lightweight nuclear device needed in the conduct of a limited nuclear war. The Communists probably would give the new device a new name, perhaps the "Peace Bomb," and proclaim to the world that its use in limited warfare would ensure world peace. If the wind did not carry radioactivity from their "Peace Bomb" to harm innocent, neutral bystanders, people would be inclined to accept the bomb's new name and the Russian claim.

Since our military unpreparedness gives the Soviet Union a good chance of winning a limited nuclear war, I believe that such wars must be expected. If wars are to be avoided, we must lower the chances of Russian victory. As a first step toward preparedness, the United States must develop small, "clean" nuclear arms that would be needed for limited nuclear conflicts.

Technical and scientific problems, however, are not the most difficult we face in creating our capability for limited warfare. Another problem is human. It will be more difficult to train the commando forces required for limited nuclear wars than it will be to develop "clean" nuclear devices. We must train men to be self-reliant, courageous, resourceful, technically capable of working with jeeps, communications systems, and atomic weapons. Each individual commando must shoulder a great responsibility. He must be able to help and if necessary to guide the fighting efforts of home-guard guerrillas in foreign lands. He should be educated in the language, habits, and histories of foreign peoples so that he can feel at home among native populations and distinguish friend from foe among the people of the embattled country. Development of such an intelligent, high-caliber commando will require a radical departure from present military training methods. This means that we must assign some specially trained commandos to each area in the world.

If any nation can organize a fighting force of this type, I believe it is the United States. Our young people grow up in a mechanical tradition, and we have trained men to repair transportation and communication equipment in the field; we also should be able to train men to assemble and operate nuclear weapons. Because the United States is a melting pot, we should have little difficulty in recruiting men for a nuclear army who would be willing to understand, accept, and appreciate the traditions of other peoples. And in America, self-reliance of the individual is a virtue; unlike the young people of Communist countries, Americans are taught to despise regimentation and to stand on their own feet. Development of the kind of army needed to fight a limited nuclear war may be impossible. But if it is possible anywhere, it is possible in the United States.

We must prepare psychologically. Since the devastation of Hiroshima, the American people have convinced themselves that any use of nuclear weapons constitutes all-out war. This erroneous notion must be corrected before we can begin to prepare for limited nuclear warfare. The American people, as well as free people throughout the world, must be educated to the fact that wars are divisible, that we can limit the scope of war, and that the use of nuclear weapons in a war limited in territory and purpose would not lead inevitably to a global nuclear disaster.

Surmounting this psychological barrier may be more difficult than any other problem we face in the necessary preparation for limited nuclear warfare. Of all inert things, the human mind may be the most inert. We must overcome this inertia, because only if we can change the way people think about nuclear weapons and nuclear wars can we ensure the stability and peace of the world.

CHAPTER SIXTEEN

The Future without Plan

PEACE MEANS MORE THAN to avoid war. Peace, like life, is an act of creation.

We can avoid war if we remain strong. But this is not enough. The world has become small, and with each passing decade all people are more dependent on each other—both for their safety and for their welfare. We must create a world community. This is the central problem of our age. Preparedness and weapons development can give us time and opportunity. The eventual outcome will depend on how we shall use this time and whether we work effectively to develop a lawful world organization.

People often ask what should have priority, weapons or constructive work for peace. I cannot help posing a similar question: What has priority, food or sleep? We cannot survive unless we have both. If we are not prepared, we cannot have an influence on the future organization of the world. If we have no clear understanding of the need for such an organization, we certainly shall not use our influence—even if we have it.

We can, of course, have a kind of peace without the hard job of military preparedness and the harder responsibility of planning for the future. We can leave these difficult tasks to others. The Russian Communists are ready and eager to unify the world. They have a practical, time-honored plan, the use of force, power, and dictation. The word *Mir* in Russian has two meanings. It means peace, and it also means the world. When Khrushchev says, "I want *Mir*," he may mean that he wants peace. He also may mean that he wants the world. He certainly means that he wants peace and the world. For us, *Mir* would be the peace of the grave.

Our plan for a world society is less practical. It is unprecedented. I am strongly tempted to believe, in sober moments, that it is impossible. We want a world organization by mutual consent, under a world law, as a partnership between equals. We want a democratic world government.

This is our ultimate goal, and the time is short. What can we do?

Our main immediate concern is to aid others and to establish understanding between nations. One of the first acts of the Kennedy administration was to propose a magnificent idea, the organization of a Peace Corps. Young men and women offered their services to help the development of underprivileged people. The drama of the Peace Corps, the ingredient that captured the public imagination, was that we would not send money, but human help. Members of the Peace Corps will live with the people whom they are helping, and their very presence should demonstrate our deep interest in the welfare of others.

It is too early to say how much the Peace Corps will accomplish, but its success is important. To give the Peace Corps the best possible chance for success, we should exempt from the draft the high-quality individuals who are willing to spend an extended period of their young lives in hard, adventurous, and dangerous work abroad.

Our government, at this writing, so far has not announced that members of the Peace Corps will be exempt from the draft. As long as this is the case, there is no clear evidence that our government is planning to establish the Peace Corps as a real weapon for winning the peace.

I hope that the Peace Corps will be taken seriously and that it will make a great contribution. But even if it should succeed, we can hardly expect it to become a really widespread activity of our people. Few can go abroad as leaders. We now lack knowledge of the countries we want to help, and not many youngsters have the capacity of acquiring the needed knowledge in a short time. And without knowledge, leadership will not produce the right results.

We should consider another possibility that is at the same time more modest and more ambitious than the Peace Corps. Let us send our children abroad not to lead but to learn. Thousands may become members of the Peace Corps and offer their effective help. But millions can and should go abroad to find out something about the many facts of this small world of which they are citizens and in which they have to survive or perish. Let us know our brethren before we presume to lead them.

One year abroad in a country that is not part of the Western civilization would do a great deal for our college students. One hardly dares to propose that a year spent in a strange and, if possible, primitive country should be made a requirement for college and university graduation. But if we could find a method that would send a million of our college-age people abroad each year, this could become a realistic psychological foundation on which the structure of a future world community might be erected.

At the same time, we should bring a million students from non-Western countries into our colleges and universities each year. Our present foreign student program has made important contributions. Despite its small size and understandable shortcomings, it provides one of the really helpful forces driving the world toward a more active and perhaps a brighter future.

The motto of the ancient world's highest educational system was "Know Thyself." Our motto should be "Know Each Other."

All this, however, can be only a beginning. We need a plan for the future, or at least an idea of where and how to begin to plan.

Well, that is just the point. I have no plan, and I can present none. I do not believe that anyone can present a reasonable plan. To function, a plan should have precedents; it should have been used successfully in many different situations. The only tried and time-honored prescription for establishing unity is conquest. This we do not want. It would destroy the very thing we want to establish. To establish unity by agreement, we must grasp each opportunity and make progress with difficult, ingenious, and often unlikely steps. We cannot have a program. We cannot predict, predetermine, or plan. We must improvise. We must be imaginative and creative. We must use the millions of heads and the millions of hearts of our democracy, and from the millions of possible approaches we must select the few which at a given moment in history have chances for success. This is why the foreign education of our youngsters is so important.

Although I cannot propose a plan, I shall outline a few possibilities for a beginning. I am not convinced that these suggestions have real merit. Anyone in our democracy might propose steps that would be more practical and more nearly possible, that would give our quest a better chance of success. There can be no doubt about our final aim. There is complete uncertainty about the road that will take us there.

The least difficult among these most difficult ways might well be the way of Atlantic Union. It has been suggested that democracies having an advanced industry and a comparatively high standard of living should form a federal union. Similarities of traditions, political institutions, and advanced technologies would reduce the difficulties of making this first step. The name of the movement, Atlantic Union, suggests Western Europe, the United States, and some countries of the British Commonwealth as participants. But the name should not be taken literally, because such a union also might include Japan and possibly other nations.

It should be clear, in any case, that Atlantic Union would not be a final answer. It would be only a first step. The trouble is that even this first step seems too difficult. We must, then, consider even less ambitious proposals.

One such proposal might be the full integration of the military forces of the NATO countries. The most important single decision would be to share our nuclear weapons and secrets. This would make it necessary to establish a common command in a strict and meaningful manner. This, however, would be only temporary. It should be followed by other steps that would cement the federal union. We need a union that would be firm, effective, and reliable in its international dealings. But within this union, there should be maximum freedom for the nation-members. We need not imagine that union would submerge the national character.

Another step leading to a union of the free democracies might be taken by making an economic arrangement. The European Common Market could serve as a starting point. The free democracies in a very short time might adopt a common currency. Customs union might follow more slowly. Tariffs on goods transported between the free democracies could be reduced gradually over ten years, to avoid severe economic shocks, and then abolished altogether. In ten years, goods could move with complete freedom, and during those ten years the difference between the standards of living in the co-operating countries might become much smaller. This may well mean that the standard of living in the United States would rise no further. At a time when all nations look at us with envy, it might be well to use our abilities and resources to increase our safety rather than our treasure and our comfort. A moratorium on keeping up with the Joneses and keeping ahead of the British, Italians, and Japanese might have some real merit.

If we could establish a close military and economic union between the free democracies, we would gain three important advantages:

We would be well on the way toward an effective federal union.

We would gain experience that could serve us well in the next step, in which less developed nations or combinations of such countries could be included in the union.

And we would gain strength. The union of free democracies could stop Communist expansion without fighting a war. It could give us time. During this time, our ideas and our organization could make further headway.

The United Nations has so many shortcomings that many are tempted to consider it only as a debating society. Yet the United Nations also has shown some strength. Its health service and its agricultural organization have relieved widespread suffering at a small cost. Its weak and incompletely organized police force performed a miracle in the Congo; it may not have been the miracle for which we prayed, but it was immeasurably better than what might have happened without help from an international organization.

Could the nucleus of the truly effective world government we need be found in the United Nations?

It seems unlikely. If government needs legislative, executive, and judicial branches, the United Nations cannot become an effective government. The existence of the veto power renders the legislative function ineffective.

But we might make limited progress in the judicial branch. The World Court at The Hague has functioned inconspicuously and well. This is true in spite of the fact that it has practically no power, and its jurisdiction depends on the litigants.

Suppose that two countries signed a treaty with a gilt edge, a clause specifying that any disagreements or misunderstandings arising from the treaty should be submitted to the World Court for a final determination. The treaty participants also would agree in the gilt-edge clause that the World Court's findings would be enforced, if necessary, by the United Nations police force under the authority of the Secretary General of the United Nations.

The Secretariat of the United Nations already possesses the rudiments of an executive branch of government. No legislative veto could stop the procedure begun by the treaty between two nations. No change of the United Nations charter would be involved. The Communists would have no effective way to stop this development. They probably would abstain from signing such a treaty, but they could not prevent the free nations from signing it.

Could such a treaty help the United States? I believe so.

Suppose that we wrote such a treaty stabilizing our relationships with Venezuela. If Venezuela should be overtaken by imitators of Castro, our oil interests would be endangered. If we tried to protect these rights by direct intervention, we would be branded as imperialists. But if we had a treaty with a gilt-edge clause that guaranteed our rights, the United Nations police force would take the necessary action.

Most important, an accumulation of treaties and valid decisions based upon these treaties could begin to build a body of effective international law. A law unenforced is much worse than useless. It undermines the authority of law. A law with a tradition of enforcement enhances that authority. In actual fact, the historical beginning of law is most usually not a covenant, not legislation, but custom supported by enforcement.

To enforce these legal decisions, the United Nations police force should become a strong and effective organization. This aim could be accomplished without excessive expense. We could provide the police force with tactical nuclear weapons, and at this one stroke the police force could become stronger than any of the world's armies except those of the United States and Russia.

It might be well to preserve the present custom and recruit personnel of the United Nations police force from the small countries. In this way, a triple alliance could be formed. The participants would be ancient: law, order, and the little man.

Where shall all these steps lead us? We still have not arrived at world government. Can we ever reach this goal without Communist Russia? And how can we imagine that the Communists ever will yield a bit of their power, their plans, their religious conviction that those plans will be realized? We certainly can have no such hopes as far as we can see at present. But we cannot see very far.

World Communism, up to now, has gone from victory to victory. There is no reason for the Russians to settle for anything less than *Mir*, the world. Before we can talk hopefully with the Russians, we must stop them. This is one reason why military preparedness and the organization of the world for peace necessarily must go hand in hand.

There is little point, at present, to discuss how we ever could agree with the Communists. It will not be easy to stop Communist expansion. We may fail in that, and we may be defeated. But if we succeed, the Communists then will have changed at least to some little extent. On our side, we will have changed. Merely to stop the expansion of Communism will require an unusual effort. To unite with other free countries will be another unusual and important experience. When the time comes to discuss world organization with the Communists, we may have gained a wider, more generous point of view.

We cannot predict whether or how we may succeed. But it is certain that unless we try, we shall fail.

Some of my good friends are Quakers. I was deeply disturbed by a remark dropped recently by one of them, a thoroughly idealistic man. He liked my suggestions concerning a lawful world-community, but he said: "Our people certainly will not change as much as you imagine."

Our nonviolent approach to a living, functioning, peaceful world requires some enormous changes. But there are some indications that changes of this type actually can occur.

These changes are in the best American tradition. This, in fact, is the tradition that has inspired true liberals throughout the world.

A very great number of Americans today desire these changes. What we lack is not imagination or generosity, but courage.

In the past, need has brought out the required courage in Americans. In the last few years the need and the danger have become even more apparent than ever before. Unless we change, we shall be changed. Unless our way of life fulfills its great potentialities in a world-wide free democracy, our way of life will disappear.

The Legacy of Hiroshima

IN A WORLD THAT IS PERHAPS ten billion years old, life has left its many-shaped traces on our planet for only half a billion years. Our special tribe, man, has existed and struggled to survive for less than a million years. In the last 10,000 years, civilizations arose and we started to change the face of the earth. But our most dramatic advances have been made during a relatively brief period: The last 300 years.

Progress in all fields of human knowledge and endeavor during these short 300 years has been breath-taking. During each of these centuries, man has learned more about himself and the universe in which he lives than ever had been known before. And the pattern of acceleration is continuing. In the last few decades we have reached out toward the stars. We are on our way to a conquest of space. Indeed, we already have brought down to the earth the innermost power of the sun and the heavenly bodies. The ancient story of Prometheus has ceased to be a legend. It has become a fact.

There are among us those who are frightened by such progress, those who would turn back. This we cannot do. We must advance into a future that is filled with uncertainties. Two things, however, are certain: One is that the story of man will not end; we shall survive. The other is that we are approaching the crossroads; the drama that began at Hiroshima will be finished before the end of this century. On the outcome depends the future of the small planet which is our home.

In a world that is so big and at the same time so insignificant, so familiar and yet so strange, preservation of a sense of proportion is not easy. It may help to look back upon the period in which man embarked upon his latest and most incredible adventures.

The human population of the earth about 10,000 years ago has been estimated at 100,000. By the time the Pharaohs began building their pyramids, the world's population had grown to a few million. When the Roman Empire was at the peak of its power, our numbers exceeded 100 million. In the history of population growth, there have been periods of stagnation and even recession. But, on the whole, the earth's population has doubled approximately once during every thousand years.

But in the middle of the 1600s, something happened. From about 1650 until today, the world's population has increased as never before. There were about 250 million people on the earth in 1650. A hundred years later, the total had grown to 500 million. A short century later, there were a billion people. Then the population increase became an explosion, and today there are almost three billion people crowding our planet.

During each of these three centuries, man has learned more about himself and the universe than could have been guessed by the most imaginative prophets. Knowledge has been breeding new knowledge, and each advance left a stimulus for further advances. What is occurring is a proliferation, a revolution, a veritable explosion of the human spirit.

Consider the world of 300 years ago. Europe was emerging from a most dreadful conflict, the Thirty Years' War. More than half of Central Europe's population had been killed—not so much by the war itself, but by epidemics that had followed in the wake of the armies. In England, the head of a king was chopped off. In France, another king still in his childhood began a reign that was to last for eighty years. Magnificent dynasties were flourishing or getting started in India and in China; their splendor surpassed that of the Sun King of France. Democracy was not established in any of the great countries of Europe or Asia, and individual freedom seemed as distant and unreal as the Kingdom of God.

There were signs of impending change. Navigators, adventurers, and pirates had sailed the oceans. The world had been explored, and the newly discovered continent of America had been attached to Western civilization. Printing and the alphabet had made available to more people a revolutionary tool: Knowledge.

This knowledge seemed safe, sound, and conservative. To philosophers and to all men of good sense, the earth appeared solid and unmoving. Everything had its natural place: The heavy earth and water below, the light air and clouds above, and the eternal crystal of the sky enclosing all. More than 2000 years before, strange ideas had been pressed against this formidable barrier of the obvious; Aristarchus of Samos had suggested that the earth was turning on its axis and racing around the sun; sober men of the scientific schools, however, had laughed at him and had forgotten him.

But now, on the threshold of the modern age, knowledge itself began to change. When Copernicus wrote, people read and wondered. When Galileo talked, people listened, objected —and finally were converted. Our ideas were in flux. Earth itself was moving.

During the hundred years between 1645 and 1745, science embarked upon a new period of critical thinking and careful looking. Newton discovered the simple fact that the laws of nature on the earth and the laws of nature in the heavens are the same, that the way in which an apple falls and the manner in which a planet moves belong to the same general and understandable scheme.

These simple laws of nature made a deep impression upon people's minds. Newton tied the happenings of our world to the ideas of space and time, of cause and effect. After Newton, the happenings around us could be described with machinelike precision. These new universal laws actually made it possible to build machines that could do useful work. This important possibility was one of Newton's legacies: Another century passed before the machines were built.

A practical problem arose during this same century: The British Isles ran out of firewood. From necessity, the English turned to a poor and dirty substitute: Coal. They soon found that in the high temperatures of coal fires, iron ores and iron itself could be treated more easily. Iron used to be expensive. Now it became cheaper than bronze. This was the real birth of the Iron Age. A serious difficulty had been solved in a way that would change the world.

At the same time, our familiarity with the living world began to increase. The recently discovered microscope was turned on a great variety of small objects. Leeuwenhoek was amazed by the unsuspected structures of living bodies and the busy populations of tiny beings that could be found in a drop of water. Linnaeus began a systematic classification of the animal and vegetable kingdoms. For the first time in history, medical men began to distinguish different kinds of diseases and to apply selective treatments.

Western science was on the move, and so was Western political strength. During these hundred years, the menace of the Moslem Empire disappeared. Central Europe recovered from the religious wars and from the ravages of religious intolerance. In France and in England the theoretical and practical foundations were laid for a new political structure: A free democracy.

During the next century, 1745 to 1845, Newton's abstract research and other scientific developments were met in history by a plentiful supply of inexpensive iron and by the enterprise of free men living in a tolerant social structure. Machines were built, and the world was launched upon the Industrial Revolution.

First in limited ways and then with an increasing generality, machines took over the burdens of human and animal muscles. More goods were produced for more people, and the general standard of living began a sharp rise. To feed the appetites of hungry machines and the increasing desires of more people with more money and more free time, merchants scoured the world for products and merchandise. Trade flourished, and nations interacted as never before. A new internationalism developed. It sometimes was friendly and co-operative. Often it was painful. No longer were India and China a match for Western civilization. The triumphant man of the West looked down on primitive people and on members of ancient cultures alike. From far-flung colonies, Europe obtained much wealth, some power, a wider horizon, and—for the future—more discord and misery than anyone could foresee.

The century literally was filled with wars and with revolutions. The Seven Years' War was fought in Europe and in distant continents. The French Revolution uprooted an old, established order, giving birth to new truths, new faiths, and new heresies. It set reason on a pedestal, wrote on its flag the rights of man, and created the idea and the reality of the modern nation-state. Massed armies of nation-states soon met on the battlefields of Napoleon and young men died, thousands of miles from home, for ideals and passions that had been unknown to their fathers. When the Napoleonic Wars ended after a dismal and deadly retreat from Russia and a semblance of the old order was re-established, the concept of the nation-state remained standing as a signpost for the future.

On our continent a more constructive revolution created the

young democracy in America. It seemed, at the time, to be an unimportant creation in a distant corner of the world. But when Alexis de Tocqueville came from France and studied this remarkable development, he concluded his penetrating and sympathetic criticism with prophetic sentences:

> There are at the present time (1835!) two great nations in the world, which started from different points, but seem to tend towards the same end. I allude to the Russians and the Americans. . . . All other nations seem to have nearly reached their natural limits . . . but these are still in the act of growth. . . . The conquests of the American are . . . gained by the plowshare; those of the Russian by the sword. The Anglo-American relies upon personal interest to accomplish his ends and gives free scope to the unguided strength and common sense of the people; the Russian centers all the authority of society in a single arm. The principal instrument of the former is freedom; of the latter, servitude. Their starting-point is different and their courses are not the same; yet each of them seems marked out by the will of Heaven to sway the destinies of half the globe.

While we reaped the sweet and bitter fruit of the past, we sowed a fertile field for the future. New sciences appeared. The way was opened to an understanding of electricity and magnetism. The secrecy and confusion of alchemy gave way to a systematic study of the transformations of matter: Chemistry. The cellular structure of living things was discovered, and mere classification of living beings was replaced by ideas of correlation, kinship, and evolution. Lamarck spun theories of how the giraffe had acquired its long neck; a few years later, an English naturalist traveling on the ship *Beagle* wrote in his notebook observations of the strange Gardens of Eden he found on Pacific isles. His notes were destined to change the position that man had assigned himself in the scheme of things.

But all this was prelude. In the next century, 1845 to 1945, more changes took place than most of us realize today; more scientific progress was made than most of us understand.

After many years of painstaking study and thought, Darwin published the work he had begun while traveling on the *Beagle*. With this one blow, the sharp lines that had separated living species became hazy. Man appeared as the first cousin of all other living beings. Before the century's end, a bridge was discovered with one pier anchored in living organisms and the other anchored in dead chemistry. The name of the bridge is the viruses.

It was unavoidable that many men of science should consider matter as the basis and explanation of everything—including man. But these materialistic philosophers had one fatal shortcoming. They knew much too little about matter itself. During the first decade of the twentieth century, a secret was discovered, a remarkable science which ties matter, chemistry, atoms, and electricity into one logical and consistent package. The secret is kept all too well. It is not guarded by the few who will not talk, but by the many who will not listen. This secret gives us a thorough and detailed command over matter. At the same time it is based upon a peculiar recognition: Matter, in its smallest parts, is not machinelike and predictable; it is capricious and subject to the laws of probability.

The great world of the stars turned out to be no less surprising than the small world of the atoms. We learned that our sun is but one of billions of sister-stars that make up the Milky Way system. In this system there may be as many planets harboring life as there are humans living on the earth. And who knows whether, someplace in this myriad of solar systems, there may not be found a surprise compared to which life itself may appear uncomplicated and commonplace. But the great Milky Way is just one of billions of other similar systems from which we are separated by the abyss of space; nothing is likely to bridge this abyss except signals, and the time required for these to carry information from sender to receiver would be measured in millions of years. To find our way in this immensity that indeed may prove infinite, we cannot use the simple markers of space and time accepted as the immutable anchors of reason and measurement. In a century during which nothing seemed to retain its familiar appearance, Einstein wrote for the astronauts a new manual of space navigation. This work of Einstein, the theory of relativity, gained universal fame. We all know that it contradicts common sense. Few realize that this theory is by no means complicated. It is simple and ties together so many old facts that one is left with the strange feeling that we are on the threshold of understanding everything.

It is impossible to compare scientific progress with practical progress. The former is sometimes not appreciated because the new science is not understood. The latter may fail to impress us because we forget how different the world used to be. Compare the twentieth century with the age of our grandparents' grandparents. In the time they required to visit friends in a neighboring state, we can travel to any place on the earth and return home. News used to travel no faster than people. Information now can be made available to all in the time needed to understand a simple piece of news. Before 1845, many people suffered unbearable pain and multitudes died of diseases which no one could explain. By 1945, we had conquered infectious disease and had learned how to eliminate pain. We can be cut up and sewed together again and benefit from the experience.

But this century of progress, along with its dazzling and practical achievements, produced a crisis. During the century's initial decades, it seemed that peace, progress, and civilization could exist side by side. But after two world wars broke the peace, the words "progress" and "civilization" sound less attractive. Were these two terrible wars accidents which were avoidable and for that reason even more tragic? Were these catastrophes the necessary consequences of the structure of our society? Were they made inevitable by the nature of the sovereign nation-state? Could the mistakes of colonialism and the hatreds of racial conflicts have been avoided? Did the iron necessity of history dictate the rise of Communism? Is the world fated to be changed by uncompromising violence? Is a gentle, gradual evolution guided by reason a mirage and a wish-dream?

These are the political questions which we have inherited from a period of magnificent progress. History gives us no answers and offers only one fact; and this fact is disquieting: During this century's two world wars, the industrial revolution transformed the art of warfare. In 1914, armies marched into battle with equipment that looked much the same as in the times of Napoleon. In 1945, the science of subatomic physics made available a totally different tool of warfare, and the sky burst open over Hiroshima.

What will science produce in the century extending from 1945 to 2045? Of all unpredictable things, science is the most unpredictable. The very nature of science is surprise. If a scientific accomplishment were not unexpected and surprising, it already would have been accomplished.

Our basic scientific ideas are in flux. Time and space are not what they used to be. Bohr's atomic theory has set limits to the oldest life line of science, the line connecting cause and effect.

Will we succeed in explaining the ultimate building blocks of our world? Or will we find that no building blocks exist? Can the laws of the physical world be derived from pure reason? Will we find the limits of our universe and will we understand the act of creation? Or will we discover that space and time have no limits and that there is no sense talking about a beginning?

Will we explain life? Or shall we learn that we never should have tried to define life? Will mechanical brains eliminate drudgery from intellectual labors? Or will electronic computers make human thought obsolete? Will we find, perhaps, that there is an element in thought which is truly human? Is it possible that by studying machines we might learn more about ourselves?

The future of science is open, and I envy those who enter it with fresh minds.

When we worry about the future, we usually do not think about science, but about the human society. And about the future of mankind, we can talk with the hope that springs from the story of the last 300 years. Amid many doubts one prediction can be made with confidence: The human race, at the end of our century and beyond, will still be here. Frequent and gloomy prophecies to the contrary are not justified. The fear of mankind's end is not based on fact. It is based on a monstrous anxiety.

The world of 2045 will be more densely populated than ever. There will be close to ten billion people on the earth. The industrial revolution will be completed, and the incredible multitudes crowding the world will live in reasonable comfort. Life will go on, and the necessities of life will be available.

In an age of many independent sovereignties, Alexis de Tocqueville predicted, correctly, that Russia and the United States each would sway the destinies of half the globe. By the year 2045, this process will have been completed. All the peoples of the world will bear allegiance to a single government. Our present uncertainties revolve around questions concerning this one government of man. What kind of government will it be? What is the road leading to a United World?

At the end of World War II, the United States was at the zenith of its power. Only we possessed nuclear weapons. Our fabulous wealth had not been diminished by the world-wide conflict. Backward nations, recognizing that the United States had grown rich and powerful through its own efforts, looked to us with the hope that our accomplishments now could be repeated on every continent. American scientists formed the vanguard in the exploration of the unknown. American history was the bible for those who devoutly believed in freedom. It seemed a foregone conclusion that the years between 1945 and 2045 would become known as the American Century.

Less than two decades later, our power is dwindling, our leadership is challenged, and our wealth is considered the result of luck. American affluence is the object of envy and contempt. American technology is being outstripped in space. The great respect that our country once enjoyed is hardly remembered.

This tragic change has been accompanied by general discouragement in the United States. A strange fact is that the discouragement did not follow the decline of our strength and prestige. It preceded the decline. We seemed to turn our eyes from an inspiring past and a challenging future. In the unfolding of human accomplishment and human power, we could see only danger—and we seemed unable to accept the fact that danger always has been a companion of change. It is of great importance to understand, if at all possible, the source of our present weakness, the cause for the eclipse of the American dream.

It is a most critical moment in the life of an individual if there is a sudden transition from protected childhood to the responsibilities of a grown man. The change may appear too difficult. The challenge may be a shock. There is a real danger, at such a moment, that the young mind may turn away from reality and its superhuman demands. The spirit may seek refuge in a make-believe world and deny the existence of the problems and difficulties that caused the dilemma.

Psychiatrists are well aware of the symptoms accompanying such a flight from reality. Memory is repressed. Meaningless substitute-actions take the place of purposeful endeavors. Rational behavior is replaced by anxiety, by feelings of guilt, by fears of improbable and fantastic calamities.

Neither logic nor any other type of scientific reasoning can justify application to a nation of the things we know about individual behavior. Yet I am reminded of these violent and dangerous growing pains of young men when I think of our difficulties in facing the atomic age. Hiroshima deprived us of the ocean barriers that had protected us. Hiroshima shattered our traditional policy of isolation. The United States was projected into the unaccustomed role of leadership in a gigantic struggle —a responsibility which the great majority of Americans did not want and for which we certainly were not prepared. This situation was created by our own actions. We had no workable plan, and we faced the problems of the atomic age with feelings of awe, guilt, fear, and anxiety.

Two years after the end of World War II, I was discussing the United States defense policies with a clergyman in Chicago. He insisted that our nation never would use nuclear weapons for mass destruction, even if that were the price of our own survival. He maintained that the deep-grained moral convictions of the American people never would permit the use of such ghastly weapons. I could make only one reply: "We actually have used them."

He said no more, leaving me with the indelible impression that he wanted to forget Hiroshima. I am convinced that many Americans feel the same way.

We argue that questions of nuclear warfare are too technical for general understanding, that they must be left to the experts. We believe that problems of nuclear explosives must be handled secretly, that they cannot be settled by public discussion. There is some validity in these arguments. But, at the same time, we are in a situation where the great mass of Americans have refused to shoulder a responsibility that belongs to the citizens of a free country. Perhaps the real reason for this behavior is that many want to avoid responsibility; the decisions that must be made are too awesome. We tolerate secrecy in a democracy and leave atomic questions to the experts because we prefer not to think about our difficult problems.

We are neglecting civilian defense. The very real possibility of a nuclear attack is too terrible even to think about. It certainly is too terrible to deal with or plan for, although preparation would eliminate the threat. Rather than concern ourselves with dangerous realities, we have substituted an imaginary danger. Worries about our unpreparedness have been replaced by fears of radioactive fallout produced by nuclear tests and dangerous only in the imagination. This is like a person relieving his tensions by the act of washing his hands again and again.

We insisted on trying to draft an agreement with the Russians to end nuclear tests. The effort was fruitless, and it was doomed from the beginning. We know that such an agreement could not be policed, and we know that it would not remove the danger of nuclear conflict. Yet we seemed eager to accept a symbol that might help us to imagine that our danger had decreased. Now it is apparent that the Soviet Union conducted secret nuclear experiments during the test-ban negotiations, increasing our danger. It is obvious that the Soviet Union prepared for an important series of atmospheric tests conducted late in 1961 even while test-ban negotiations were in progress. But many Americans, unwilling to face these facts of Russian duplicity, continue to seek a test-ban treaty that would be unenforceable but that would stand as a comforting symbol.

At the same time, we have continued to raise our standard of living. The great majority of the people in the world are starving, but we have managed to increase our own well-being by almost 50 per cent in less than two decades. Although our survival is closely allied with the fate of all men in all parts of our world, we prefer to live as if we alone existed.

In a dangerous situation, we have chosen the most dangerous of courses. We have chosen not to face our danger.

What needs to be done will not be easy to do. But whatever the difficulties, a few tasks clearly must be accomplished.

We should be prepared to survive an all-out nuclear attack.

We can and we should have adequate shelters for our entire population.

We should have plans and stockpiles so that after an all-out attack, we could recover. If we are adequately prepared, the attack never will come.

We should abandon all plans to deter Communist expansion with the threat of massive retaliation. We should, however, maintain secure retaliatory forces to make sure that any all-out attack against our nation could be answered with a crushing counterblow.

We should be prepared to respond to limited aggression at the same level at which the attack is made. We can and should limit the area and aims of such conflicts. We cannot and must not try to limit the use of weapons.

We should develop our tactical nuclear weapons and our mobile forces to the point where concentrations of invading armies can be defeated and other strictly military targets can be wiped out. For the winning of a limited war, we must rely on the local people fighting to defend their freedom.

We should accelerate scientific and technical efforts that will lead to future military strength. We need more work on developments of nuclear explosives. Only with continued preparedness can we ensure peace long enough to build the foundations of a stable world order.

We should give full support to peaceful research in many fields, including meteorology, oceanography, and the use of nuclear explosives in geographical engineering, to release the riches of the earth and speed the day when all peoples can share in the fruits of the industrial revolution.

We should pursue the exploration of space and rally the interest and work of other nations to make, together with us, a united effort in man's latest adventure.

We should strive for a gradual abandonment of governmental secrecy in scientific and technical fields so that our people once again can have a full voice in the affairs of our nation.

We should improve science education so the United States might regain the scientific leadership which we are certain to lose.

We should teach our children the languages, histories, and customs of our neighbors so that they can understand people with whom our fate inevitably is linked.

We should abandon our goal of a further increase in our standard of living. We must look first to the improvement of the backward nations and to our own survival. Indeed, we are not likely to survive unless we help those who are starving and assume leadership in the Revolution of Rising Expectations.

We should mobilize the almost inexhaustible energies of the United States and the free world to win the peace as we won the war. Under proper leadership, our creative effort can be more than doubled.

We should strive to establish a just and secure Government of Man, a world-wide government to which all owe allegiance and which guarantees freedom.

Establishment of such a world government would be difficult even if we had centuries in which to make it effective. But we have only decades. I believe no single man has the ingenuity and knowledge to propose a workable plan. Our only hope is that the countless people of all the free countries will have the determination, the moderation, the imagination, and the selflessness to complete, in peace, the greatest revolution in the history of mankind.

America, by itself, cannot be successful in this undertaking. But unless we contribute fully to the peaceful co-operation and the development of a lawful world community, our way of life will end during this century.

World government, in any case, will be established. If we are unsuccessful in obtaining its establishment by consent, it will be established by force—and the doctrine of the future then will be the Communist doctrine.

Will the individual human being be the measure of all values in the world society of the future? Or will that society itself be the source and the goal of all endeavor? These are the paramount questions of our time.

If our ideas of freedom are to survive, we must change. Our job seems impossibly difficult. We must bring out the best in the free individuals. Only then can we hope that the future will belong to the free. It is hardly credible that the camel will go through the needle's eye; but we can at least be confident that after it has emerged from its ordeal, it no longer will be the same crude and clumsy creature.

The job of the Communists is easier. The world has been transformed by force in the past, and it may be transformed by violence again in the future. The Communists claim that if they win in this transformation, the state will wither away and all will be happy and content. But when it comes to the details of this vision of the millennium, Communist theorists are somewhat reticent.

No one can be sure how a mature Communist society would operate. But I am tempted to guess, and I shall imagine the best. In the Communist society, the individual will be a new and re-educated being. He will subordinate himself voluntarily to the collective welfare. He will not only accept, but he will actively seek his specialized function in which he can best serve, not his own interests or the welfare of his neighbor, but that higher organism that will embrace all mankind. For a Communist, the idea that a human is but a cell in the social body has a real, practical meaning: The human cells can and should fulfill their individual functions in a perfect manner, but the cell really does not matter. Only the whole society matters.

This picture has grandeur, and it may become axiomatic in the world of tomorrow. But, to my mind, our own goals not only are preferable, but belong to a world of incomparably wider and more splendid horizon. If you realize that billions of human beings have the same potentialities that you have yourself, and if you remember how rarely any of us has accomplished in the past what he could have achieved, then you get an inkling of what man might be and do if he can avoid becoming a cell. A plan may be good, an organization may be great, but a single human being can be infinitely better. And the idea of humanism will not be fully realized until it can be applied to all of us equally.

Do we have a chance? It is the meaning and the legacy of Hiroshima that the crisis and the decision will come soon—much too soon.

Nobody knows what will happen. Freedom may survive, and the world of the future may be a better place than we can imagine today. Or freedom may be suppressed, and not even its memory will remain. Our future will be determined decisively during the last decades of the twentieth century.

Index